Members with food at the Boston Food Co-op. Photo by William Ronco, reprinted courtesy of *Working Papers*.

FOOD CO-OPS

AN ALTERNATIVE TO
SHOPPING IN SUPERMARKETS

WILLIAM RONCO

BEACON PRESS   BOSTON

Copyright © 1974 by William Ronco

Beacon Press books are published under the auspices
of the Unitarian Universalist Association

Simultaneous publication in Canada by Saunders of Toronto, Ltd.

Published in simultaneous hardcover and paperback editions

Printed in the United States of America

9 8 7 6 5 4 3 2 1

DISCOUNTS TO CO - OPS

Library of Congress Cataloging in Publication Data

Ronco, William.
   Food co-ops.
   Bibliography: pp. 181-183.
   1. Cooperative societies – United States. 2. Food
industry and trade – United States. I. Title.
HD3284.R55   334'.5   74 - 211
ISBN 0 - 8070 - 0880 - X
ISBN 0 - 8070 - 0881 - 1 (pbk.)

To my wife, Wilma Lilley Ronco,
and the memory of my grandfather, William Pommerank

Weighing out produce at the Central Square Co-op in Cambridge, Massachusetts. Photo by William Ronco, reprinted courtesy of *Working Papers.*

CONTENTS

William Ronco (right) talks with Roger Auerbach, produce buyer for the New England Food Co-op Organization. Photo by Jacki Schmerz.

PREFACE

Food co-ops are genuine peoples' organizations. They
reflect their members' needs, interests, politics, neuroses,
fetishes. Accordingly, I've tried to write about co-ops
in a way that will allow free rein for the expression of peoples'
experiences with co-ops. Instead of offering my directions for
co-op organization I've tried to recount the relevant experiences
of co-ops (read people) themselves. I've added some of my own
observations and in some cases included theories and findings
of social scientists to help provide perspective on the experiences
of the co-ops.

The first of the five chapters of this book describes various
specific food co-ops in operation, pointing out the potential
savings and time commitments involved, the organizational possibilities, the national scope and economic breadth of food co-op
activity.

The second chapter describes how co-ops start, beginning with
the initial organizational meetings of a group in Concord, Massachusetts. The chapter relates how the Concord co-op handled basic
issues like space acquisition, bookkeeping, financing, and organizational form. A detailed description of wholesale buying techniques
is included in this chapter.

The third chapter relates how food co-ops develop and change
over time, what trends seem to emerge from the growth of
various co-ops, and what can be done to keep co-ops responsive,
flexible, and successful.

The fourth chapter reviews some of the links between food
co-ops and various meanings of the word "politics."

The final chapter traces recent (since 1970) co-op history
and compares it with the experiences of co-ops in the 1930s
and in the previous century. The chapter features a description of

utopian experiments and theories and their ties with early and recent co-ops.

Appendix A at the end of the book includes several newsletters/notices put out by food co-op themselves. Appendix B is a list of wholesalers compiled from questionnaires I sent to co-ops (see below). Appendix C is a listing of about 1,000 food co-ops across the nation.

I collected most of the information in this book in interviews and discussions in the Boston area in 1973 and 1974 and in visits to Chicago, Minneapolis-St. Paul, Washington, D.C., Madison, Wisconsin, and New York City in the winter of 1973-74. (I first saw the clenched fist and carrot symbol in the Minneapolis - St. Paul co-ops.) Prior to the trip, I sent questionnaires to about 140 food co-ops in a list compiled and given to me by Don Lubin of the Boston Food Co-op. About half of the co-ops responded to the questionnaire, most with careful, some with wonderfully detailed replies. Some people responded with invitations to "come see our co-op," which, in some cases, I did.

I wish to thank the people who helped me in the researching of this book: Mark Sherman, Diane Brown, Bruce Singer, Roger Auerbach, Dave Zinner, and the numerous and consistently friendly co-op members I spoke to and corresponded with in the past year.

Several people read portions of the manuscript and provided (though I may not have received it as such at the time) invariably constructive criticism: Mary Corcoran, Jerome Murphy, Diane Pitkalis, John Case, Nancy Lyons, Gail Howrigan, and Gregory Jackson. Mary Jo Bane commented on the whole manuscript and provided needed advice and much-appreciated support throughout. Dr. Bane and others at the Cambridge (Massachusetts) Policy Studies Institute were instrumental in having me write the article on food co-ops for "Working Papers," which was the precursor of this book.

Finally, I want to thank my wife, Wilma Lilley Ronco, for her help in every aspect of preparing the manuscript.

Final accounting at the Needham (Massachusetts) Food Co-op.
Photo by William Ronco.

The Selby Food Co-op in Minneapolis-St. Paul. Photo by William Ronco.

Getting "carded" at the Boston Food Co-op. Photo by Jacki Schmerz.

Check-out at the Boston Food Co-op. Photo by Jacki Schmerz.

Wholesale buying at the New England Produce Center. Photo by
William Ronco, reprinted courtesy of *Working Papers*.

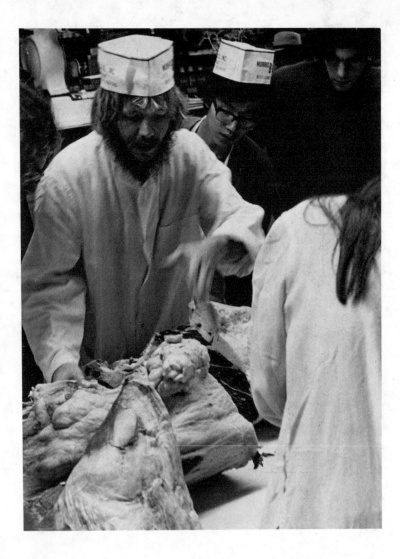

Terry Molner makes a fine point at Boston Food Co-op's
Meatcutters' Collective. Photo by William Ronco.

Browsing at the Stone Soup co-op in Washington, D.C.
Photo by William Ronco.

Taking inventory at the Boston Food Co-op. Photo by Jacki Schmerz.

Early days of the Fitchburg (Massachusetts) co-op. Photo
reprinted from *The Story of a Cooperative* by Savele
Syrjala, United Cooperative Society, Fitchburg,
Massachusetts.

Food to be bagged at the Broadway Co-op in Somerville, Massachusetts. Photo by Jacki Schmerz.

Chapter One

MORE THAN CHEAP FOOD

utside an aging, weathered, wood-frame church, bleak gray clouds predict that a chilling winter rain is on the way. But Mrs. Nancy Littlehale, busy inside the United Methodist Church in Somerville (Massachusetts), is oblivious. She's directing a food distribution operation as she's done on other mornings, every Tuesday, for over a year. Mrs. Littlehale, mother of three, is "bagging coordinator" for the Broadway Food Co-op in Somerville. She has been responsible for seeing that the food gotten by the fifty-family co-op from the wholesale market moves from its packing crates into the bags of co-op members. On this particular day Mrs. Littlehale has an added responsibility. While acting as bagging coordinator, she is being filmed by CBS for a nationwide Saturday news special.

CBS's interest was spurred by the recent growth of food cooperatives and the increasingly important promise that co-ops make: high-quality food for low prices. The weekend news team is in town for four days. In addition to the relatively small Broadway Co-op, they're taking a look at the larger (5,000+ members and an inventory including produce, meat, fish, dairy goods) store run by the Boston Food Co-op.

Before filming the bagging operation the news team had been at the wholesale produce market where the co-op buys its food. Later in the day they will film the families who come in to pick up the orders made up by Mrs. Littlehale and her crew. While the film crew follows with lights, camera, and a baseball bat of a microphone, the bagging crew proceeds with its work. The day's crew, several women and some children on their school vacation, open crates, take the produce, and put it into numbered shopping bags lined up around the inside of the church. Mrs. Littlehale explains how the co-op works to a slightly bewildered member of the news team.

She explains how the fifty families pick up order sheets for the following week's food, along with the day's completed order awaiting them in the church. On Friday, they drop off the orders and money to cover what they estimate (based on this week's price) the food will cost at "collection points"—homes of members in the area. On Monday night a member of the co-op calls in the total order (now averaging $300) to Roger Auerbach, who buys at the wholesale produce market for more than twenty similar groups in eastern New England. A crew of co-op volunteers with a truck will meet Roger at the market on the following Tuesday to pick up what he buys and bring it back to the co-op. When they unload it, Mrs. Littlehale will see that it gets re-bagged as the orders families submitted.

Mrs. Littlehale is one of ten coordinators who take control of co-op functions. Other coordinators handle bookkeeping, trucking, ordering. One coordinator specializes in seeing that every co-op member is assigned some sort of job. Each member must work at the co-op. Mrs. Littlehale explains that most members work from two to three-and-one-half hours a month, depending on their "jobs." The co-op depends on volunteer labor to keep its prices down. It charges no overhead and therefore sells food for the same prices it pays for it. The day (in February 1974) that I visited, I drew up this comparison between its prices and the prices at the supermarket down the block:

	Co-op	Supermarket
Bananas	$.09 lb.	$ .18 lb.
Eggplant	.29 lb.	.39 lb.
Mushrooms	.50 qt.	.59 pt.
Eggs (X lg.)	.74 doz.	1.03 doz.
Grapefruit	.14	2/.59
Tomatoes	.24 lb.	.69/12 oz.

The list reflects the concentration of the co-op on produce. It also handles meat, but can't quite compete with supermarket "specials."

Mrs. Littlehale notes that she and the other coordinators put in more time than other members because they like to. "I'm a lousy organizer," she confessed, "but I like to get out of the house. I really enjoy it, besides saving the money."

TIME AND MONEY

Mrs. Littlehale reported that she saved five or six dollars on her weekly grocery bill, an amount not unusual among co-op members. Prices at food co-ops are lower than at supermarkets, but how much lower varies widely. Co-op produce prices are consistently much lower because supermarkets charge a high percentage markup on produce to cover spoilage losses and refrigeration costs. When co-ops handle meat, dairy, and baked goods the savings are still good but not quite as spectacular as the savings on produce. Only co-ops with very high volumes who buy in large quantities are able to get any savings at all on canned and packaged food. Supermarkets don't mark these up much because they sell fast and don't spoil. Some co-ops carry these items at prices no better than the supermarkets to save members extra shopping trips.

Prices at the Somerville co-op are typical for co-ops in the area. Listed below are some price comparisons done by other Boston area co-ops. (As of this writing the lists are a few months old and I can see that inflation has already made some of the prices items of nostalgia. The comparisons and percentage savings are still, however, fairly accurate.)

Lynn, Massachusetts, food co-op (taken during summer of 1973):

	Supermarket	Co-op
Potatoes (10 lbs.)	$ .98	$ .55
Onions (1 lb.)	.30	.12
String beans (1 lb.)	.49	.25
Tomatoes (1 lb.)	.59	.27
Winesap apples (6)	.83	.36
Carrots (1 lb.)	.25	.11
Peaches (1 lb.)	.33	.16
Cucumbers (each)	.13	.05
Sliced bologna (1 lb.)	.99	.89
Sliced imp. ham (1 lb.)	2.36	1.59
Hamburg (medium, 1 lb.)	.99	.80
Centercut pork chops (1 lb.)	1.38	.97
Top of the round steak (1 lb.)	1.79	1.49

Worcester, Massachusetts, food co-op (taken during September 1973):

	Supermarket	Co-op
Carrots (pkg.)	$.22	$.16
Celery (pkg.)	.48	.23
Cucumbers (each)	.24	.09
Onions (1 lb.)	.16	.09
Green peppers (1 lb.)	.38	.17
Tomatoes (1 lb.)	.38-.48	.18
Apples (1 lb.)	.19	.16
Bananas (1 lb.)	.16	.14
Oranges (each)	.14	.08
Large eggs (doz.)	.93	.83

Boston, Massachusetts, food co-op (taken during March 1974):

	Supermarket	Co-op
Navel oranges (each)	$ .10	$ .07
Asparagus (1 lb.)	.79	.54
Spinach (10 oz. pkg.)	.39	.29
Honey (1 lb.)	1.58	.55
Whole chicken (1 lb.)	.59	.46
Ground beef (1 lb.)	1.05	1.03
Italian bread (1 lb. loaf)	.50	.35
Frozen cod fillet (1 lb.)	1.29	.86
Vermont cheddar cheese (1 lb.)	1.49	1.10
Large eggs (doz.)	.94	.72

Price comparisons are really only a partial consideration in calculating co-op savings. The kind and quality of the food and the time demands of co-op participation must also be taken into account. Many people, for example, find that several weeks after joining a co-op their total grocery expenditures drop considerably even though they may be buying more produce at the co-op than they did at the supermarket. This happens because they start using produce in place of other items—fruit replaces candy and snacks for children, fresh vegetables replace expensive frozen vegetables. Some families use co-op produce in main dishes, replacing meat with vegetable dishes once or twice a week.

Higher quality food is another benefit of co-op shopping. From the most wildeyed Greenwich Villagers to the most conservative New England women, co-op members consistently remarked to me about the high-quality produce they get. Co-ops get the food from produce terminals to people faster than any supermarket, and the food they get is usually the top-quality stuff that the supermarkets wrap in special paper to show off. "We figure we're saving so much," a New York co-oper commented, "we might as well go first class."

Most co-ops can work it out so that the time members put in does not wear away price differentials. In co-ops like the Boston Food Co-op, with its predetermined time commitments (two hours per month) the amount of savings (five to ten dollars on a weekly family order of twenty-five dollars) far outweighs the time put in by most members. Smaller co-ops that may demand more time can approach a point where the savings aren't worth the bother. Research conducted by Ronald Curhan and Edward Wertheim of the Boston University Business School found that members of smaller cooperatives reported they spent an average of 1½ hours weekly running their co-ops and more time doing co-op shopping.[1] This average figure, however, includes wide variation ranging from people who seldom fulfill their work requirements to people who put in extra time because, like Mrs. Littlehale, they enjoy it. And the averages were calculated on the basis of a 1971-72 survey. Since then many co-ops have refined organizational techniques and gained in efficiency. The Broadway Co-op, for example, simply requires that each member carry out some job. The amount of time put in varies according to the job. Mrs. Littlehale thought that most members worked between three and four hours each month.

The whole issue of how much time co-ops require is more pressing to people who don't belong to co-ops than to co-op members who know that it's more a matter of give and take than of statistical averages. In all co-ops, some members work a lot and some don't. Judging from the people I've met, the ones who do are usually motivated more by a desire to belong and participate than the obligation to the organization per se. In co-ops where poor organization makes unrealistic demands of members it is a simple matter to drop out. With co-ops growing and expanding it is also relatively easy to find a co-op that works.

THE NATIONAL PICTURE

The story of the Broadway Co-op is no doubt a great human-interest story. No wonder the CBS news staff could get excited about it. But the story in Somerville goes beyond the human-interest angle, for what's going on there is being duplicated literally all over the country. The directory in this book (tabulated by the Food Co-op Conference, Midwest Region) lists nearly 1,000 food co-ops well distributed throughout the nation.

From uncertain roots in the political activism and unrest of the late 1960s, food co-ops have developed a broad base of support, involvement, and activity. Assisted, certainly, by rising supermarket prices, co-ops have been adopted by a broad range of Americans. Some areas of the country have carried out cooperative development to impressive lengths. There is a lot of activity in Boston, New York, Washington, Chicago, and along the West Coast. Minneapolis is a veritable co-op heaven, with more than ten co-op stores, a warehouse, restaurant, bakery, and hardware store. One observer claims that Minneapolis's co-ops do over $1 1/3 million in business annually, provide subsistence wages for over sixty people and buy crops from twenty farmers.[2] It's hard to determine what about a city promotes co-ops. Easy access to wholesale markets helps, as does space amenable to co-op use (such as free use of demolition-scheduled buildings or low rents) and people likely to join up. The student population helped get things off the ground in Boston, and extremely high supermarket prices boosted co-ops in New York. Minneapolis's co-op growth is partly due to long-standing midwestern populist cooperative tradition.

But none of these places could have been accurately predicted four or five years ago. The most influential factor in predicting co-op development seems to be not the passive background characteristics of the city but the character of the city's early co-op experiments. Though some have more than others, all cities have a population with some economic and social interests in co-ops and some helpful economic support. If early co-ops build on these and reach out to other areas in the cities, they can strongly influence local co-op growth.

Co-ops have marked their growth not only in numbers but by increased cooperation among co-ops. They have banded together regionally, and recently, nationally. Some have even blazed trails past all middlemen direct to farmers and producers. Food co-ops in the Boston area, for example, combine their buying strength at the wholesale produce market. Acting as a representative of the New England Food Cooperative Organization (NEFCO), Roger Auerbach makes the 5 A.M. trek to the New England Produce Market every day, buying for twenty-five to thirty co-ops each week. Roger describes himself as an "ex-lawyer." Actually he's a graduate of Boston University Law School and a member of the Massachusetts Bar. While working as a lawyer for HUD, he began buying produce as a volunteer one day a week for the Mission Hill Food Co-op. As frustrations with government bureaucracy and the court system increased and as a commitment to the cooperative way of life increased, Roger quit the government and law to become a full-time manager at the Boston Food Co-op and is now a full-time buyer and coordinator for NEFCO.

Roger's personal relationships with wholesalers are backed with formidable amounts of cash (as of this writing, NEFCO business is $10,000 - $12,000 per week). NEFCO's financial strength enables him to buy in larger quantities, thus saving some money, and his daily presence at the market ensures that he is on top of the ever-changing quality/price outlook. In addition, Roger is often able to help co-ops coordinate orders so that they can buy together in wholesale quantities (i.e., cases). People from the co-ops accompany Roger on his rounds of the market, taking part in the backslapping, hand-shaking, produce tasting, and sampling of the coffee and donuts supplied by the larger wholesalers. The Broadway Co-op, which participates in this arrangement, finds it can offer better prices and quality than it could through a previous deal with a private concessioner who worked at the market. "We like it because it helps the other co-ops, too," a member noted.

Washington, D.C., co-ops use a similar arrangement. A woman buyer regularly accompanies the two women in the truck collective to the market several times a week. Because the wholesale market for D.C. co-ops is in Baltimore, co-ops had enough to gain in sharing transportation to foster the development of the truck collective.

OTHER KINDS OF CO-OPS

If you ask for directions to the local food co-op in cities around the country, you can't be sure about what sort of place you may find. In St. Louis or New York City, you might be directed to someone's apartment or to a vacant hallway. In Minneapolis you might be directed to a storefront, in any suburban area to a garage or backyard. Once you went inside the apartment (hallway, storefront, etc.) you might not recognize what people are doing.

Grab Bags

A small group of people in a New York City hallway run an almost unrecognizable co-op. They have no order forms, few people, not that much food. The members of this co-op might explain that in their organization there are no order forms because there are no orders. People pay a lump sum each week and divide up whatever produce the buyer of the week brings back. They can count on lettuce and tomatoes usually, but after that it's anybody's guess. "It's great for us," a member of such a co-op told me, "we're all friends on this floor of the building and we all eat pretty much the same kinds of food. When we put five dollars in every week we know we'll get our money's worth. We don't care much about what kind of produce we get. We're more interested in being sure that we get a nice assortment of fresh fruits and vegetables every week. In a way it's even nice to not know what kind of fruit you'll get. We're usually pleasantly surprised." The members of this kind of group often call it a co-op. They share the work of buying, bagging, and collecting money. They don't make any effort to have the co-op replace a substantial amount of supermarket shopping. In fact, they often have to buy produce at the supermarket to fill the gaps in their grab-bag orders. Nonetheless, the co-op is important to them because it provides them with a weekly base of food that is particularly hard for them to get in the supermarkets. The simplicity of their organization and the small amount of work required of members balance out some of this kind of co-op's limitations.

In parts of metropolitan Boston you would probably recognize that you're in a co-op. The Mission Hill Co-op, the North Cambridge Co-op, the Boston College, and numerous others

look pretty much the same as the Broadway Co-op. They are
all housed in different buildings, of course, but the crates of
vegetables, the scales, the bags, and the extreme amounts of
activity are unmistakably co-op. Some of the other co-ops are
indeed almost organizational duplicates of the Broadway group,
but a number that look the same in operations are not at all the
same in organization.

The co-op in suburban Marshfield, for example, is small
enough to be run without a committee of coordinators.
The twenty members simply run the group themselves, changing
job assignments as they choose (often weekly). The larger
Needham co-op and a number of other suburban co-ops run
almost the same as the Marshfield group.

Blocs

The Mission Hill group is a co-op of co-ops. It looks different
from the others in its dollar volume and inventory. A look at
Mission Hill on distribution day reveals three or four times
as much produce being subdivided as one finds back in
Somerville. Such activity could obviously get to be quite unwieldy
for an organization like Somerville's. Mission Hill handles higher
volume by using a bloc organization. It is made up of (at this
time) twenty blocs, really twenty small co-ops.

Each bloc contains seven to fifteen families and operates
itself as a small co-op. Some of the blocs come from
pre-existing groups that join the larger group, some are old blocs
that split or new combinations of older blocs. A few were
started with assistance from people in the co-op.

The blocs are usually very community-oriented, drawing
from one or two streets in a neighborhood or a small neighborhood organization. Every week members bring their orders to
the home of a fellow member, who collects and summarizes
orders each week. Then the day before distribution someone from
the bloc house (inevitably called the bloc head by many) calls
or brings the order to the major distribution point. At the end
of the next day, someone from the bloc picks up its order,
brings it back to the bloc house, and distributes it to the members.

The central distribution work of the co-op rotates among blocs.
At Mission Hill, for example, each of the twenty blocs takes a
turn at coming to the main distribution point and working out
the order for the whole co-op. Once every twenty weeks,
each bloc must accompany the buyer to Chelsea, bring

the food back, and distribute it according to orders submitted
by the twenty blocs. Bloc members can forget a lot over twenty
weeks, so there are usually one or two co-op coordinators on hand
to help out with questions. The central distribution differs
little from the order-making work of the Somerville co-op,
but the large scale complicates things. Bloc co-ops' dollar volumes
and membership totals are both four or five times greater than
those of single co-ops like Somerville. Mission Hill, for example,
has a weekly dollar volume of $1,500 vs. Somerville's $300.

Bloc co-ops can reduce the work loads of average members.
The weekly chores of distribution within the blocs are easily
managed. The small units also help promote group solidarity and
the social rewards many people look for in co-ops. Most members
seldom have to participate in major distribution work. When they
do, they can plan to set aside the time that central distribution
requires. The bloc organization helps give the co-op increased
economic strength while enabling it to remain "small." Although
the number of people involved in individual blocs is small,
the collection of blocs creates an economic strength impossible
for any single group. The economic strength can enable the co-op
to expand its inventory into perishables which need refrigeration
(difficult to manage with a small group) and to help new
blocs get started. Many bloc co-ops have almost no inter-bloc
interaction, except perhaps an occasional party. They concentrate
instead on making individual blocs strong.

Branches

Worcester's Community Stomach Co-op uses a branch system
similar to the bloc system. Like the bloc system, the branch
arrangement provides both for intimacy among small groups of
people and greater economic strength. The need for small co-ops
to affiliate is even greater in Worcester than it is close to Boston
because of the greater distance (about forty-five miles) to the
wholesale produce market.

There are seven branches in Community Stomach at present,
each with fifteen to forty active families. The co-op's weekly
dollar volume is around $500, down a bit from the $1,000
averages of several months ago. "Organizational problems—it
happens to everybody," their financial coordinator, Terry Dix,
explained. "We'll bounce back, we always do." About 100
families order through the co-op at any one time and about
150 are active overall.

Each branch voluntarily contributes people to central committees for shipping, purchasing, finance, publishing, etc. These committees take care of operations for the whole co-op. The committees are supplemented by locals (organizations of two or three branches) and general membership meetings. The general meetings are run like New England town meetings, with an effort to establish direct democracy. The quarterly meetings set price and product policy and establish committees and programs to deal with problems and new ideas.

"Each branch is responsible for its own affairs," Terry explained. Branches operate like blocs, except that branches are often larger and a bit more structured. A pamphlet put out by Community Stomach estimates that each member should work from 1½ to 3 hours every three weeks. Branches are housed in community centers and churches in several Worcester neighborhoods rather than in houses because of the size of the organizations.

The central committee system eliminates the arrangement in bloc co-ops of blocs having to distribute for the whole co-op. The committees handle the buying, transportation, and finances each week for the whole co-op. They spread the responsibilities so that work is more evenly distributed than in bloc systems. This sometimes makes for a less hectic organization—bloc people who've tried to run a large co-op for a day often get washed out. But the committee system entails greater organization. Branches must submit working schedules to the locals for review. The locals (consisting of several branches) check to see that all branch members are on the schedule and involved in the organization. The central committees themselves rely on the branches for manpower.

Some favor the branch system because it spreads responsibility more evenly throughout a co-op's membership, but others feel the extra organization required is not worth the extra work. Bloc co-op members know that they need only one "blowout" day over a large time period, and may be able to arrange their schedules around such a commitment. People working regularly, however, may find it easier to spread their commitments out during their leisure time.

All the weekly co-ops (called "food conspiracies" in some areas), from the New York City grab-bag types to bloc and branch co-ops, usually supply only a portion of most families' food requirements. Families do not live by produce alone, and even those co-ops that include cheese, dairy goods, and meats in

their inventories can't enable their members to completely
stay away from supermarkets. They can supply a large quantity
of some items at significantly reduced prices, and this is enough to
make them important for many families.

Storefronts

Some co-op enthusiasts go beyond the small inventories
available in weekly arrangements by setting up storefronts.
There is as much variation among these as there is among weekly
co-ops. One kind of storefront is the kind that grows out of
a successful pre-order co-op. Some of the bloc co-ops in
Cambridge are considering such a move. The Boston Food Co-op
has undergone such a change and has done quite well.

A Membership Storefront

BFC (as affectionately referred to by locals) started several
years ago with a $10,000 grant from the Student Union of
Boston University which paid for initial inventory, supplies, and
equipment. The co-op also used the grant to rent a university
building (an old warehouse) accessible to the student community.
The co-op severed ties with the university early in its history
but continued to rent the conveniently located building.
The initial organization of the co-op was a pre-order closely
resembling the Broadway Co-op. Each member submitted orders in
advance for food to be picked up later in the week. Many more
people joined the co-op, enabling the inventory to expand and the
pre-order system to run several days a week. Throughout all this,
all members were required to work two hours per month.

The organization finally reached a point where the errors
involved in calculating and tallying pre-orders were no greater than
the errors involved in guessing what people wanted, so they
eliminated the pre-order system. The co-op stopped having people
order and just opened its doors (somewhat cautiously). Members
were so enthusiastic about the idea of not having to order that
they overlooked inadequacies in inventory. The inadequacies
disappeared as the buyers got a better reading on what to expect
from the membership, and the organization has been developing
ever since.

Currently, BFC's weekly dollar volume is upwards of $23,000,
about that of a small supermarket. The board of directors (a mixed
group elected by the membership) recently voted to seal off
membership of about 4,000 members because the operation was

getting too big—too much to manage in the crowded space and too
big to be what members felt was a real co-op.

A BFC Shopping Expedition

You don't find the Boston Food Co-op unless you're looking
for it. Its entrance is on an alley called Babbitt Street in an
area of the city near the Back Bay most people refer to by the
name of its largest occupant—B.U. (colloquial for Boston University). It isn't that the co-op is hidden from public view—thousands
(from inside it seems like millions) of cars pass within ten feet
of the back of the building, where the Massachusetts Turnpike
extension slices through the city. But as there is no special exit
for the co-op, people have to come in through the alley sandwiched
between the turnpike and Commonwealth Avenue via a side street
off "Comm. Ave." The alley itself is a slalom run of potholes
lined with illegally parked cars which get towed at the whim of
local landlords. In the winter the alley is a Sahara of thick, brown
snow, a pawn in a philosophy of snow removal referred to by
some as "the Lord giveth and the Lord taketh away."

Cars that survive the obstacle course are rewarded with a
gift of free parking if (that's a big if) the lot has room and they
display a co-op decal. Cars without decals are often towed by
the university (the co-op rents the building and the lot from B.U.).
Whether the lot is full is not an emperical question—its capacity
is measured not in square feet but in members' flexible perceptions.
Depending on prevailing moods, capacity can be anywhere between
fifteen and more than twenty cars. Overflow from the lot is
faced with the impossible task of finding a space on the street.

Some co-op members avoid the driving/parking crunch
by using the ironically named rapid transit system on Comm. Ave.
Trolley service is regular and cheap if not quiet and uncrowded.
It is not uncommon to see a contingent of commuters standing
sentry over boxes of produce, waiting for a trolley.

The co-op building is a drab brick sample of the industrial
architecture of earlier decades. The outside is brightened by a
cavernous metal garbage receptacle that gets taken away and
replaced with an empty duplicate as needs require. Deliveries are
made at the large garage door through which members exit.
The entrance, several feet to the right, is a plain single door.
All the windows are covered by silver wired tape carrying the
alarm system, installed after a rash of robberies.

Members ascend a short flight of steps paralleling a platform

where recently emptied cardboard crates are stacked. Where
possible, the crates are used in lieu of bags. Members are
encouraged to bring in used boxes so that the co-op doesn't have
to buy a lot of bags. The boxes also replace shopping carts—
a member carries the boxes around in the store until, as they are
filling it like a picnic basket, it gets too heavy. Then the box
usually gets placed on the long table which lines up to the
cashier. With the box in place, members roam the store,
bringing armfuls of items back to the box. Although the boxes
are usually strong, some come apart in the middle of shopping,
sending oranges rolling around on the floor and jars crashing
to oblivion. Spinach boxes are notorious for this.

Armed with an empty box or two, members pass by the
broken meat grinder and enter a reception room. Filled bulletin
boards line the wall above an unconnected sink. Notices and
posters reach far beyond the borders of the bulletin board
onto the wall, over the doorway to the "store," and along
the wall perpendicular to the sink. The room is cluttered, but
in an orderly way. Things look as if they belong in their
places. The tables and floor are clean.

Someone there, usually a volunteer, sits at a table opposite
the bulletin board wall to greet members and check their
membership cards. People coming in are "carded" and their
names are checked in a large file to see if they have fulfilled
their work requirements. People who haven't met their two hour
per month work commitment for over a month or who have
no card are let in at the discretion of the door tender. Recently,
with the co-op's membership limited, door people have been
rather strict with people who have no cards. The work requirement's flexibility changes with the door tender, the mood of the
day, the tide. Members must work only when they shop at the
co-op, and needn't make up for months spent out of town.
Members mark their own cards as they complete their requirements.

Some members come in couples or teams, dividing into worker
and shopper components at the store. While one person shops,
the other sees a store manager for referral to whatever work
needs to be done at the moment. They may end up bagging
granola or flour, sweeping the floor, cutting cheese, or stocking
the shelves. The co-op is encouraging members to do this on
a planned basis. Stocking shelves and cleaning meat counters is
pleasant enough work in the atmosphere of the store, but the
irregularity of volunteer scheduling means that the store

management runs on a feast or famine supply of workers.
The feast is particularly evident when members cram to get
their time in on the last few days of the month. The co-op is
beginning to ask members to sign up for regular monthly work
brigades or for outside-the-store work like the granola collective.
Posters in the reception room advertise various free services
(piano lessons, tax preparation) offered to members by other
members as a way of filling their work requirements.

The real shopping begins when members enter the store.
The meat and fish counters to the right of the entry display a
full complement of beef and chicken cuts, luncheon meats and
cheeses, and seafood. Some people are initially intimidated by
the meat display—they half expect a butcher to serve them
and worry that perhaps they're not allowed behind the counters.
But no, there isn't an attendant. There may, however, be
someone on hand to answer questions about what cuts of meat
are available, how they might be prepared, etc. Most of the meat
is pre-cut, weighed, labeled, and priced so that members can
just pick it up and go. The luncheon meats come both in sliced
portions and unsliced chunks. Some imported cheeses are displayed
with the luncheon meats, as are lox and chicken livers.

The fish freezer at the rear of the meat department contains
an assortment of whitefish and shrimp. Shrimp and fishcakes are
pre-measured, but the frozen fish often is not. Members themselves
must weigh the fish packs on one of the nearby scales and
put prices on.

Proceeding past the meat department, members pass the
new bulk spice department. A scale is set up there amidst several
large jars filled with loose spices. The spices must be weighed,
measured out, and priced much the same as the fish. The bulk
spices are sold for very little money when compared with
supermarket spice tins. A sign over the spice jars informs members
that a more efficient spice rack is under construction.

The dairy cases come next on the tour. The lower halves
are filled with an assortment of cheeses ranging from Vermont
extra sharp cheddar through Syrian braided. Pieces of cheese
are enclosed in clear plastic wrap, having been weighed, priced,
and cut from a large cheese block by volunteers. The upper
parts of the cooler contain milk, butter, sour cream, and yogurt.
A particularly interesting item is the "Miracle Yogurt" sold in
quart containers and priced much below the other brands.
A close look at the label reveals the legend, "It's a miracle if it

tastes good" and a short list of ingredients conspicuously lacking
sugar or preservatives. (It actually does taste quite good.)
The address on the label is a residence near the co-op. According
to local myth, Miracle started out as a yogurt equivalent of
bathtub gin.

Moving along, members pass a low stand of bottled oils
and small bags of loose herbs for tea. Opposite the herbs is
a deep freezer used for frozen orange juice concentrate. The
freezer seems to be often empty because members' taste for
orange juice consistently outpaces the expectations of co-op buyers.
Fresh oranges and lemons are next to the freezer along with a
poster indicating that members should not choose lemons on
the basis of looks. The poster indicates that the "ugly lemons"
are as good, if not better, than their waxed-and-painted
counterparts.

One of the high points of the co-op is behind the oranges—
a walk-in cooler. The cooler is over seven feet high and the size
of a small room inside. A sign on the door reads: "Please keep
this door shut tightly. Thanks—The Compressor." Back-up
supplies of cheese, yogurt, some meat, poultry, and perishable
produce are kept in this walk-in cooler. Nonperishable produce
is displayed on rustic stands along the rear wall, near the windows
overlooking the turnpike. Two high rows of shelves nearer the
front of the store house canned goods and packaged items.
A rack of grain bins separates the packaged goods from the
produce. The grain is displayed in plastic bags, pre-measured and
priced by volunteers. Bread, bagels, cake, and crackers are near
the grain.

The new bulk oils section is near the center of the store.
These were established in spite of paranoia about the spills born
when a BFC member witnessed the upending of a fifty-five gallon
drum of peanut butter in Minneapolis. The bulk items on display
aren't in such large containers but there is still considerable worry
and careful instructions posted above the cans. Using the bulk
system is a bit complicated, but it can yield savings that can't
be matched. Posters encourage members to bring their own jars.
If people don't bring their own containers they are usually not
able to buy in bulk as jars are seldom available at the co-op.
Some resourceful members solve this dilemma by drinking a quart
of orange juice while they're shopping and using the emptied jar
for other liquids to be brought home.

Instructions for the bulk liquids direct members to weigh a

jar before filling it, then to fill it, then subtract the weight of
the jar before calculating the price. The mathematics are not
difficult and the scale is marked to give continuous price readouts
for all possible weights. Actually getting the liquids out of the
nondescript metal tins is a dramatic process. Oils are gravity
siphoned through plastic tubing, regulated with clamps. The honey
pours thickly from a tilted metal can directly past a flap valve.
Bulk liquid soap is available in the same way.

When members' orders are complete, they line up at the cash
registers, pay, and go. The cashier tallies all the items, which are
marked at the price the co-op pays for them. At the end of the
tally, a 10 percent surcharge is added to cover the co-op's
operating expenses. The cashier sells co-op pens, buttons, and
decals. Checks are accepted.

There is usually a lot of activity in the storefront during
shopping hours. A radio perched on one of the meat cases
provides suitable background music. Volunteers stroll around,
unpacking crates, trying futilely to answer shoppers' questions,
and keeping the shelves stocked. There's a lot of conversation—
questions, comments, small talk—while waiting in line. Even for
old-timers, co-op prices and marketing techniques are never-ending
topics. Conversation seems to be the norm, even among strangers.
Signs and posters for everything add to the atmosphere. A banner
thanking Roger Auerbach for his service to the co-op remains
posted over the vegetable section months after the party that
was given in his honor. A sign near the granola notes: "This
granola isn't just heavenly, it's ethereal. Tho get thum for
breakfast." A standard federal poster for base price information
near the meat counter has been filled in to read: "For further
information on the base prices in this store, contact *the
President at the White House* . . . ." There's a coffee pot and
some cups near the cashiers and a "muncheez jar" on the meat
counter for contributions for snacks eaten while shopping.

Most people end their shopping tours at the cashiers, but if
they can navigate the winding, narrow metal stairs, some visit
the free store downstairs. The free store offers what the name
implies—free things. Co-op members are asked to bring in
their surplus clothes, books, dishes, whatever. They may take
whatever they want. An embryonic carpentry shop and a
small meeting room are also located in the basement.

Community Stores

Some co-ops don't require membership or participation. They are just storefronts which offer discounts to volunteer workers or encourage community participation in other ways. There are more than ten such storefronts in the Minneapolis-St. Paul area, each organized in a way that doesn't exactly duplicate any other. Some are run by small (ten to fifteen) member collectives that do most of the work and sometimes reimburse themselves for their efforts. When such payment exists it is usually quite low—normally $30 for three shifts. Each shift lasts from six to ten hours. For some people the payment is a sole means of support—it can be done, especially if people live communally. People who belong to food co-ops run as collectives are involved on a scale much different from that of people in participatory co-ops. For many of their members, work collectives are full-time jobs.

Co-op stores that aren't run by collectives are organized and operated by volunteers, often with extremely intricate scheduling. It is difficult to imagine, when looking at or shopping in one of these stores that there is no manager, no paid staff. Some storefronts have work teams for each day of the week; others set up specific committees for co-op functions (bread purchasing, store maintenance, bookkeeping); still others use combinations of approaches. I couldn't quite understand how the stores can operate since people who try to operate similar stores on a profit-making basis often can't do it. Most of the co-ops are in onetime Ma and Pa stores that went out of business. But it does work. The people show up, the work gets done, and the stores look good. Workers are a mix of "I've lived here all my life" older folks and younger transients, with increasing numbers of neighborhood people on the way in. The volunteers come with a variety of motives not unlike those of the people who belong to buying clubs. Many of them put in less time than members of buying clubs and have the benefits of a store open daily. Although they may become big and impersonal, the stores can still offer people social benefits and economic gains. A storefront can be used more often than a weekly co-op, and for more kinds of food. It belongs to all the shoppers and it can be a focal point for neighborhood activities.

Green Grass Grocery in St. Paul is a good example of a storefront run by volunteers. Its major responsibilities are handled by coordinators assigned to various store functions—meat, bread, grains, bookkeeping coordinators, etc. Each oversees the handling of a product from purchase to sale. Other people can work with a coordinator or simply come to the storefront and see what needs to be done. The coordinators were originally a small group of neighborhood people (about ten of them) involved in other community work.

The coordinators are a mixed group reflecting the heterogeneity of the neighborhood. Students and young people handle some functions, a woman in her fifties is the vegetable coordinator; an ex-bookkeeper in his sixties is the financial coordinator. All the coordinators are volunteers, but there is an expectation that the co-op will be able to provide wages for some of them.

There is no manager, but a person who works for the community agency wanders in and out of the storefront frequently. Who's minding the store is established by a schedule at weekly meetings which also review problems, ideas, and the need for new products. Storekeepers are signed up from the group of coordinators and from the community in general.

People who work at the co-op, whether as storekeepers or interested volunteers, pay 10 percent less for their food than the normal 20 percent markup. When I visited the store, the cashier asked each customer, "Are you a worker?" and "Would you like to be a worker?" explaining what work involved and provided. A card file recording the time (three hours per month qualify a worker for the discount) put in by each worker contained 150 names when I visited the store.

While there is no membership *per se* in the co-op, shoppers hold a status different from that in regular corner stores. "If you want to help us make decisions, come to our meetings," a descriptive flyer invites. "Everyone is welcome." Besides decision-making and help in store operations, customers are requested to "bring your own sacks, egg cartons, and other containers" and to "please fill your own container and weigh your own purchases." (For a fuller description of Green Grass see Appendix A.)

Green Grass made an active attempt to get shoppers to participate in store operations by offering a differential discount policy and asking people to drop by, but some storefronts operate without any attempt to involve the community in store operations. Stores run as work collectives, for example, may only survey community needs informally and run the co-op

on their own. At Stone Soup in Washington, D.C., Steve Clark
explained that volunteers are welcomed, but a collective of ten
people actually runs the store. Stone Soup does not try for
much community involvement. "The most important aspect is
that the people who work here control the business," he
points out. Stone Soup maintains a payroll of $100 a week
for each of the ten members of the collective. The collective
feels that its significance lies not so much in providing high
food quality, low prices, and a different store environment as in
creating viable jobs in an alternative economy.

While most people involved with storefronts agree that they
should relate to their respective communities, there is little
agreement on what the relationship should look like. Bruce
Singer, who is working on organizing the Washington, D.C.,
Warehouse, told me that there is considerable disagreement over
the meaning of "community ownership," a phrase which many
area co-ops claim applies to them.

For example, each of the ten members of Stone Soup
receives a substantial paycheck from the proceeds of sales.
Like Green Grass, Minneapolis's Powderhorn Food Community
has no paid staff. But instead of coordinators it has a collection
of voluntary collectives that manage individual areas and
coordinate to manage the store. Both are successful on their
own terms, but the terms are quite different.

Though they are quite different, Stone Soup and Powderhorn,
Boston Food Co-op, Community Stomach, and Broadway Food
Co-op all call themselves co-ops. The label is accurate in that they
all involve a degree of cooperation among some people, but
misleading and confusing to the uninitiated. The use of the co-op
name also is upsetting to some of the people in the Cooperative
League of the U.S.A. The Cooperative League is the organization
that links a variety of cooperative services in the U.S. It includes
credit unions, farmers' co-ops, mutual insurance companies, and to
further confuse the naming of Stone Soup, Powderhorn, etc., a
chain of cooperative supermarkets.

Cooperative League

A 1971 Cooperative League fact sheet indicated that there were
257 food and home supplies co-ops with 560,791 total member
families and a total yearly dollar volume of $441 million. The
Greenbelt supermarkets in the Washington, D.C., area are co-ops
and there are a number in New York City, New England, and the

Midwest. The co-op in Berkeley, California is particularly well-developed. It's no wonder that these organizations frequently look with scorn on the smaller new co-ops and refer to them as "buying clubs." Cooperative League supermarkets are sometimes called "Twin Pines" after their trademark or "Rochdale" after their history (see later chapters). They often don't look much different from regular supermarkets, though a number of them stress consumerism. Their prices are the same as regular supermarket prices. They call themselves cooperatives because they are owned by their memberships, and they distribute whatever profits they earn to members as a yearly patronage refund based on what members spend. Unlike the new co-ops, members don't participate in the store operations except to elect a board of directors. Members can establish consumer education committees and work on starting other co-ops.

European and other foreign co-ops generally follow the League model for organization. Co-ops in other countries have acquired formidable economic clout. Swedish co-ops handle 15 percent of the nation's total retail trade and 25 percent of the food business. Co-ops account for 9 percent of England's retail trade.[2] But co-ops have developed differently in those countries from the way they've evolved in the U.S. The state of co-op development in different countries is symptomatic of different political cultures.

I asked Art Danforth, executive treasurer of the League, to clarify the difference between a co-op and a regular chain-store supermarket. He explained that both returned profits to a group of people—a co-op to its members, a corporation to its share-holders—but co-op membership was more spread out than corporation shareholders. "Sure, a lot of people own shares in supermarkets, but a very few people own a lot of shares." Share ownership in a co-op is limited in the amount available to each member and spread out, making the co-op a sort of people's corporation. The co-ops further differ from regular supermarkets in that their employees and managers are motivated by consumerism. Managers of regular supermarkets are accountable to shareholders; managers of co-op supermarkets are accountable to members who are usually shoppers.

But co-op supermarkets in practice don't always follow the theories. Mr. Danforth, referring to the concept of store management's accountability, commented, "We don't push that button hard enough." There is little to set some co-op supermarkets

apart from regular supermarkets. This is partly because, at the
urging of new laws and profitable concepts, regular supermarkets
are item pricing and showing well-advertised but questionable
concern for consumer interests. The distinction is further
blurred by the co-ops themselves, which are simply too big,
too prosperous, too impersonal, and too much like supermarkets.
There are some exceptions to this (exceptions are the rule for
all co-ops), but the overall image of co-op supermarkets among
members of the new co-ops is one of big business. One "buying
club" member remarked, "Buying clubs my foot. We're more
cooperative than those supermarkets could ever hope to be."

Links between the old and new co-ops are at this time
only beginning to take shape. The new co-ops began and
developed largely on their own, and what help they did get
from outside institutions included almost no support from
the older co-ops. The links being formed now and the
reasons behind them are described in the chapter on co-op
history. There is also some overlap in the emerging paths of
new and old co-ops. Both are trying to expand, to involve
greater numbers of people. The Cooperative League helps fund
such agencies as the Council for Self-Help Development in
New York City, which tries to initiate supermarket-type co-ops
in low-income areas. Members of New York City's newer
co-ops are trying to serve the same people by helping them set up
"buying clubs." The League and the new co-ops also overlap
in NASCO (North American Student Cooperatives Organization),
an arm of the League which reaches out to students and interacts
with many new midwestern co-ops.

A particularly interesting "new" form of co-ops will probably
inspire further overlap. The League is currently supporting a co-op
form called direct charge that is of considerable interest to the
new co-ops. Direct-charge co-ops have been most successful in
Canada, particularly in British Columbia. They sell all items at cost,
without any markup. They cover necessary operating costs
(and more) by charging each member a set amount—perhaps two
or three dollars per week per family. The direct charge (of two or
three dollars) gives the co-op a guaranteed financial base that it
can use to expand inventories and operations. Unlike regular co-op
supermarkets, direct-charge co-ops offer shoppers lower prices.
Newsletters from co-ops in British Columbia read like rags-to-
riches stories and cover reviews of new items like color television
sets. As of this writing, several people are experimenting with

direct-charge co-ops in western Massachusetts while other new
co-ops in the area look on with interest.

Whatever problems people have differentiating between the old
co-op supermarkets and regular stores don't seem to exist for
the new co-ops. Prices are much lower at the new co-ops;
people participate in actually running the new co-ops. Also, the
new food co-ops look different from "regular" supermarkets and
stores. Weekly co-ops are run wherever small groups of people
have the ingenuity to find the space—garages, basements, apartment
hallways, church halls, etc. The small spaces ensure that weekly
co-ops will look different from supermarkets, but the differences
extend 'way beyond the spaces they inhabit. The tone of business
is friendlier, warmer, looser. There's more conversation. Business
aspects like bookkeeping, supplies, and equipment are handled
with as much ingenuity as spacefinding. Some weekly co-ops
use baby scales to weigh produce and old Salvation Army
refrigerators to store meat. Even co-ops that have storefronts
have a way of being different. They're usually located in
unconventional buildings, often in unconventional neighborhoods.
Madison, Wisconsin's, Whole Earth Learning Community has a
prominent location next door to a do-it-yourself nude photography
studio (models provided). Boston's Mission Hill co-op is near
an alleged gambling front that figured prominently in a recent
newspaper expose. The buildings themselves may have
intricacies that make life more interesting, like the lock of
Minneapolis's Powderhorn co-op. A newsletter (January 1974)
instructs members:

(T)here is a trick to it. Most of us have found it workable when we
do as follows – 1. insert the key. 2. put toe of foot against the bottom
of the door and push in. 3. lean knee of same leg into the door and
4. turn key.

Even the internal store operations are different. Displays in
cardboard boxes, on plain metal shelves, with huge bulk
containers and outdated refrigeration machinery would give
supermarket managers nightmares. Even the business operations
are—different. The large pigeonhole filing slots above the
coordinator's desk at the North Country Co-op in Minneapolis
bear such labels as "Deposits and error correction slips;
more bank shit; food research; relief shit," etc.

Although the kind of people involved in food co-ops is
diversifying to include more families and fewer young and

"fringe" people, there is still a substantial and active core of
people that Middle America would classify as "different."
Ronald Wolff of Oakland's Alternative Foodstore sums up the
store's environment:

Many workers at the Alternative have meager mathematical abilities,
which causes hassles at the scales and check-out counter. Same
with our customers. We are in a low-income artsy-craftsy neighborhood—
many gays, genuine loonies, older people as well as young, spaced-out
hippies, etc. A smattering of the cosmos, you could say.

FARM DEALS

Though wholesale markets offer low prices and entertainment,
many co-ops are trying to bypass them and deal directly with
farmers. These attempts have met with mixed success and are
not really feasible for a single small co-op. Groups of co-ops
seem to do better. Eighteen New York City co-ops dealt extensively with the Natural Organic Farmers Association in the
summer of 1973. There were some problems with consistency/
uniformity ("The farmers kept using different-sized boxes,"
one man observed.) and delivery ("Sometimes they just couldn't
get the food ready in time."). Basic food production was
tooth and nail, since most of the farmers in the association were
amateurs, transplanted city folk. "They called us up one week
and said, 'Sorry, but all your food is dead,' " one New Yorker
told me. But the overall experience was a successful one and
people are looking forward to more business in the coming year.
    New England's experience with direct farm dealing was on
a smaller scale, but was set up in an interesting way. A
sympathetic New Hampshire landholder gave over some acreage
for free use by co-ops. A farming group formed with members
from several co-ops and sold farm shares for $10.00 to members
of various co-ops. Shareholders were entitled to a share of
whatever the weekly harvest was. The weekly harvests had
mixed yields, to say the least, but most people agreed that they
got their money's worth. The farm was in operation in the
summer of 1972 but not 1973 because there was a farmer
shortage—co-ops members who ran the farm previously wanted a
year off. In the coming year links will be made with more
established local farmers.
    With their location, it's of little wonder that the midwestern
co-ops seem to be making the greatest strides in farmer

relationships. According to Paul Schultz, who works for the
American Friends Service Committee organizing farmers to sell
to co-ops, the farmer-co-op network in the Illinois-Michigan-
Wisconsin area now includes forty farmers. Though he didn't have
full figures when we talked, he was certain that one farm in
Michigan had done $5,000 in co-op business in the summer of
1973. The farmers in the league are not career farmers. Mr.
Schultz believes they can be categorized into equal-sized groups
of established farmers—those with three to six years experience—
and newcomers. "There are many part-time farmers," he reports.
Mr. Schultz tries to get co-ops to draw up contracts with farmers
by holding meetings bringing co-ops and farmers together. Because
of the uncertainties of food production the contract is primarily a
statement of intent. "There's a lot of give and take on both sides,"
he noted. Although this sort of ordering process can only be done
well by co-ops who can project with some minimal accuracy what
their produce needs will be, groups of small co-ops can assemble
enough volume and flexibility to make a farm deal worthwhile.

As of this writing, co-ops along the east coast are planning
inter-co-op farm deals for the summer of 1974. These will, if
successful, link Boston, Connecticut, New York, and Washington,
D.C., co-ops with farms in the southeast.

Dealing directly with farmers can provide, in addition to lower
prices and better food, a way for co-ops to bypass another link in
the standard economy of food distribution. No wholesalers are
involved. Direct dealing with farmers can also make it easier for
those co-ops interested in organic foods to make their needs felt
more directly. A co-op member in Washington, D.C., told me
of local plans to use direct farm deals to influence the economics
of production. He thought it would be a good idea to have farmers
set prices by their needs rather than by the unpredictable forces
of the supply-demand market. Consumer co-ops dealing directly
with farms can guarantee an income base that would enable
farmers to bypass the normal market system. Establishing farmer
relations often adds a side benefit, too. Co-op members in New
York, New England, and the midwest all reported some use
of the farms by city folk interested in "going up the country,"
"working on a real farm," or just getting an opportunity to
get out of the city for a bit. Farmers welcomed the free labor,
providing barn or tent space, and in some cases, food.

Where possible, Paul Schultz thinks it sound practice for
consumer co-ops to deal with producer co-ops and collectives.

He believes that the shared principle of "people wanting more
control over their lives" will be strengthened if producer and
consumer co-ops support each other. At present, small producers'
co-ops seem willing to deal with the new food co-ops. (Co-ops in
New York are currently trying to link up with black farmers in
the South, as some Chicago co-ops have already reportedly begun
to do.) The older, more established producer co-ops, however,
have become high-volume businesses, indistinguishable in most
ways from regular corporations more interested in money than
in forwarding co-operative principles. (The milk producers of
campaign contribution fame are co-ops.)

Different areas of the country offer varying benefits and
hindrances in produce buying. Physical proximity between farms
and co-ops helps minimize delivery and communication problems.
Also, wholesale market structures in different areas spawn
numerous co-operative "solutions." The cooperative buying done
by Roger Auerbach for NEFCO is made more worthwhile by
the extreme inbreeding and dislike of outsiders at the New
England Produce Center. In Chicago, a wholesaler who has taken
an active interest in co-ops reaps financial gains from the
organization he has helped start. Minneapolis co-ops, which are
advanced in cooperation among themselves, don't cooperate
to buy produce because the local produce centers are small and
fairly open. New York co-ops combat costly and troublesome
city transportation to the Hunt's Point market by subscribing to a
co-op delivery run. Midwestern co-ops generally have an easier
time with wholesalers simply because, as was mentioned before,
the word "co-op" is not new or suspicious in the midwest.

SUPPORT INDUSTRIES

Food co-ops have contributed economic and moral support
for burgeoning spin-off "industries" in various parts of the country.
Co-op warehouses service the metropolitan areas of Minneapolis,
Chicago, New York, Washington, and several places on the
West Coast. There are bakeries that are closely tied to the
co-ops in Minneapolis and Rochester. Two trucking collectives
serve midwestern co-ops and two more are being planned by
Washington, D.C., and Boston co-ops. Minneapolis has a co-op
restaurant and a co-op dry goods/hardware store.

Though they may be called co-ops, the support industries are
usually work collectives. From about three to ten people each

use the industry as a source of livelihood. The collectives are usually anti-profit and closely linked to food co-ops in the area. Often the collectives encourage customers to volunteer in running the operation, but there are no requirements. Most collectives seem to try to "break down traditional economic roles" as they put it, encouraging workers to relate closely to customers.

Warehouses

Warehouses enable co-ops to benefit from economies of scale, by coordinating buying at a scale involving many groups and saving much money. Also, warehouses can store items so that co-ops can devote precious floor space to other tasks.

The People's Warehouse in Minneapolis recently moved to a building which it is buying. It raised an $18,000 down payment toward the full $70,000 price by soliciting loans and charging co-ops a 10 percent overhead on the goods they buy. The warehouse is in a mixed-use part of the city. It looks very much like a warehouse, except that it is exceptionally clean and well-ordered. There are 6,000 square feet of space in the building (4,000 ft. for storage, 2,000 ft. for other uses), filled with assorted grain bags piled on trucking pallets. There's room for a flour mill (under construction as of this writing). The spice room houses large shelves filled with jars of bulk spices and the small office houses harried workers. A sign on the office door reads: "Food prices high? Eat the rich." Access from the warehouse to cars and trucks is easy via a loading platform.

An eight-person collective runs the warehouse. Each person works three ten-hour shifts per week. Workers earn $30 per week, enough for most of them to make ends meet if they live cheaply. Rents and other living expenses are not high in Minneapolis, but $30 per week is still a minimal amount. When I visited in late December 1973, one of the members told me that collective members were usually able to get along on the low salaries, but there were occasional problems. "We were doing fine until Thanksgiving," she remarked. "Now we're all about a week behind."

The collective could afford to pay itself more money, but members are adamant about keeping wages low to set an example of nonmaterialistic living. "The important thing is not that it's $30 or any other specific amount, but that it's a 'people's wage,' geared to real needs." This is an important part of what the group tries to communicate to the rest of society.

The group feels that special needs of members should be
responded to with pay increases where necessary, but that such
increases should be made on the basis of individual needs rather
than salary policies.

The warehouse collective was enjoying a run of economic
strength when I visited. Warehouse economics seem generally
to come in runs. The collective scrimps and saves in order
to place large orders, then they rake the money in as co-ops
buy out the inventory. This feast-or-famine approach was
bringing them a $1,200 monthly surplus above operating costs.
They were busy at work plowing the surplus back into more
bulk orders and building payments.

The collective's success comes from its ability to supply the
co-ops with high-quality goods at low prices. It is able to do
this better than any single co-op because that's all it does.
Its members don't have to worry about retail sales or store
management. They can concentrate on getting the best deals,
on identifying and building strong relationships with small local
producers and large, faraway producers. Producer links are
cherished and valuable. They have significant effects on the
availability, quality, and price of the food that comes in.
The warehouse collective can also develop more efficient and
sensitive ways of distributing food to the co-ops, serving them
better than any profit-making distributor would want to or
could. The warehouse caters to existing co-ops and helps new
co-ops get started by providing credit for new inventory.

The inventory developed by the warehouse concentrates
on beans, grains, and other dry bulk food items. Some nonfoods
(Tampax) and a substantial spice collection round out the stock.
The collective steers clear of produce because they feel it is
too hard to keep the produce fresh. Also, the availability of
produce in the Minneapolis area does not enable co-ops to
significantly deflate market prices.

Warehouses in other areas do not always replicate the
Minneapolis model. Chicago's Cornucopia warehouse is run by
a collective and stresses the distribution of produce rather than
grains. People's Warehouse in New York hit a high point of
activity in the summer of 1973 when it coordinated produce
shipments from organic farmers in southern New England direct
to New York City co-ops and day care centers. Their work
enabled some fifteen co-ops and thirty day care centers to
bypass the Hunt's Point wholesale market during the growing

season. The New York warehouse was not run as a
collective but as an arm of local co-ops. Each co-op
participating in the warehouse was to supply one volunteer to
keep the warehouse going.

Both the Chicago and New York warehouses have had some
difficulties. Cornucopia's neglect to account for spoilage in crates
of produce it subdivides for smaller groups has led it to absorb
losses and face financial troubles. New York's group has been
moved about by a fickle landlord (urban renewal) who can't make
long-lasting decisions on which buildings it will demolish. Winter
months severed connections with frozen eastern farmers, and the
low volume of the co-ops stopped the warehouse from making
"big deals" with large southern and western producers. As of this
writing, the warehouse houses the remains of a mixed-quality
organic orange shipment from Texas and a lot of loose floor-
boards. The remnants of the organization have been taken up by
one person who buys for and delivers to several city co-ops for a
slight markup charge. The future of the New York warehouse
looks bleak. Enthusiasm is down since the warehouse has been
unable to live up to expectations during the winter. The crushing
blow may be delivered by the Southern New England farmers
organization that provided the bulk of New York's produce in
the summer of 1973. At this point it appears that the farmers
may deal exclusively with the expanding New England co-ops.

Several people in the Washington, D.C., area are trying to
get a new warehouse started. Bruce Singer, who is leading the
effort, informed me that the warehouse would begin by carrying
grains and dry goods and hopefully move on to produce and
possibly meat and cheese. He was being supported by the
Glut and Stone Soup storefronts in his efforts, and was trying to
set up the warehouse to serve them and other new stores on
the horizon. He was also interested in having the warehouse
take an active role in helping suburban buying-club-type co-ops.
When we spoke, he hadn't yet settled on a building. He had
spent several months carefully researching wholesale buying
and selling mechanisms and establishing relationships with
wholesalers in the area. He located wholesalers by tracing food
that co-ops bought from local wholesalers back to the people
that sold to them. Some of these were brokers who handled
other items, too. In most cases he reported that people were
willing to talk and interested in dealing with the warehouse.

Mr. Singer was unsure of the structure of the warehouse with

regard to participation from co-ops and the forming of a
collective. He thinks people should be added as the need arises
and there are too many variables to make specific plans. He does
plan to develop close ties with nearby farmers wherever
possible.

The warehouses overall add a kind of synergism to co-ops
they work with. By establishing physically separate facilities
from the co-ops, the warehouses are able to pursue the business
of wholesale buying more competently, unhindered by the
distractions of co-op operations. They can also gear themselves
to helping co-ops, something most co-ops would like to do but
can't because of their own problems. Though their organizational
form has not been completely ironed out, they can be economically viable and they're quite valuable for co-ops.

Bakeries

Co-op bakeries that I know of are at this time doing business
in Rochester, New York, and Minneapolis. Groups of people are
doing co-op-related baking in Boston and other areas with some
plans for broader operations, but the Rochester and Minneapolis
bakeries are the most established. The mechanics of bakery
production/operation make baking a relatively easy task for
co-op groups. Canning, freezing, freeze-drying, etc. all require
much more complicated equipment. Baking can be done in
places like churches that have institutional ovens and in
neighborhood, small-scale bakery facilities. Baked goods are often
particularly appealing to co-op members because they're
inexpensive and because they can be manufactured to suit
the tastes of purchasers, i.e., not bland, and conspicuously
lacking preservatives and other questionable ingredients.

The People's Company bakery in Minneapolis is closely
linked to co-ops in the area. It supplies them with most of
what it produces—a total of about 500 loaves of bread daily,
along with granola, cookies, and large sheet cakes which they
cut up and sell by the piece. The bakery also sells some items
at its storefront. Depending on the weather, the day, the
bakery takes in between $200 and $500 daily. I sampled some
of the bread varieties, the cookies, and the cake and was
much impressed. The bakery looks much like the "normal"
bakery it was ten or twenty years ago in pre-co-op days, though
there are some distinguishing characteristics. It's in a mixed-use
neighborhood across the street from a bank and near a large

Sears store and a movie theater. The building is not much wider
than the bars and luncheonettes on the block, and the low
aluminum walls and large mural on the window of a clenched fist
holding a sheaf of wheat suggest that it is not a typical
neighborhood bakery.

Inside there are some display counters, mirrors on some of
the walls, and a waiting-room sofa. When I visited, several people
were sitting on the sofa, chatting or reading, apparently not
waiting for anything but enjoying the bakery as a social gathering
place. The displays were about half-filled, mostly with cookies
and pieces of cakes. The modest display area opened into a large,
clean back workroom. Several large stainless steel refrigerators
lined the right wall adjacent to a "nerve center" where inventories,
orders, and sales records were kept. Long work tables, dough
mixers, coating racks, ingredients in bulk (flour sacks, etc.) and
of course ovens filled the rest of the space.

There was little activity in the bakery during my visit at
mid-day because as one worker explained, "We do all our work
early in the morning so we can get the goods out to the co-ops
and because the ovens make the place hot." A few workers were
cleaning up. One person was using the massive chopping block
and what appeared to be a dough cutter to chop some fresh
vegetables into an interesting-looking salad.

One worker stopped cleaning up to describe how the bakery
operates: "It's a nonprofit partnership. There are about twenty
people in the partnership and fifteen regular workers. The regulars
get first choice of three eight-to-ten-hour work shifts a week.
The length of the shifts depends on what we bake, how much,
and whether you get stoned. People sign up for shifts at meetings
on Sundays. There are five or six substitutes, too. New people
start out as volunteers. There're usually plenty of people around to
work in the winter, but we have problems during the summer.
We sometimes have problems getting experienced people, too."

The bakery workers didn't seem to be as dedicated to bare
subsistence-level living as the warehouse people. The worker
explained: "Thirty dollars a week is really not enough for most
people. They make up the difference between the thirty and what
they need by taking on other part-time work, or doing a full-time
outside work jag for a few months. One woman makes hats
that sell at 'The Dry Goods,' another woman works at Mill City
Co-op and here. Oh, and there are very few students—only one
in the bakery group."

The biggest and most persistent problem that the bakery has is personnel. Aside from seasonal shortages and surpluses, there is much turnover during most of the year. The turnover cuts down on the strength of interpersonal relationships and reduces the efficiency of the workers. This doesn't critically hamper the way the bakery functions—friendliness helps compensate for seniority and the work isn't all that technical. Also, there are almost always enough people to bake the bread. Turnover is nonetheless a bother because it disrupts organization.

The bakery serves a unique purpose for the co-ops in that it provides them with a product of higher quality and at lower prices than they could get on the regular wholesale market. The bakery also adds an extra dimension of independence to the co-ops' operations—they can bypass other bread producers completely if they want. The bakery itself benefits from the independence, creating a micro-economy in co-op circles. It buys most of its ingredients from the warehouse and sells to the co-ops and occasionally to the co-op restaurant.

Trucking Collectives

All co-ops need some way of bringing what they buy to their members. Sometimes the distance between a co-op and the places it buys from is formidable. In many cases, deliveries to co-ops are so geographically scattered and chronologically sporadic that the co-ops have to rely on paid trucking services. Weekly or daily produce runs are often handled by the co-op itself with a bought, rented, or borrowed truck. But the trucking business is complicated, bothersome, and somewhat grueling, so many co-ops seek out other ways of taking care of it.

The co-op in Needham, Massachusetts, pays a driver to bring a van into the Chelsea Wholesale Market, load it with the produce bought by the NEFCO buyer, and bring it back to the co-op's church basement operations center. A man in New York City combines delivery service with wholesale buying at the Hunt's Point for co-ops that have a difficult time getting to the market.

Trucking collectives involve more people and operate on a larger scale than these delivery services. The two-woman trucking collective in Washington, D.C., for example, makes frequent runs to the wholesale market in Baltimore, taking care of the orders of several D.C. area co-ops. The increasingly independent col-

lective began as an attachment to one of the co-ops, branching
out from produce runs to summertime farm runs and other
delivery needs.

Midwestern trucking collectives are making significant strides
in linking co-ops with each other and with producers. The I.C.C.
collective specializes in a loop around Lake Michigan that includes
co-ops, warehouses, producers, and farmers in Ann Arbor, Chicago,
Milwaukee, Madison, Minneapolis, and the rural areas in between.
In an article in *Network*, the magazine of Madison, Wisconsin's,
Whole Earth Learning Community, Ken Crocker described a trip
that included: dropping off soy-oil, sunflower, and sesame seeds at
the Quercus Alba Bakery in Oregon, Wisconsin; unloading goods
at the Ann Arbor warehouse; making a side trip to northern
Michigan in a rented truck; buying wholesale produce at the
Water Street market in Chicago; picking up goods at Sinai Kosher
Market; picking up dry goods at Foods for Life in suburban
Chicago; dropping off goods at the Fertile Dirt restaurant and
Outpost Co-op in Milwaukee; picking up dry milk at Pabst Farms
near Milwaukee; picking up apple cider and returning to Madison.[3]

The Dick-Freeman Trucking Company ("the straight name
for a workers' collective in Bloomington, Illinois," according to
Ed Dick) recently broke from its midwestern routes to coordinate
with six midwest co-ops the purchase and shipment of 38,000
pounds of organic oranges, dates, raisins, and almonds from
California to Minneapolis, Chicago, Milwaukee, and Ann Arbor.
They've also shipped grain from the warehouse in Minneapolis
to other co-op warehouses in Seattle, Washington, and Rochester,
New York. Dick-Freeman is a very active collective. They have
a 1972 Diamond Reo tractor and a refrigerated trailer which
they use for a variety of work, not all of it co-op. At present
co-ops don't have enough volume to keep them busy, but they
do co-op runs whenever possible and are planning for expansion
in that area.

Co-op members in the Boston area are planning for some sort
of cooperative trucking to handle the increased activity of NEFCO,
and the Washington, D.C., co-ops are reviewing the status of
their trucking arrangement for the same reason. Trucking support
for co-ops doesn't seem to have developed as much as the
warehouses and bakeries, probably because of the expenses and
economics of trucking as a service. "The economics of trucking
demand that you keep rolling," observes Ed Dick. With such
pressures it's difficult to establish a strong organization. The

truckers are accordingly loose. There is probably enough activity
among co-ops to sustain cooperative truckers, but the specifics
seem to need working out.

Restaurants, Dry Goods, Etc.

Variations on the collective theme are endless, and they may
not always develop from food co-ops. In the Boston area, about
forty-five work collectives evolved in the past few years. The
collectives are organized around a wide variety of services.
There are some organic restaurants, a health foods store, musicians
groups, an auto repair garage, a carpentry service, and so on.
They are generally made up of small groups of people who enjoy
their work and are more interested in having control over their
work than in earning large salaries. Some of them do earn
considerably more than "people's wages," but a number are
anti-profit. They are linked to local food co-ops only by the
fact that many collective members also belonged to co-ops. In
late 1973 as the work collectives began to develop a "collective
of collectives," they also began making more formal links to
food co-ops. There are some informal links (some of the
restaurants buy from the co-ops) but great potential is over
the hill.

There are some collectives in Minneapolis that are unaffiliated
with the co-ops, but the network seems closer (because Minneapolis is smaller?). There seems to be greater interchanging among
people in the groups. Also, the largest collectives were fall-outs
of co-ops. The warehouse, the bakery, the restaurant, and
the dry-goods store were all spin-offs of food co-ops and food
co-op people.

Chapter Two

STARTING A FOOD CO-OP

Although largely unrecognized, or at least undiscussed, starting a food co-op is not unlike attending an orgy. Neither requires any experience. At both, people interact with others, perhaps making new friends and often discovering new ways of doing things. The experience is usually enjoyable, but it takes a bit of energy. And of course, the possibilities are infinite.

Most articles, pamphlets, and handbooks on how to start a food co-op unfortunately omit this last point. There are lots of ways to start successful co-ops, plenty of room for innovation and new ideas. The only ingredients necessary to start a food co-op are: a group of people, some space to put them in, some of their money to buy food, someone to sell them the food, and some way for them to distribute the food back among the group. The specifics are open to much discussion among the groups themselves. The number of members can range from five to five thousand and more; space for co-op operations can range from a double-parked car to a store that looks like a supermarket. None of these is better than any other except in very specific ways—each co-op offers its members particular advantages and disadvantages.

The beginnings of most of the food co-ops I know of originated with one person or a small group of people. This isn't the most cooperative way of starting, but it seems to be the most feasible. The odds against twenty families simultaneously deciding to have a food co-op appear high, and someone has to get things going. The people I've met who were the "prime movers" for their co-ops constitute a diverse group. There are some experienced organizers, some with a good deal of co-op experience, but a number with no experience whatever. Some of the most competently run co-ops I've seen were started by people who had neither any experience organizing people nor any prior knowledge of food wholesaling and distribution. A suburban Massachusetts woman told me, "I just refused to pay those supermarket prices, so I decided I'd organize a co-op." With co-ops, pure motivation can carry people fairly well until competency catches up.

It's possible to start a co-op of just about any size or form and there are a lot of similarities among all the possibilities. But there are some basic differences between storefront co-ops and "floating" or weekly co-ops. Storefronts require much more organization and much more total effort, though they can yield much more. By being open daily and carrying a large inventory they can serve many food needs of many people. The physical facility itself, a tangible thing, can be a visible focal point of organization within a community, a resource to the neighborhood. Moreover, a store can support employees, creating an alternative for workers as well as an alternative for shoppers.

Not everyone wants to be so organized, though. Storefronts can get out of hand, removed from most of the people who use them. Weekly co-ops ("floating crap games," one suburban Boston woman called them) usually provide greater intimacy, greater control, and less bother overall. Small buying club co-ops can provide greater social and economic rewards for less involvement. Many people don't want to live co-op, they just want to have a co-op.

First Meetings of a Weekly Co-op

I sat in on one of the starting-up meetings of the co-op in Concord, Massachusetts. The Concord Co-op was initiated by Ben Kellman, a member of the Board of Directors of the Boston Food Co-op. Ben had moved to Concord and was interested both in bringing a co-op to the town and in making it easier to do the shopping for his own family. He worked from the beginning with friends in the neighborhood. They made up a number of posters announcing a meeting and put them up in the center of town and at some other co-ops. They also contacted some other nearby co-ops that had established waiting lists when their membership began to mushroom. They set up two meetings before their planned beginning date— the first to serve as a general introduction to the idea, the organization, and the people who showed up; the second to go through a "dry run" of a distribution.

The first meeting went fairly well. It drew thirty-five people from mixed age, education, and income groups and

an encouraging amount of enthusiasm. The second meeting drew
some of the same people and a number of new faces.

The atmosphere at the second meeting was cordial. About
thirty people were jammed into the living room of a house
designed for twenty less. Looking around at all the newcomers
settling into spaces on the floor, one of the hosts commented,
"We should have these people over all the time." The meeting got
off to an amiable start when someone suggested that everyone
introduce themselves and say a sentence about themselves. "Maybe
some people don't want to talk about themselves," a person
commented from the floor. "There's a sentence," replied the first
person. "Next?"

Ben gave a general introduction to the co-op ("We're forming
ourselves out of a need for fair food prices and for dealing with
people we like") He went on to discuss a $5.00 nonrefundable
membership fee and the material goods it would buy (a scale,
an adding machine). He surveyed the group to try to determine
which hours of distribution would be best to begin with—an
all-day or an evening-only schedule. ("Our weeks are pretty full,"
one man cautioned when Ben spoke about an all-day operation.)

Then Ben went on to discuss the various ways in which
people could put in time to run the co-op. There was a tentative
schedule of jobs, the amount of time necessary to do them,
and when they had to be done. "You don't need to actually help
distribute food to participate in the co-op," he explained. Some
jobs can be done at home, at night, away from the co-op.
"Everybody should be able to do every job," he added, explaining
an apprenticeship program in which inexperienced people would
work with people who had been doing a job for some time.

People had a number of questions about the mechanics of
paying in advance for the food, but there seemed to be a general
acceptance that things would work out and a general willingness
to try the whole idea. People made comments frequently, but
the core of what Ben presented was accepted without serious
questioning. Ben stressed that the organization should be flexible
to meet unforeseen tactical problems and new needs of members.
"We've got to let each other know when there are problems.
There are no customers here—everybody's a member."

Then he got to the part of the meeting people were waiting
for. You could actually see smiles break out as he brought out
a poster-sized duplicate of an order form. "You'll all be getting
one of these tonight, so we ought to go over what's available

on the market and how you can order it." He explained the
straightforward mechanics of ordering and went down an item-
by-item listing of the produce.

A good deal of time was devoted to discussion of the
logistics of the membership fee. The debate centered on whether
the fee should be assessed per member, per family, or per
the number of people in a family. People with different home
situations took predictable sides but with a prevailing tone that
the end result must be fair for everyone. The end result was
that the fee would be on a basis of $3.00 per individual member.

The meeting ended at about 10:00 with enthusiasm and
readiness for "order day." It worked well as a preparation,
and "order day" turned out to be not much more confused
than distribution day at established co-ops. The meetings worked
well for the Concord group, but the Concord group had some
unique factors operating in its favor.

To begin with, the Concord co-op had a ready supply of
members in the waiting lists of the other co-ops. In areas where
co-op activity is at a lower level, it's often difficult to find
enough people to make a co-op work.

In *Rules for Radicals*, Saul Alinsky illuminates the difficulty
in getting people to organize through a parable of the ten-
dollar bill. He describes how he once walked four blocks
around the Biltmore Hotel in Los Angeles, trying to give away
a ten-dollar bill. None of the fourteen people he encountered
would take it because it was "beyond the range of their
experience" to have a stranger offer them money. Alinsky
suggests that beginning organizations work within their members'
range of experience, fixing on clearly identified shared goals
and common interests.[1]

Typically, people who want to organize a co-op spread the
idea around among friends and neighbors first. Often, though,
friends don't live close enough or have their schedules worked
out similarly enough to get into the same co-op. Neighbors
also are not necessarily automatic joiners. A woman who
organized a co-op in Marshfield, Massachusetts, told me that
when she put notices of her first meeting in the mailboxes
of all the houses on the suburban residential circle where her
house is, she got no responses. She then decided to advertise
in the local suburban newspaper and got fifteen responses—
enough to get things underway.

Other co-ops have stirred up initial interest by putting up flyers or posters in laundromats and even in supermarkets. A woman in Somerville, Massachusetts, went door to door with a low-key, friendly appeal. People who are still active in the co-op told me that a lot of the people joined initially because they liked the woman who came around.

Some of the people who organized co-ops in New York had great success in getting people out to the first meeting by circulating a flyer that featured low food prices. The flyer indicated that two or three popular food items would be available at a very low cost at the meeting. Prices were prominently displayed on the flyer. People coming to the meeting were able to buy the food after hearing a short talk on the co-op. The majority of the people who came didn't stay in the co-op, but many more people than would have responded to a plain flyer came out.

In addition to a relatively large supply of members, the Concord group had considerable food and co-op experience spread among its members. The Concord group was able to bypass many of the normal problems of buying by hooking up with an ongoing, sympathetic produce-buying service (Roger Auerbach's at NEFCO). Co-ops that don't have these kinds of experience grow their own. It's a good idea for new co-ops to contact a nearby co-op, possibly using the directory in this book. Other co-ops have invaluable perspective and knowledge of local conditions. One or two members must make cautious trips to the market to reconnoiter the wholesaler situation. A core of the group may have to work hard to establish credibility and trust among new members. It's a rare group of people that isn't wary of giving its food money to strangers. So some co-ops build in elaborate financial safeguards.

The Concord core group had a fairly accurate preconception of how large their membership would be and enough knowledge about different co-op forms to set up a manageable framework. Other new groups try in vain to adapt unsuitable co-op forms to their needs. Ben presented, and the group accepted, a number of organizational points that could have gone a number of other ways.

OTHER KINDS OF CO-OPS

The core Concord group chose to have the membership consider a co-op in which each person does a particular job, people

work every week, and there is a pre-paying ordering system.
A smaller group might have chosen the "five-dollar grab-bag"
approach. For this, each member of the group would get five
dollars' worth of whatever food the buyer was motivated
to buy that week. The "grab-bag" approach seems to work well
in groups where people have similar food tastes and don't
rely too heavily on the kind of food they get.

A larger group than in Concord might have split in half along
neighborhood or common interest lines, forming subgroups
(or blocs) which alternate co-op operations. Elaborate bloc
systems with numerous blocs are not uncommon, but they're
not easy to start. They usually grow out of the joining
together of small co-ops like the Concord group. Once established, co-ops with several blocs can encourage and assist the
development of new blocs.

The organizational structure set up by the Concord group,
however, seems to work well for a beginning group of fifteen
to twenty families, offering them a greater variety of food
than the "grab-bag" approach. The structure of the Concord
group also can fairly easily accommodate a number (usually up
to fifty before it starts to get out of hand) of additional members.

SPACE

The Concord group got started by using a garage attached
to a house. The garage was big enough, provided everyone didn't
come for their food at the same time. Garages are popular
locations, but they can get awfully cold in the winter. Some
co-ops use basements or members' dens during cold weather.
The Community Stomach co-op in Worcester, Massachusetts,
advises in a bulletin:

Find a place. A very clean room, approximately 20 x 20, with access
to a sink for washing, is what you'll need. Churches, community centers,
schools and people's homes are used.

Small co-ops are frequently able to distribute from a
living room. Apartment buildings usually have an available nook
or cranny. Apartment hallways and elevator waiting areas make
for congenial co-op spaces, too, if the building management
is supportive or unknowing. An award for ingenuity in co-op
space should go to the woman in New York City who
distributes her co-op's orders from a double-parked car in

front of the members' apartment building. On rainy days, they use
the building's awning walkway for shelter.

Space in homes or garages can get quite messy in use for
co-ops, so a lot of groups search immediately for an external
location. Church basements are a favorite choice because they
often have institutional-type storage space available, they're clean
and easy to keep clean, and they're relatively easy to obtain.
Some churches are becoming increasingly supportive of community
interaction and activities, and food co-ops qualify. Church members
have some claim to use of their churches for co-op purposes,
but nonmembers haven't done badly either. Despite churches'
willingness to help food co-ops, one co-op member reported:
"We've always had a problem with churches that you have to
come to them every few weeks and tell them what wonderful
people they are." Colleges have a variety of potentials for space
and may have motivations similar to those of the church in
supporting community activities.

Neighborhood agencies, antipoverty boards, and urban renewal
commissions in various parts of the country have all supplied
co-ops with space. Public agencies can provde low-cost space,
but they may want affiliation with or control of the co-op they
help, and their help may justifiably scare off some people. Even
public agencies that don't seek control of the co-op can seldom
offer more than temporary use of low-quality space. Buildings
earmarked for demolition are not uncommon co-op spaces.

Rents at church, college, or public facilities can be quite low
or even free. Some co-op members feel that rented space is
good not only for maintenance but because it provides a more
collective identification of the space. The co-op meets not in
one person's garage but in its own shared location.

Rental space with only the most basic kinds of physical
attributes (a door, a window, some tables, basic cleanliness)
can keep many co-op members happy. But a secondary effect of
renting space is that the co-op becomes more visible. The garage
operation that no one cared about can easily become the church
basement co-op that the local health department wants to clean up.

MONEY

All food co-ops need money to get started. Few wholesalers
will give a new food co-op's buyer credit, and the co-op needs
to cover other expenses for operating and supplies. Beginning co-ops

may try to raise initial expenses by charging a membership fee
which they may want to designate as refundable if a co-op
member leaves. Co-ops that think they'll have additional
expenses may solicit loans; co-ops with anticipated small initial
outlays may decide to try to cover expenses with a percentage
surcharge on their orders. The Marshfield co-op charges a high
(twenty dollars) membership fee and 10 percent surcharge until
a member accumulates a forty-dollar balance. This may seem
high, but the group prefers it to prepaying each week and
the coordinator says the amount is necessary to cover what people
order. "The bill is fantastic," she reports. It gets to $500 when
the under-twenty-member co-op does a meat order every third
week. All co-ops have to decide if members will pay for their
orders in advance or simply order in advance and pay when they
pick up the food. Co-ops that prepay their food orders supply
the money necessary for the group to deal with wholesalers.
When co-ops don't prepay their orders, they must raise the
money in some other way—membership dues, fees, loans, etc.

The Concord Co-op used a three-dollar membership fee
to cover the cost of initial supplies and build up a slight
reserve. It established a 10 percent markup on all items to cover
operating overhead costs. Some co-ops like to start bigger, building
up a larger capital reserve and a bigger inventory, or to just
fund themselves differently.

Co-ops that try to keep a low financial profile may scrounge
their initial supplies. The co-op in Marshfield, Massachusetts,
uses a baby scale to weigh its produce and a salvaged adding
machine to handle its calculations. Resourceful people can
start a co-op with no capital and no membership fee, but most
co-op members I spoke with thought it was sound organizational
practice to elicit a financial commitment from people at the outset.

Co-ops that don't use prepayment systems may feel they
need a substantial bank balance to tide them over between
payment and order. They can raise this with high member fees
or by taking out loans or soliciting gifts. Usually membership
fees are refundable, but some co-ops (particularly those with
financial difficulties) hold on to them. Co-ops that don't
prepay (and some that do) use member fees to cover losses
if people don't show up to get their orders. Tight bookkeeping
and financial control can reduce the need for high membership
fees if that's what the members want.

The recurring costs of co-op operation can be as variable as.

start-up costs. The major sources of costs for small co-ops are transportation, spoilage/shrinkage, and basic financial mismanagement. All these can be controlled or varied. A co-op in residential Needham, Massachusetts, started with stationwagon transportation supplied by members. As it grew, it added more stationwagons until it discovered it was cheaper to rent a truck. A co-op in working-class Somerville, Massachusetts, solicited and got free use of a van owned by a local university interested in the community.

Food spoilage can be disastrous for a small co-op, as can minor pilferage and poor bookkeeping. All these can be minimized, but it's almost impossible to eliminate them completely. Most co-ops charge a markup fee on their costs. These are usually around 10 percent for small co-ops, though a co-op may charge more if it is in debt or if its operating costs are high. The Somerville co-op, serving about fifty families, proudly charges no markup. "Write that down," one member advised me. They get free transportation, free use of a church basement, and free miscellaneous supplies (newsletter paper, etc.) from a local community organization. "Whenever we're in a hole, we bake a bunch of cakes and sell them when we distribute the food," a member explained. They also run occasional cake sales to raise contributions in lieu of rent for the church.

Money handling in most small co-ops is done by check because checks are "neater" and provide permanent records. Money is harder to keep track of, but is preferred by co-ops whose members' checks bounce frequently or who want to start fresh and clean up the books each week.

Co-ops that levy a markup fee and manage themselves with a degree of competency are likely to build up a surplus beyond the amount of "cushion" members might think useful to get the co-op through hard times. This surplus, sometimes called the "bump" fund, can be donated to a voted-on worthy cause. The North Cambridge Co-op newsletter warns, lest the bump get too big, that "It is harder for a camel to go through the eye of a needle than for a rich food co-op to go to heaven." The use of "bump" funds is a favorite topic of debate.

SCHEDULING

Even though food co-ops like to promote an informal atmosphere, they usually have to work out a schedule so that all the work gets done and distributed equitably among the membership.

A well-thought-out schedule can balance the work that must be done so that no one has to put in an excessive amount of time. Schedules need to be tailored to the individual needs and problems of members, but the experiences of some co-ops bring but some common problems and innovative solutions.

Scheduling for the Concord Co-op was straightforward. The day for distribution was chosen with consideration to when the members could meet most conveniently and when the NEFCO buying service could most ably accommodate them. One co-op distributes on Fridays because, being payday, Friday is when members find it easiest to pay. Other co-ops distribute when they get their most important deliveries or when they can use their hall or basement space.

Scheduling on distribution days must take into consideration when food comes in, how long it takes to prepare it for members, when members pick it up, and when members are available to work. The West (Greenwich) Village Co-op in New York City displays a schedule every week and requests members to sign up next to a time slot. Calls and personal pleas help fill open slots. The West Village Co-op doesn't start distributing until relatively late in the day because they subscribe to a buying/trucking service run by a person who works with the People's Warehouse. West Village's schedule begins at 11 A.M. when members pack dry goods and nonperishables on hand from the co-op's (meager) inventory. Concerted activity begins at 1 P.M. when the produce delivery arrives. (One P.M. is when the produce is supposed to arrive. When I visited, delivery was over an hour late and the members who were there worried that the whole schedule would be put back.)

During the work shifts from eleven until two and two until five, volunteers are supposed to break down the bulk orders and make up members' orders according to the checklists members prepare and submit in advance. This involves more than just picking items from one pile and putting them in another. One enterprising regular packer drew up and had printed a sheet containing notes for packers. The sheet describes where orders should be, how to get the bags necessary to pack the order ("hustling from supermarkets . . . outright purchase . . . or recycling"), and how to figure unit pricing (price per pound = total price divided by number of pounds received). Prices are posted on a blackboard next to a list of the food items received. Food items that are not received in full quantity are distributed as much as possible in proportion to the amount ordered.

With the packing itself, the sheet advises: "Please don't put soft items (tomatoes, strawberries, etc.) under all the hard and heavies. Then softies become squishies." The sheet suggests that packers mark each order with the adjusted (the price paid in advance is an estimate based on the prior week) price as they fill it. Then, "For the orders which are complete (including cheese and eggs) you can fill in the Total Price—that is if your head is not too messed up already."

The actual handling of the food involves some intricacies, too. Oranges, lettuce heads, and other items sold by number are easy to distribute—workers simply open the large crates, count out the oranges, and put them in the bags or boxes that contain members' orders. The Somerville Co-op simplifies this matter by assigning a number to each participating family and writing the family's name and number on large grocery bags recycled from prior supermarket use. They line the bags up around the walls of the church where they meet. They then open up the bulk crates, remove the produce, and, following the order slips from members, put it in members' shopping bags. Some items are sold by weight, though, and they require that co-op workers dig into the large crate and sift out the amount that members want. String beans, potatoes, and bananas are among the produce that must be weighed. This can be done simply with a large scoop and a produce scale, both relatively easy to acquire. Workers usually scoop produce into paper bags placed on the scales, then put the bagged produce into members' order boxes. The weighing and bagging can be done as an operation separate from making up the orders. With produce pre-bagged, workers making up orders can work more smoothly.

Larger co-ops organize the packing by cross-referencing the information on people's orders to cards indexed by item. The Mission Hill co-op uses this system. They make up separate index cards for each item, avocadoes and asparagus through zucchini. Then they note, say, on the asparagus card, every person (or bloc) who gets asparagus. When the bulk order comes in, they distribute the asparagus according to the card, then go on to the beets card, etc. One thing they have to be careful of is to break the alphabetical order of items and people occasionally, so that Mr. Zebulon doesn't get stuck with all the loose ends and surplus.

The "Store" shift at West Village, working from five to eight, distributes the food to the members and collects the money. The interchange is a co-op version of the checkout line with a few differences from the supermarket type. There's a lot of conversation and no one's in a hurry—co-ops and hurrying don't mix. There's a lot of questioning. "What happened to the squash this week? Can we get rhubarb soon?" If things aren't right, people want to know why, and they want things fixed. They're likely to end up fixing things themselves, of course. The store shift also distributes order forms for the next week.

Clean-up of the church basement goes from eight to nine. From nine until whenever, a final work crew collates the orders for the following week, making up one bulk order from the single orders submitted by members.

This whole process sounds much more polished than it is. Typically, there are complications at every imaginable level. Some work crews are understaffed, some overstaffed. Breaking down the bulk order is a confusing and messy process. The produce does not come in plastic bags, and it must be handled and weighed. The cheese must be cut. Things may be dropped or spilled. People who don't get what they ordered may be most disappointed or upset.

Many other small co-ops organize their schedules in ways resembling West Village's schedules. Most co-ops start earlier, as they must get to a wholesale market. The Marshfield Co-op and a number of others take members' orders by phone the day before distribution day because many people can't prepare a good order a week in advance. The Needham Co-op uses a local card/gift shop as a "drop" for order blanks so that members won't have to take a lot of time organizing the order over the telephone. The shop owner was ecstatic to have forty regular visitors each week. Some co-ops try to do as much work as possible on nondistribution days to help spread the work out and make distribution day run smoothly.

PARTICIPATION

Members participated in the West Village and Concord co-ops by signing up for work shifts. Some of the more involved work, like bookkeeping or wholesale buying, is done by a group of regulars. Both co-ops ask members to work for a certain amount of time (one hour each week for Concord, three for West Village) but neither gets the full amount. Neither co-op expects or needs full participation to get the work done, but both strive to have as many members as possible involved in the operation of the group. Everyone doesn't have to be there at once, but if work is spread more evenly, everyone will have to do less. Besides, the whole point of a co-op is to work together.

The Somerville Co-op and a number of others organize the work into teams or subgroups. The Somerville Co-op has ten of these—a bookkeeping group, a transportation group, a packing group, etc. It even has one group which specializes in handling complaints. Each group is "led" by a coordinator, thus breaking the fifty-member group into smaller groups where it is easier to maintain more personal contact. The ten coordinators meet weekly to discuss general problems in addition to running their "shop." Some co-ops that have job teams make a point of rotating jobs so that, to the greatest extent possible, everyone knows everything. Some co-ops reject the job team idea entirely because they feel it is too bureaucratic and too narrow.

The Marshfield Co-op has established an elaborate point system for participation in response to the justifiable common complaint that some jobs take longer than others. They figured out how many jobs were necessary to run the co-op and assigned a point value to each job based on a combination of how long the job takes and how much of a bother the job is. They calculated the resulting number of job points for a week's operation, then for three month's operation. Then they divided the total number of points by the number of members they had, determining, for example, that in a three month period each member had to earn X number of points. The three-month time span gives members flexibility for piling up or easing off, and things overall work out well.

The Marshfield plan combines points with a schedule. The information sheet they give to new members includes this schedule:

Drive (pick up and bring to co-op) - produce	7 pts.	Be here by 11 A.M. Thurs.
Drive - bread and meat	6 pts.	Be here by 11 A.M. Thurs.
Drive - fish	5 pts.	Be here by 11 A.M. Thurs.
Cashier	4 pts.	11:00 - 2:30 Thurs.
Packer	4 pts.	11:00 - 1:00 Thurs.
Clean-up	2 pts.	2:15 - done
Take telephone orders	4 pts.	1:00 - 4:00 Tues.

Participation is one of the key factors that sets co-ops apart
from supermarkets. If, in the initial organization of a co-op,
the means of member participation are not carefully worked into
co-op operation, the co-op won't be much of an alternative to
anything. Often it's easier for a small group of people to do
the bulk of the work than to try and involve more members. But
the best long-run approach for a co-op is full participation.

This does not mean that a food co-op must become a major
component in the lives of all its members. If a co-op is well
organized and everyone does the work they're supposed to,
each member can get by spending about the same amount of
time at the co-op as in one extra weekly run to the supermarket.
In the Marshfield Co-op, for example, each of the twenty members
had to earn twenty-five points in a three-month period—five
bread runs in thirteen weeks, or six weeks of taking calls or
being cashier. Other co-ops vary widely in requirements. Some
co-ops have trouble getting people to work because their
schedules concentrate the work at hours that are awkward for
the people the co-op is trying to attract. Generally it seems
that co-ops that spell out clearly from the beginning how many
hours are expected of members do best in getting what they need.

BOOKKEEPING

Bookkeeping is one of those neglected co-op jobs that has
a great deal of importance. Financial problems need to be identified
and cleared up before they get out of hand. Good bookkeeping
can keep a co-op on top of financial matters. It's very difficult to
have bookkeeping done by a group of people because it involves
a singular kind of understanding and continuity. The Good Food
Co-op in the East (Greenwich) Village of New York City tried
a multiple approach after they discovered that they had a
substantial shortage. With their system, four copies were kept
of every transaction of money—money or money food. Each

person involved kept a copy, a record drawer got a copy, and a witness or bystander got a copy. If it's set up well, the bookkeeping job can be handled by one person without making a lifetime commitment.

The goal in bookkeeping is not to create pretty columns but to set things up simply so that people know where the co-op stands financially and every transaction is recorded. "We've done it very simply," Alex DiVincenti told me at the West Village Co-op. "A real bookkeeper would pass out cold if he saw our system, but it covers things for us." She showed me the forms that she keeps in a small, looseleaf notebook. One form, covering the week's activity, is broken down by these page headings:

Quantity Ordered	Quantity Received	Selling Price
Apple juice - 7 cases of 6 (½ gal.) bottles	@ $5.50/case, 7 cases $38.50	$.97

This list includes all current prices and the prices of items carried over in inventory. This form is used to keep tabs on volume, ordering, and price sheets.

Another form, also kept each week, describes the financial situation of the co-op. It is broken down along these headings:

Income	Spent	Owed
$614.80 (total brought forward from previous week)	_____ (cheese)	("If people owe for their order or loose ends, we keep track here.")
- 407.44 (total from "Spent")	_____ (dry goods)	
207.36	_____ (eggs)	
+386.89 (total sales)	_____ (bill to church)	
594.25	_____ (miscellaneous)	
+ 10.38 (sales of surplus)		
604.63	$407.44	

The final $604.63 figure is the total balance of the co-op's account. It will be used in the following week to buy the food. The figure is about $100 short of what would be in the till if all the member fees were intact. Losses in weighing, operating costs, and outright pilferage have reduced the total. If the co-op were to disband, each member would get an equal share of the balance.

The Marshfield co-op's bookkeeper categorized her system as a nonsystem. "I have a book where I keep records of everything that

comes in and goes out, but I don't think anyone would recognize
it as a bookkeeping system," she observed. For the twenty-
member co-op, she finds it relatively easy to keep records for
each member. Each person is kept track of on a page with
these headings:

date	cash-check	order	sub-total (cost of goods)	10% overhd	total
12-7	cash	groceries, bread	$4.88	.49	$5.37

She fills in the categories and keeps a running tally of everyone
for each week that the co-op is in operation.

Terry Dix, who keeps the books for the Worcester Co-op
suggests that a slightly more complicated system works better
for larger co-ops. Terry spent time in Boston University's
Business School, so he has more experience than most co-op
bookkeepers. Though he had a course in bookkeeping, he points
out that "It sure doesn't show. We should have gotten the
books a long time ago to where they are now." Where they
are now is a double-entry ledger system which helps eliminate
mistakes and shows where the money goes.

The system is called double-entry because it involves
noting each transaction with these categories:

date	description	debit	credit

The remainder of the book contains pages with recurring areas
of transaction like truck, equipment, accounts payable, accounts
receivable, membership, and operating gains and losses. The
system keeps an accurate picture of the co-op overall and of
various aspects of co-op activity. Problem areas and sudden
changes can be quickly identified.

Probably neither Terry's system nor Alex's system will fit
any other co-op, but they may be used as guides. Another good
source of a guide is the bookkeeping section in the Buying Club
Manual put out by the Cooperative League. Some co-ops work
with a bookkeeper to set up an initial framework that meets
their needs.

STOREFRONTS STARTING UP

Though many storefronts grow out of floating co-ops or federations of floating co-ops, it's entirely possible to start a co-op storefront from scratch. The organization operates on a larger scale but storefronts must deal with many of the same considerations as buying clubs.

I visited the Green Grass Grocery (not to be confused with the Good Grits store on the other side of town) in St. Paul shortly after the storefront opened. The storefront is in a former blue-collar neighborhood in St. Paul. With no other stores in the immediate area except one scheduled to be demolished for urban renewal, the storefront is not really in competition with other businesses. The building is clean and airy. The co-op shares the rent with a community agency in the adjacent office, paying $100 a month while the agency pays $200. Staff and interested folk associated with the neighborhood agency provided the initial impetus for organization.

The initial core group of about ten people raised enough money to open up the store by running a neighborhood festival and securing a loan from the landlord. The storefront needed little more fixing up than a paint job. It already contained shelves, a sink, and a walk-in cooler. The co-op added a lounge with two donated sofas near the entrance. One member set out to paint a wall mural of the founding group. Initial funds also went toward the purchase of the store's beginning inventory.

The number of people interested in running the co-op grew to about fifteen, each of whom took on one aspect of the co-op's operation. As with the Somerville Co-op, there is a bookkeeping coordinator, but other coordinators work with food items rather than single aspects of operation. The meat, cheese, and dry goods coordinators, for example, each oversees the total picture of operations for those food items. New coordinators join the organization as new product areas are added. Recently, the people who have suggested adding various products have ended up being the coordinator for the product.

After one month of operation, the co-op seemed to be on a fairly solid footing. Its approximate $100/day volume was covering expenses. The storefront looked good. The flow of customers that I saw included several newcomers, shy at first, who responded warmly to the conversation attempted by the

shopkeeper. Some were confused by the weighing processes and
the prospect of getting their own peanut butter from a tap
on a fifty-gallon drum. But overall, their curiosity and
the appeal of the store carried new people through uncertainties.
I would bet that they'll come back. The co-op had recently
received some good publicity in a column in the local newspaper. The storefront looked friendly and inviting and the
overall situation seemed promising.

STARTING WORK COLLECTIVES

Though many of the same logistic principles apply for
storefront space, financing, and management, it's a wholly
different proposition to start a work collective co-op than to
start a participatory one. Work collectives concentrate participation and responsibility among a much smaller number of
people, making the personalities and interrelationships of a
work collective take on greater importance. There is less room
for nonworkers, more problems for people who don't relate
to the group. The same people who get along well in a two-hour
weekly co-op might tear each other's hair out if they had to
work together in longer, more concentrated doses.

Aside from people issues, the tactical issues are also on
a different plane. The issue of saving money on food is replaced
by the need to earn enough money to survive. Pay scales,
lifestyles, take on great importance. Scheduling and decision-
making must also be worked out. Simple tactical problems that
workers in traditional jobs take for granted must be dealt with.
Withholding taxes must be calculated; insurance must be
considered. Some areas have an abundance of such assistance
available from local groups. Legal aid societies, where they exist,
are important resources. The United Methodist Volunteer Service
(offices at 475 Riverside Drive, Rm. 344, New York, N.Y.,
c/o Randle Dew) has provided free leadership training, health,
and life insurance for some people involved in alternate
institution-building like work collectives.

Money for Storefronts

Often more money is involved in setting up storefronts
than Green Grass needed. With its low rents and assistance
from other co-ops and the warehouse, the Minneapolis-St. Paul
area is a good one for starting a co-op. For some co-ops capital

must be raised to cover rents, equipment, and possibly the labor
of the people doing the start-up work. The issue of capital
acquisition, then, usually must be carried beyond members' dues.
The Boston Food Co-op got started with a healthy $10,000 grant
from the student activity fund at Boston University. Stone Soup
got their operation underway in Washington, D.C., with $20,000
in loans from sympathetic individual and institutional supporters.
Most of the new Minneapolis-St. Paul co-ops have started with
loans. John Gauci, Executive Director of the Council for
Self-Help Development in New York City, has been trying to
start a food co-op supermarket in the Brownsville section of
Brooklyn. His group has thus far raised $10,000 in fifty shares
sold to 2,000 families. Many of the members pay five dollars
a month toward the total. He feels that the high share amount is
justified because it will more likely lead members to shop at
and support the co-op.

Storefronts usually don't have the financial problems that
accompany preorder or prepaying co-ops because storefronts
usually stock an inventory of items. There is a whole other set of
problems, though, in maintaining an inventory that matches the
shopping needs of members. Oversupplies may spoil; undersupplies
will disappoint members. When the Boston Food Co-op changed
from a preorder to a straight stocking system, there were few
problems. The inconsistencies in inventory were no greater than
the inconsistencies in figuring out the large number of preorders
that had been coming in.

Storefront starting costs can vary a great deal depending on
the availability of space, supplies, operating equipment, and
interested people. Many materials can be scrounged or impro-
vised, but corner-cutting may have harmful effects in the long run.
Inventories can be built up on credit if co-op workers put up
a strong enough argument with wholesalers. Co-op warehouses can
make early storefront weeks a bit easier by providing credit,
technical help, and moral support. "We never could have opened
without the help of the Warehouse," a member of Green Grass
told me.

Most storefronts handle more money than most buying clubs.
A $10,000 weekly volume is not unusual. The mere existence
of a higher level of money activity leads almost inevitably to
more concern with money and more work to keep track of it.
Co-op finances can get to be a real distraction.

STOREFRONT SPACE

Storefronts are easier to describe than buying clubs because they can be pointed to and have their picture taken. Like Green Grass in St. Paul, many co-op storefronts are former corner groceries already containing important equipment. Like the Santa Cruz Consumers' Co-op with its "little old antique store," many are more improvisational. Convenient storefronts have easy access for deliveries and member entry/egress, adequate space for shopping and display, and basic structural soundness and aesthetic appeal. Most, if not all, municipalities have building codes, enforced in widely varying degrees, which require some local research.

In order for a storefront to get the most from its physical plant, it needs refrigeration equipment. This can be expensive to acquire, maintain, and run. Storefronts also need storage space to take advantage of economies of scale with some food items.

The availability of storefronts imperfectly parallels normal real estate market considerations. When co-ops pay rent, they must cope with normal local market conditions. In Minneapolis, for example, co-ops can rent a storefront for about $140/month. In Boston or New York, well. . . . But many co-ops get special deals. The Boston Redevelopment Authority allowed the Mission Hill Co-op to use a condemned billiard supply store gratis for several years. The Good Food Co-op in the East (Greenwich) Village uses a storefront owned by the city and located by Cooper Square, a community organization. Colleges, churches, and private "interested folks" join urban renewal agencies as possible sources of free space, though there is some danger of strings attached in all of these.

Even at a very low level, there is a potential for conflict over co-op space. People at the West Village Co-op in New York told me about a woman a few blocks away who organized neighborhood people in a food co-op that would be housed in her gift shop. At the first meeting of the co-op, the neighborhood people rebelled at the donor's attempt to take over the co-op, cancelled the woman's self-appointment as manager, and caused an immediate and emotional turmoil about hypocrisy vs. getting thrown out on the street.

The opening of a storefront in a neighborhood is not unlike the opening of a new grocery store. People located within the area have a new competitor. Some co-ops say they don't want to hurt small businessmen, but when they carry similar items they can't avoid it. This consideration, and worries about centralization, have led the Boston Food Co-op to lengthy, anguished debate about the sort of building they should move to. A large building could double as a warehouse and help establish the co-op as a powerful economic force. Moving to a number of small buildings would help the co-op relate better to neighborhoods.

Storefronts suffer from logistic and tactical problems that floating co-ops avoid. There are occasional, sometimes expensive thefts. Someone capable must always be present to mind the store. The storefronts that I visited in New York had a persistent wino problem. Frequently enough to be bothersome, people would wander in off the street, look around, and try to panhandle a banana.

VISIBILITY'S REWARDS

Storefronts have a way of getting attention. They're a favorite feature topic of Sunday newspapers. Floating co-ops get publicity, but seldom as much. The publicity is often cutesy and demeaning, like "oh look what the hippies are doing now," as a woman pointed out to me in Washington, D.C. The same woman told me that her co-op had refused to appear in any articles because the newspaper wanted to put the articles in its "Style" section. Publicity may bring more members, as when Minneapolis's North Country Co-op was the subject of a TV news special. TV coverage of Glut's co-op operation in Washington, D.C., was followed by a call from Dun & Bradstreet asking if Glut wished to be listed. In many cases, though, publicity inspires a deluge of inspectors from the assortment of local agencies that may hold forth in an area.

Agency inspections of co-ops demonstrate well a point that one of my political science instructors beat into the ground: the essence of a law is not what's written on the books, it's the tone of enforcement that matters. The tone of enforcement of laws that apply to co-ops resides with a band of inspectors whose moods and sentiments are much less predictable than the weather. Steve Clark, who works at Stone Soup in Washington, D.C., told me how members of the collective once stayed up until 3 A.M. to ready the building for a health department inspection. The previous inspection had downgraded the co-op for several items, and the group wanted a good rating. A different inspector came, however, and stressed completely different things.

Most health department inspections I've heard of have been of the firm but fair type. I've seldom heard of any intentional bothering or hostility, even from groups that I don't think would proffer a warm welcome to inspectors. I've never heard of a co-op being closed down due to health inspections. Usually whatever is wrong can be remedied in time for the next inspection. Sometimes the point of staying clean is blurred when co-ops strive to meet the sometimes irrational checklists of health departments. Many of the problems co-ops face with inspections are due to new laws that require stainless steel work surfaces and other germ-resistant equipment. Though there is truth behind some of the laws (wooden butcher block tables do promote bacterial growth), it is rumored in co-op circles that some of the laws are a product of a powerful restaurant equipment lobby.

In some towns, co-ops are inspected separately for health aspects and structural aspects. Some towns have separate inspections for dairy, meat, and general retail. Some require co-ops to purchase licenses. Some require nothing. A few co-ops take the initiative in calling local agencies, but most follow the adage of letting sleeping dogs lie.

Visibility, high volume, and high risks lead some co-ops to incorporate. Some small co-ops worry about liability, too. Would a member using his or her garage be covered by the usual homeowners' insurance if another member slipped on an avocado and sued? I haven't come across any precedents, but some buying clubs who were worried enough to talk with their insurance agents reported that there should be no problems. The buying clubs' informality and nonbusiness status mean that they would probably be viewed as social gatherings. The Framingham, Massachusetts, claims office of Allstate Insurance confirmed this. Storefronts are usually more concerned with liability because they have more (people, money, equipment, activity) to be liable for.

State laws regarding the mechanics of incorporation vary, but in most cases it is a relatively easy and inexpensive process. The state fee may be between $25 and $100 and co-op members can do the filing themselves or enlist the sometimes complimentary assistance of an interested lawyer. Individual and local considerations lead most new co-ops to incorporate not as co-ops or corporations but as nonprofit organizations. Art Danforth of the Cooperative League doesn't think that co-ops could qualify for nonprofit status under close scrutiny. He showed me a recent court ruling that a Philadelphia buying club could not be categorized as nonprofit because "the organization is operated primarily for the private benefit of members and any benefits to the community are not sufficient to meet the requirement of the regulations that the organization be operated primarily for the common good and general welfare of the community." (6691, Rev. Rul. 73-349, IRB 1973-35.7 [Code Sec. 561]).

Roger Auerbach, NEFCO's buyer and a recent law school graduate, shook his head in disbelief when he learned of the Philadelphia decision. "I'd like to argue that one myself," he mused. He doesn't feel that the decision is a precedent. Even if it were, many co-ops would not meet the criteria set forth in the case. Each co-op has unique conditions and relations with the community, and nonprofit status is determined on an individual basis.

Co-ops that don't grant membership or that don't try for nonprofit status as a social welfare organization may meet with different results. Some co-ops feel that incorporation laws don't do much to reduce liability anyway. North Country Co-op in Minneapolis decided to disincorporate as a co-op and simply form as an association. In any case, the incorporation issue is open to debate and should be reviewed carefully and individually by each co-op.

ANTICIPATING PROBLEMS

When dealing with problems in food co-op organizations, it seems that the best defense is an offense. Successful co-ops recognize and solve problems cooperatively.

A handbook produced by the Community Stomach co-op in Worcester, Massachusetts, advises:

Make some decisions.... You'll need to make some decisions about how [you're] going to operate. What happens when members don't show up for work? If work slots can't be filled or other mistakes are being made.... What is done? If money problems arise, who's responsible and how will it be made up?

Some co-ops have found it helpful to establish policy for issues such as those raised by the Worcester group. Any policy must be flexible, of course, to meet members' changing needs. Co-ops often express policy in a handout sheet for new members like those in Appendix A of this book. Producing such a sheet can help members of a new co-op crystallize their expectations and expose conflicts.

Another tactic which helps some co-ops is selective imitation of supermarket techniques. For example, many co-ops have found it easier to have members prepack bulk goods into standardized or prepriced amounts to speed things up on distribution day. If co-ops emulate some supermarket financial tactics (by dealing with co-op services and firms, for example), they can help strengthen co-ops' overall economic position. Supermarkets also provide good standards for health and safety. In their quest for "personality" or "good vibes" too many co-ops confuse dirt with good feelings. Clean suburban co-ops sometimes store meat for hours without refrigerating it. Even the best-intentioned co-ops can fall into slipshod food-handling habits. One case of food poisoning or one rotten roast is usually enough to remind groups that they're handling food, not rocks. But it shouldn't get that far. Some co-ops appoint cleanliness coordinators to make sure that it doesn't, but the best way to keep a co-op clean and healthy is to make cleanliness an aspect of every food handling job in the co-op.

Member turnover is a fairly accurate barometer of a co-op's success. Co-op coordinators and true believers often ignore changes in the membership, looking instead at overall co-op size. This is not a healthy policy. A co-op that shows a stable size but is filled with new faces every week has to eventually reach the end of its rope. Besides, it's important to keep turnover rates low in order to build strong relationships between members and the co-op.

Aside from the problems already covered in this chapter, co-ops have to respond to their members' particular needs and priorities. A co-op that works well on Manhattan's Lower East Side might never get off the ground in New England. In addition, the co-op must tailor itself to the different needs and expectations of its membership. Mission Hill lost a bloc of elderly citizens because the older folks couldn't put up with the uncertainties of the co-op's substitution policy. "It's fine for everyone else," a member explained, "but if we give them hard, crisp apples instead of the mushy bananas they ordered, they can't even eat them."

Order substitutions and run-of-the-mill administrative snafus seem to be the leading culprits in making people leave co-ops. Chuck Fager explained in an article in Boston's *Real Paper*:

Anybody who has juggled the forms, addresses and schedules for a few weeks knows that going to a capitalist supermarket is infinitely simpler [than shopping at a co-op]. And the avoidance of skilled management doesn't produce the charm of amateurism; it leaves people with no cucumbers and a box of dates when they ordered and paid for figs.[2]

Co-ops can minimize order substitutions through a combination of careful shopping, tactful subdividing of orders, and a shared understanding that substitutes are sometimes inevitable. Even the largest supermarkets occasionally run out of some things.

Co-ops can minimize administrative snafus by balancing the organizational factors described in this chapter against a background of understanding. It needn't be a struggle. It can work; it's working in a lot of places. A little planning, work, and understanding can get a co-op off to a solid start.

WHAT AND HOW TO STOCK

The kinds of food that a co-op stocks reflect members' needs and strongly influence the overall organization of the co-op. The decision of what food to stock is a complicated one rooted in the savings possible with different food items, the mechanics of food handling, and storage and ethical/political considerations. Local food availability and wholesaling structures also influence what a co-op can handle.

Vegetables/Fruit/Produce: Ecstasy Among the Eggplants

Fresh fruit, produce, and vegetables are the mainstay of most buying clubs, and with good reason. They are readily available in many areas of the nation and, of all food items, they usually provide the greatest savings over supermarket prices. Supermarkets have to have a high markup on produce prices to cover spoilage and storage. In addition to low prices, co-op buying clubs can usually provide fresher vegetables than supermarkets because buying clubs buy and sell their merchandise on the same day.

Skillful produce buying depends on an understanding of local wholesaling mechanisms and an understanding of produce itself. Local wholesaling mechanisms can appear complicated, even mystical to the uninitiated. And sometimes the initiation is costly and torturous.

Most large cities have some sort of wholesale produce distribution center. There are seventy-five such centers located in the United States. The larger the city, the larger the center. The wholesale market in an area can be located by checking with the local United States Agriculture Department offices, asking wholesale fruit or vegetable dealers listed in the Yellow Pages, restaurants, or other co-ops. Other co-ops are likely to provide the most useful information. Boston's Chelsea Market draws trucks from Massachusetts, Maine, Vermont, New Hampshire, Rhode Island, and Connecticut. Food comes in to the center by truck, train, and airplane.

At Boston and other large cities, some people who receive the food specialize in one or two items. That way, they can maintain a relatively simple high-volume operation. They are not, however, always happy to do business with a low-volume food co-op. The people who are more likely to deal with co-ops have greater selections and less volume. There are usually some of these people at the largest markets. At the majority of markets, most wholesalers are of the latter type: they have a large selection and will deal with co-ops.

Produce business is usually done by the crate. Different items are packed in different ways to constitute a crate—dozens, pounds, or bushels may be the standard used. Wholesalers tend to view crate-breaking with great disfavor because it "disrupts things." This sometimes causes problems for small co-ops since they do not always have enough volume to get a full crate of some items. The newsletter of one small co-op summed up the situation: "Artichokes come in cases of 48. Can we, as a co-op, eat 48 artichokes?" Some wholesale markets house concessioners who solve this problem by selling broken (partial) crates for a proportionately higher price. Two of the co-ops I visited in New York City solved the problem by pooling their broken crate orders. Many co-ops simply try to come as close as possible to a full crate order, and then leave the surpluse conspicuously displayed for sale when people come to pick up their orders.

In Boston and Chicago, cooperative solutions have evolved to meet the crate-breaking problem. Cornucopia, a warehouse on the west side of Chicago, deals primarily with co-ops. It breaks cases of produce and stocks a variety of other items as well. The Boston Food Co-op absorbs into its regular inventory broken cases for smaller co-op buying clubs.

Wholesale produce markets have an undeniable mystique which complicates rational buying. The mystique is caused in part by the predawn business hours common to most markets. Co-op buyers who are not accustomed to the early hours wander bleary-eyed and short-winded through the market trying to maintain a semblance of personal order. The early hours are necessary in order to get food back to the retailers who shop at the market and the best food is always sold earliest. Besides, early market hours enable people who work from nine to five to participate in co-op operations.

The market mystique is enhanced by the sheer volume of food being passed around. Crates of crates, truckloads, whole railroad cars of food get broken down and moved around. "You haven't lived until you've seen an entire railroad car filled with spinach," I've been told.

The mystique of the early hours and vast amounts of food is rounded out into a total experience by the markets' cast of characters. Produce wholesalers are a varied but invariably colorful breed. Simultaneously crying about the inequities handed them by their suppliers and fleecing inexperienced buyers for all they're worth, the wholesalers conduct business in an intense way. "It's tough," a woman in New York's Chelsea Co-op told me. "They smile at you and talk to you. Then you get back to the co-op and see that they showed you one thing and sold you something else." Standard transactions are packed with emotion. Still, the woman felt that "Those guys are all right. You've just got to get to know them." She showed me the surplus crate of oranges that one wholesaler gave her co-op because "he likes the co-ops." Another co-op reported, "The man sold us some green tomatoes and they just never turned red." A man in a Chicago co-op described the situation more bluntly: "You just have to be prepared to get screwed for a while until you learn what's going on."

Until the recent growth of co-ops, business at the wholesale markets was carried on almost exclusively among males. The co-op-backed presence of even a few women is a phenomenon that wholesalers rank with Watergate or the gas shortage. "A few years ago, I didn't sell to any women," a Boston wholesaler told me over a stack of lemon crates. "Now there's a few every day. They only buy a little, but I don't mind dealing with

them one bit." The women who deal with him and other wholesalers know he doesn't mind, and know that his interests are
not in the area of equality in women's status. "The market is
very chauvinistic," a friend at Boston Food Co-op explained.
She described how she seriously disrupted normal business
one day when she didn't wear a bra. She concluded, "It was
sort of fun—they're basically nice guys. But I wouldn't want
to do it again."

Although wholesale markets are fascinating places, few people
can make regular commitments to take care of the shopping
each week. It can be a very pleasant experience once every
month or two, but on a regular basis it's usually too much.
Some co-ops deal with this by rotating the buying among blocs
or among a buying team. This spreads the responsibility well
but contradicts the strong buyer-seller relationships that form
the basis of most transactions at the market. Spreading out
produce buying also builds a degree of ignorance into the
buying process because food quality and prices change frequently
and drastically. Some co-ops appoint and pay a member to
take care of buying. Some co-ops, like branch co-ops, establish
committees that carry out key functions like buying for
extended periods. Thinking that it's worth their money to bypass
time lost in comparison shopping, many co-ops simply buy
from concessioners at the wholesale markets. Dealing with one
concessioner who buys up everyone else's loose ends isn't as
cheap as shopping the whole market, but it takes a lot less
time. The best buying arrangement for most co-ops is a
cooperative one if such an arrangement is available. The system
used by New England co-ops wherein Roger Auerbach buys
for twenty-five to thirty co-ops each week provides even
small co-ops with the lowest prices and the best quality food.

Aside from the mechanics of local market structures,
co-op produce buyers also need to be well versed in produce.
Not only the volume, but the selection, too, of produce
available at the markets is staggering. Buyers have to know
both what a Hubbard squash is and what makes one Hubbard
squash better than another. Making full use of the large available
selection can introduce members to "new" fresh produce.
One suburban Massachusetts co-op built up its volume by
featuring a crate of "exotic vegies" and accompanying recipe
each week.

Tips on measures of food quality and freshness are best

picked up from fellow co-opers. One general rule that I've come across in several places is "Buy fresh fruit in season." A more detailed approach is set forth in *Packet for the Bride,* a collection of booklets put together by the Government Printing Office.[3] If co-op members can channel their tastes along with natural growing cycles, they will inevitably get the highest quality produce at the lowest prices. Fresh produce bought out of season may be the object of additives and preservatives and/or the recipient of a lengthy, stifling ride in freight transit. Some co-ops try hard to get organic produce, and frequently do well in lowering the unpayable prices usually attached to organic goods.

Grains

Grains seem to occupy second place in co-op sales activity. Like vegetables, grains can be sold by a co-op for a price much lower than regular store prices. (High grain markups are the product of profit-taking and limited competition in retail grain sellers.) In addition, there is little problem in spoilage, so there is no concern with "broken crates." Even small co-ops can sell a fifty-pound bag's-worth of many grains.

The mechanics of grain buying are not much like those of produce buying. There are no regional markets. A few large grain wholesalers account for much national grain sales. Sales can be worked out by order and delivered to a co-op.

Grains and oils suffer from even less exposure and public understanding than exotic vegetables. Most co-op people, and especially those in the East, would be hard put to describe what to do with barley. Sales of wheatberries (which can be ground into flour) at the Boston Food Co-op were so slow that they were not reordered. Interest in grains is increasing, however, because they offer variety and, in some cases, high protein content for a low price. Soybeans, mung beans, and lentils are being used increasingly as substitutes for high-cost meat products.

Co-ops with a high enough sales volume can order much of their grain directly from large producers. Smaller co-ops can team up for orders or buy from nearby retailers willing to sell in bulk. Transportation charges must be weighed against economies of scale.

Once ordered, grains are received and handled by co-ops much differently than produce. Since there is no spoilage problem, a grain order does not have to be fully sold out in any one week. Surpluses can simply be kept on hand until they are sold. This does, however, require that suitable storage be available,

not always an easy requirement for co-ops that meet once weekly
in rotating locations. Even co-ops that have space available find
that grain storage is not without problems. "Mice like grain!
Please keep the floor clean," a sign reminds workers in the
Boston Food Co-op grain room. Storage of half-filled fifty-pound
bags of grains engenders some special problems. At a co-op
in New York's West (Greenwich) Village, I sat in on a small
group discussion on how cat food found its way into the lentils.
Some co-ops fight the battle of the (loose) bulk by prebagging
grains in premeasured amounts. A number of Minneapolis co-ops
use large plastic trash barrels to store loose grains.

Though I am unaware of any grain-buying plan like the
NEFCO produce buying arrangement, I do know of several
co-op warehouses whose primary stock is grains. Of these,
the one with which I am most familiar (and the one which
has attained nearly legendary status in co-op circles) is the
People's Warehouse in Minneapolis. The warehouse, which is
described in greater detail in another part of this book, was an
outgrowth of the thirteen or so co-op storefronts in Minneapolis-
St. Paul. It supplies the grain needs of the co-ops better than
any one co-op can because it can get very low prices with its
high volume. Also, since it specializes in grains and doesn't
have to worry about regular co-op hassles, the warehouse can
and does develop links with large producers.

Other Items: Dairy, Bakery, Groceries, and Meat
These items are all subject to wide variations in availability
and potential savings according to what area of the country
a co-op is in. Generally, co-ops can make local connections
similar to those used by small stores and restaurants for
dairy, bakery, and meat goods. Choice of a supplier reflects
co-op members' interests: some co-ops interested primarily
in low prices get their bread from a surplus day-old store;
some co-ops interested primarily in food quality get their
bread directly from small ethnic bakeries. Groceries (canned goods,
etc.) are shunned by most co-ops because of both a general
lack of interest and an inability of co-ops to save much, if
anything, over supermarket prices. Still, the Boston Food Co-op
carries groceries to enable members to avoid extra trips to the
supermarket for the same items. Some co-ops succeed with
nonfood items such as books, grinders, and craft work done
by co-op members. Vermont's Northeast Kingdom food co-op

did a bulk cross-country ski equipment order in the winter of 1973. With these items, all that is usually necessary to get wholesale prices is a minimum order that meets the wholesalers' requirements. Wholesalers for these and other nonfood items can be located in the Yellow Pages or by asking local retailers who their supplier is.

In addition to food prices and quality, co-ops may be concerned with other aspects of wholesalers' business. Credit and mode of payment are important considerations for co-ops with small volumes. A wholesaler can make life much easier for a co-op if he delivers the food promptly and reliably or extends credit when needed. Some wholesalers can supply co-ops with material goodies. A soft drink wholesaler who gets enough co-op business can supply display coolers that would cost a co-op a considerable sum.

Some co-ops are discovering that the nature of most of the wholesaler's business influence their dealings with him. The Boston Food Co-op recently dropped a milk wholesaler who dealt primarily in large orders for one who dealt primarily in small store orders. With the latter, they found that their order was more important and entitled them to better service and some assurance that in times of shortages they might get extra consideration. Some people at the Boston Food Co-op believe that food shortages are destined to become an increasingly important concern in numerous aspects of co-op activity.

WHOLESALERS AND FOOD ACQUISITION: GENERAL CONSIDERATIONS

The experience of most co-ops point out two rules of thumb with regard to wholesalers and food acquisition: (1) food acquisition is primarily a local endeavor and (2) co-ops benefit when they join together in getting food.

When food acquisition is viewed as a local endeavor, co-ops build local resources for acquiring food and establish themselves as part of a community. Every area of the country offers some indigenous advantages for co-ops. Co-ops can benefit individually and collectively by integrating into local business and community operations. The wholesaler list provided in this book (Appendix B) is intended as a guide to people's experiences and a last resort for co-ops that have difficulties finding wholesalers in their community.

Co-ops benefit when they join together in getting food because

they often can get lower prices. Equally important, however, is
the increased communication that inevitably comes about and
the economic solidification of co-op forces.

Before actual acquisition of food, co-ops typically do a lot
of soul-searching. Logistics and handling of some food items
is too much of a bother for some co-ops. The need for a
freezer or refrigerator can block a co-op from handling some
items. One asset which has been an invaluable help to the
Minneapolis-St. Paul co-ops has been the involvement (interest
and free labor) of a refrigerator mechanic. In addition to
tactical problems, many co-ops are concerned about the political
and ethical issues raised by the food they carry. A number of
co-ops, for example, won't carry lettuce unless they are certain
that it is United Farm Workers lettuce. Some co-ops search
hard for organic produce. Co-op buyers scour the markets for
unwaxed cucumbers and unpainted oranges. Minneapolis co-op
members had a difficult time believing that the Boston Food
Co-op carried meat and Coca-Cola. Some co-ops use food as
an extension of their members' politics, and with good reason.
If co-op members choose, they can make a strong economic
statement in their buying habits. Food politics along these
lines can also wreak havoc with a membership holding split
views on the subject. The important thing is to at least realize
that decisions of what the co-op should stock have implications
beyond simple logistics and considerations of whether the item
needs to be refrigerated or not.

The way in which stocking decisions are made is important,
too. A note in the newsletter of the Powderhorn Food
Community in Minneapolis asks: "Which is more important?
The *decision* to carry a new product or . . . the process which
we go through in making that decision?" New products decisions
are good vehicles for broad-scale participation. Decisions are
subject to frequent changes as the co-op itself changes. They can
serve as an expression of members' interests while providing
good food ideas.

It's perhaps too easy for a co-op to get sidetracked on
the intricacies of buying, but such digressions need not occur.
Co-ops have as much legitimacy as wholesalers' customers
as any retail food distribution service. Diane Brown, a member
of Washington, D.C.'s, Glut collective, urges that "It's important
not to feel intimidated by wholesalers and not to get distracted
by problems with wholesalers. The important thing is to get

going, to open up and establish yourself as a place where people can get good food at good prices." Relationships with wholesalers need not, perhaps should not, be permanent. As wholesaling is almost as changeable as co-op organization, food acquisition must keep up the pace.

Chapter Three

DEVELOPING AN ONGOING CO-OP ORGANIZATION

The Mission Hill co-op has been around as long or
longer than most co-ops in the Boston area, so it seemed
that their experience might be an object lesson in
how co-ops grow. Nancy Perrelli has been the co-op's produce
buyer for over a year, and she's also been involved in the Boston
Food Co-op as a cashier. I spoke with her in the Mission Hill
storefront, which seems to get more filled with refrigerators
and more beset by physical problems (the ceiling is falling in)
as time goes on. It was a Thursday, which is Mission Hill's
distribution day, so there were a number of people in the storefront accepting deliveries and breaking down large amounts
of crated produce into orders assembled by the blocs. The
operation was, except for an occasional unfindable item (the
truck crew had neglected to pick up the avocadoes that Nancy
bought) smooth and low-key. There was no question that the
work would get done and the food co-op would carry on again
next week.

Ms. Perrelli and I settled down on the worn shelving used
by the former tenant (a billiard supply house) after being ousted
from the front window desk by diligent members. She had a
difficult time pinning down the exact beginnings of the co-op.
"A lot of people have different memories," she explained.
After some thought and consultation with Rich Mansfield, who
was coordinating much of the work that day, she concluded
that the co-op began with a buying club operation in 1969.
There seem to have been several small neighborhood operations
which grew and joined together, first in backyards and then
in a storefront on the Fenway. One of the original groups
arose from the antiwar demonstrations centered on Hemenway
Street, where a sizable number of students and radicals lived.

Many students were involved, and there was much overlap with war organizing. "We were called the People's Revolutionary Food Co-op," recalled Rich, "and there wasn't anybody who would mess with us." The storefront was a temporary gift from a local business, but it was a real problem. "There were always drunks sleeping there and the place smelled strange," Richard reminisced. At any rate, it didn't last, for one reason or another.

Shortly thereafter, the Fenway group left (was pushed from?) the store and joined forces with a group from the Mission Hill area, operating from a garage. By that time there were about fifteen blocs, including some from Beacon Hill and Allston, both rather distant from the distribution point. Deliveries were done from Chelsea Market "with as many vans as we could get our hands on from members." The dollar volume then was about $500 each week, but there were still problems. The garage served adequately as a space, but was located near a housing project that had an oversupply of hostility. Some local youths burned the garage down, and the operation moved to Ms. Perrelli's basement.

It was then that Roger Auerbach and Saul Chadis took an interest in the buying operations for the co-op. Until that time, buying had been done mostly through one or two people at the produce market who dealt with the co-op's low volume by keeping prices high and food quality questionable. Saul and Roger made a concerted effort to buy from the larger wholesalers and crack the market situation that closed co-ops out. They began to have some success. The co-op continued to grow, with dollar volume increasing from $600 to $700 each week. The operation got increasingly complex, and the co-op began to search for another location. "We got too big and people kept hitting their heads on the pipes," Ms. Perrelli explained.

All the members engaged in a search mission for a new home for the co-op and one came up with the storefront in which the co-op is still housed. The building, which belongs to the Boston Redevelopment Authority, is due for demolition whenever the Authority finalizes its plans for the area. Although this is not likely to happen soon because of shifting federal priorities, Ms. Perrelli thinks that the co-op ought to move from the dingy accommodations. At any rate, the co-op survived the move without losing members or organizational skill.

What harmed Mission Hill most, in terms of membership, was the opening of the Boston Food Co-op. "And we'll lose more to the Jamaica Plain group when they open their storefront," Ms. Perrelli added. Still, Mission Hill has a stable operation of about fifteen blocs and may weather the opening of the new co-op as it weathered other problems. It has lasted through five summers and the accompanying massive attrition of student members, winters with disproportionately high activity (the co-op ran duplicate operations twice weekly in the winter of 1972 to accommodate its high volume), a merging, unmerging, and remerging with the Fenway Co-op, and a shift in membership from predominantly students to predominantly families.

Paced by activity in the numerous blocs, change came to the Mission Hill Co-op slowly. Some of the blocs have withered, combined with others, or simply disappeared. The Divine Light Mission (of Guru Maharaj Ji fame) bloc broke off and formed a co-op in itself. So did the Jamaica Plain bloc. A number of the people in the Allston-Brighton bloc are now in the Allston-Brighton Co-op. There was a new bloc run by co-op members for residents of a housing project for the elderly and another new bloc representing a drug treatment rehabilitation halfway house. Activity within the blocs has slowed over time. Monthly covered dish dinners are now rarities; they were once standard. Ms. Perrelli speculated, "I think this change has a lot to do with changing political interest. It sort of just went slowly away." Some of the blocs located close to others have recently joined forces to form neighborhood organizations. One of these, a group of blocs on the "back" of Mission Hill, is now working closely with an advocate planner to develop alternate plans for the area's redevelopment.

The greatest surge in Mission Hill's growth occurred in the earliest period, 1969-71, with the change of the co-op from a single-area co-op to a multi-bloc development and addition of new blocs. Since then, overall operation has been stable, with the addition of new blocs balancing fairly well the dissolution of some older blocs. Individual bloc operations have been more tumultuous, with frequent collaborations and dissolutions. Within and between blocs, membership has ebbed and flowed with the coming and going of students and other transients. People who stayed in the area often changed blocs while honoring the long-standing Boston custom of moving every September. Some members dabbled with the Boston Food Co-op, found it "too big," and returned to Mission Hill. Some dabbled with a return to supermarket shopping but simply couldn't face it, knowing that the co-op is in operation.

Co-op people have gone on to new involvements. Ms. Perrelli is active at the Boston Food Co-op as a paid cashier. Roger went on to work at Boston Food Co-op as produce buyer, then was hired buyer for NEFCO. He has helped numerous co-ops get started and keep going. His friend Saul now works occasionally unloading trucks at Chelsea for Boston Banana, a wholesaler.

Co-op organization has gotten a bit more formal. When Saul and Roger left in 1972 they urged that the next produce buyer be paid for his/her trouble because of the amount of work and the amount of personal commitment involved. Ms. Perrelli receives $25 weekly for her predawn buying expeditions. In the fall of 1973, co-op members voted to provide five dollars of "free" food to the co-op's bookkeeper, coordinator, cheese buyer, and the Tuesday and Thursday coordinators and the newsletter editor for the same reasons. Three area head positions were created to provide a sort of ombudsman service on the overall functioning of the co-op. The co-op added a number of new products over the years (cheese, yogurt, and breads) as it got refrigeration equipment, and helped a subsidiary monthly grain co-op get underway a few months ago. Current plans involve hooking up with the Boston Food Co-op's meat collective. Use of truck rentals replaced the solicitation of members' vans about a year ago.

With the truck rentals and paid positions the co-op's organization has grown increasingly sophisticated, but it is still no supermarket. The mechanism that has held the co-op together since most people can remember is the biweekly meeting. A representative from each bloc is required to attend. ("If they don't, they get a warning, and if they don't show at the next one they get a telephone call and a threat that they'll have to leave the co-op. At the next one, they show up," reports Ms. Perrelli.) The meeting is run partly on an agenda covering timely problems and issues and partly on a looser "general" format. Aside from the meeting, the co-op sponsors parties at Christmas, Halloween, or "whenever we get up for it." A weekly newsletter also helps unite the blocs and between-bloc interests.

One major change that has come to the co-op is the shift in membership away from students and younger people to families and "neighborhood people." This change reflects similar developments in co-ops in other areas. It happened in Mission Hill as a premeditated act. In the summer of 1973 co-op members

undertook a door-to-door recruitment effort to bring in more
families because of a general feeling that more families should be
involved. The door-to-door approach paid off and the family
groups soon came to form the most stable constituency of the
co-op. Part of the effort to get new people involved in the
co-op lives on in an advertising committee which is preparing
articles for community newspapers.

The co-op has had high and low points with membership,
sales, and organization following a seasonal pattern. Summers are
low points, when many people are away on vacation or on
transient schedules that take them out of the city. During the
summer the co-op operations fall back on "old stand-bys."
Fall usually brings an influx of students and recurring interest
in the co-op from families, too, as they settle into more patterned
weekly routines. During the cooler weather the co-op's volume
and range of related activities increase.

The overriding product of the Mission Hill Co-op's progression
through the years is stability and a consciousness of what makes
the co-op work. Problems get solved; operation is smooth.
If membership drops or some aspect of the organization goes sour,
there are people on hand who can and do take care of the
situation. There is not a weekly questioning of whether the
co-op will be around next week, but a long-range reflective
concern over what will happen to the co-op when new storefronts
open and how the co-op should grow over time.

Because of its longevity and expertise, the Mission Hill Co-op
makes a justifiable claim as an authority on food co-op operations.
It is one of the few co-ops in the area that does not use the
NEFCO buying service, but pays to have its own produce buyer.
Ms. Perrelli feels that it is important for a co-op of Mission
Hill's size to have its own buyer, in spite of the work and
personal inconvenience involved, because it brings the co-op
"that much closer" to full control of its operation and helps
make the co-op "tighter" overall.

The co-op's expertise, however, may be a detriment in some
respects. Co-op members know that their system works and are
quite unwilling, possibly even fearful, of experimenting with
new ideas. Ms. Perrelli told me how the co-op couldn't seriously
discuss the notion of opening its own storefront on a daily basis
"because, well, they just didn't think they could do it, and it
didn't seem like a good idea politically, cutting off some of
the neighborhood involved in the co-op to serve one neighborhood

better." Ms. Perrelli believes that the regular storefront idea deserves more careful consideration because the bloc form limits the kind of food the co-op can carry and the kind of relationship the co-op can have to members. A storefront would enable members to use the co-op every day, and for more items than weekly arrangement. Other co-op members are wary of the storefront approach because they feel incapable of maintaining the organization and because they "don't want to look like the Boston Food Co-op" (which is "too big").

GROWTH PATTERNS

Other co-ops have developed in ways so similar to Mission Hill as to be noteworthy. See, for example, the notes on the Broadway (New York City) Local Food Co-op in Appendix A. Looking back on the description of Mission Hill, I can see that the words don't really do justice to the existing level of activity. "The addition of new blocs balancing the dissolution of old blocs" really means long, anguished hours involving emotional meetings spent deciphering sloppy orders or arguing fine organizational points with friends who hold positions that are diametrically opposed. An editor at Boston's *Real Paper* said that her co-op was like "Peyton Place with vegetables." In the questionnaire responses to my mail survey, several co-ops indicated that their response to the "How has your co-op grown and changed?" question would occupy a book in itself. Several other co-ops indicated that they just couldn't begin to answer the question because it was so involved.

Those co-ops that did answer the question, along with the numerous co-ops I visited, point out some organizational trends which are somewhat troublesome. "Moved from a more casual approach to a fairly tightly structured one," notes the 300 Riverside Drive Co-op in New York, along with the note that they expanded their stock to include cheese and eggs. (The 300 Riverside Drive Co-op is a small—$100 weekly—buying club.) "Got a health department permit, a bank account, our own truck, and a fine bureaucracy," observed a newsletter of New York's Broadway Local Food Co-op. At the Santa Cruz Consumers' Co-op storefront, where "from $50 per week, our gross sales escalated to $1,500 per day! at times," a member observed, "Our growth has necessitated vital structural changes. We realized our need for a board of directors when the co-op decided to purchase the Way of Life Herb Store. . . . And we recently moved, the board playing the vital roles of finding and approving our new home. Also, we have two orderers rather than just one." Numerous co-ops chart their growth through increases in the variety of food they offer. "There are plans to double the size of the inventory if a new building can be found," notes the New Pioneer Food Co-op in Iowa City. "We've expanded products and services available," explains the Northside Buyers' Club in Peoria.

The path of Mission Hill from single organization to multi-bloc is typical of a lot of co-ops, but there are exceptions. Some co-ops resist joining up as blocs in larger co-ops if they want to maintain a strong identification with members or with "the community." The decision to join up often rests in the demands made by the larger co-op. Some, set up to promote bloc identity as much as possible, enable a co-op to maintain its sense of self.

Individual co-op growth and development is not independent of regional growth and development. Mission Hill's current form reflects the state of co-ops in the Boston area. It benefits from advances in buying technique and regional unity; it creates its organizational profile in relation to other co-ops in the area. Regional co-op buying services or organizational assistance can boost individual co-op growth tremendously.

MONEY

Co-ops often measure growth and change in terms of dollar volume because money activity fairly accurately depicts the level of all activity within a co-op. In addition to being a barometer, money can be the root of a barrage of problems.

For most co-ops, financial trouble means a shortage of money. This can occur through incompetent buying, wholesaler and delivery shortages, waste, and a variety of operational expenses (new equipment, transportation, or rent cost increases, etc.). It can also be caused, and this really hurts, by theft, plain and simple. "We were getting ripped off" is the lament of more co-ops than involved people like to admit. Some theft is petty stuff—food items sneaked into a bag, or short payments on an order—but some is serious dipping into the till. Even petty theft can have very serious consequences for a small co-op, throwing the group into debt and disillusioning the members. The best way for co-ops to prevent theft is by being a co-op as much as possible. A tightly knit group provides a strategic hedge against shrinkage because everyone knows what everyone else is doing. Still more important, a close group also creates psychological barriers. People are much more willing to steal from strangers than from friends.

Aside from theft, many co-ops are plagued by a devil-may-care attitude about money among the membership. Financial tightrope walking is a co-op tradition to the extent that a strong financial base is anathema to some groups. After the initial wave of co-op growth many co-ops got so used to financial instability that it became a way of life for them—they had been around long enough in a precarious state to become convinced that they were immortal. Since then, some co-ops have folded, and money management has become a more serious issue. A healthy financial profile does not have to be the *raison d'être* of a food co-op, but it does warrant real concern.

Bookkeeping problems lie at the heart of many co-op financial problems. Some co-ops don't know they're in debt or being stolen from because they don't know where the money goes. If co-ops have difficulty keeping track of their money, they need to remedy the situation quickly because money problems can all too easily multiply within short periods of time. Once a co-op has a workable system of bookkeeping set up, it should stick with the system so that it can spot changes and problems. A bookkeeping system that changes every month won't do the job of showing where the money goes much better than no bookkeeping system at all.

Keeping track of money is not a mystical chore. It may seem that way when bills come in, payments go out, or orders come with wrong amounts of money. But money management is not difficult—it just requires a little organization. Further, it's important not to let money management get out of hand. The co-op has better things to do.

PHYSICAL FACILITIES

Storefront co-ops may see growth as the expansion of their physical facilities. Getting a new refrigerator can increase the service provided by the co-op and elicit new membership interested in the larger inventory. Sometimes co-ops have to pay for such equipment: Glut, in Mt. Rainier, Maryland, recently laid out $1,500 for a stand-up sliding door milk cooler. The Alternative Natural Foodstore in Oakland got their cooler in a better deal: "We scored

one refrigerator case for $95—at a fish market; someone had
their eyes open and made an offer on the spot—no ad or anything.
Our produce case was probably done similarly." Physical facilities
may include items less obvious than coolers. There is a need for
shelving and display areas, often constructed ingeniously, though
rustically, by volunteers. Some physical facilities, like cash
registers, are controversial because they represent to some people
the degeneration of a co-op into a regular supermarket. The
anti-cash register faction at the Boston Food Co-op held out for
months until money shrinkage and unbearably long lines at
the rickety adding machines convinced members that cash
registers were a necessity.

Like interior physical facilities, the space in which a co-op
is housed is likely to play a key role in co-op development over
time. Inadequate basements or garages may cramp operations
to the extent of slowing things down and discouraging membership.
Conversely, moving to new quarters can bring on a burst of
enthusiasm to "get the place fixed up." In the course of co-op
growth, the organization may move from a private basement to
a form of rented space, in which case the considerations in
the "Space" section of Chapter Two apply. Co-ops that move
to rented space instead of starting there have the advantage of
an ongoing organization to weather the change. Often such
a move has little effect on how things run. Mission Hill, for
example, suffered little in bouncing from garage to basement
to storefront because, as a bloc organization co-op, it saw most
of its interaction with members within blocs rather than at
the all-co-op level. When the blocs changed locale there were
more far-reaching effects, however. Similarly, there are important
effects for a small co-op when it moves from one member's
apartment to another's, or to a hallway or other common space.
The configuration of the meeting space and the facilities available
do a lot to the organization at an operational level. Whether
or not the host's refrigerator is large, for example, can determine
if the co-op will handle perishable items. A simple added facility
like a coffee pot can favorably influence group interaction.

Staff

A major area of growth for co-ops is the addition of paid
staff. At Mission Hill, people were remunerated for bookkeeping,
coordinator, and area head positions with free food while the
produce buyer earned $25 each week for her work. Other co-ops

set up similar kinds of pay scales. It is most usual for bookkeepers to receive some sort of pay because of the inordinately involving and time-consuming work they must do. Bookkeeping, unlike produce weighing or order makeup is not a task that every co-op member can do. Even if the co-op were composed entirely of accountants, it would probably not be a good idea to change bookkeepers each week because some continuity is necessary. Transactions have a way of spreading themselves over time, requiring for the sake of accuracy that whoever fulfills the bookkeeping position is around to keep track of them. Some co-ops establish the position of coordinator in the same way.

Establishing paid positions often effects major ramifications within the organization. In a small co-op the "employee" almost unavoidably becomes an organizational superstar, someone who is omnipresent at all co-op activities and hence an authority. Moreover, people in the organization may allow their own participation to lapse since, well, "It's her job—let her do it." There is an inevitable ambiguity in the difference in roles between member and employee and a degree of upset in the balance of power in the group overall. Some groups react to this by setting up very conservative job definitions and tasks, unconsciously creating a form of alienated labor within the co-op. Others try to promote workers' control among employees. A number of co-ops treat the matter of paid staff with a hands-off approach, rotating as much work as possible, even bookkeeping, among numbers of people.

Sheer Numbers

Changes in membership totals bother many co-ops. When membership is down, some products become harder to get as economies of scale shrivel. Also, a co-op that loses members is not apt to be a happy place, especially if efforts are being made to keep members in. Severe membership reductions often catalyze dissolutions and mergers. Membership expansion can bring problems, too, if the organization is geared to working with smaller groups. Some co-ops fantasize an ideal co-op size, but co-ops can work at any size if they organize carefully. The best argument I've heard for an ideal size co-op is the grab-bag co-op in New York that tries to stick with twelve members because most of the crates they buy come with twelve items inside.

Some people worry about turnover in co-ops. Turnover is a

real problem for co-ops whose membership base is predominantly students or other transients. For more stable groups, turnover may not be such an issue. The Marshfield Co-op numbers its turnover in one or two members every few months of a total group of fifteen. New York City co-ops organized by working- and middle-class people report an attrition rate of one or two members per year. Even among these, there are many who turn up in other co-ops. Often people who do leave are not disillusioned (notwithstanding the *Real Paper* article discussed in Chapter Two) or upset by co-ops, but unable to work out tactical or scheduling problems.

One conclusion about membership size that makes sense is that size has strong effects on co-op operations. "We could really feel the difference when we went from fifty families to seventy," a woman told me at one New York co-op. "With the space we have available, the bookkeeping work, and making up everybody's orders, sixty is just our capacity." Space, book- keeping, the amount of time people want to put into the co-op, and the way the co-op is set up all affect the workable, comforta- ble capacity a co-op has. (There is, incidentally, a big difference between what's workable and what's comfortable.) A happy, sixty-family, job-specific co-op may have to break into blocs in order to comfortably accommodate more families. A large co-op of many blocs may have to open a storefront in order to handle new blocs. The co-ops in Cambridge, Massachusetts, have aligned and realigned blocs several times in varying configurations of North, South, and Central co-op to keep the size comfortable.

Some co-ops make conscious attempts to limit membership. "If we get too big," a Cambridge woman explained, "we'll miss what the whole point of the co-op is. If I can't know everyone in the group, I might as well be shopping in the supermarket." Some suburban Massachusetts co-ops have established cut-off limits at whatever number of families— forty or fifty—began to make everyone nervous. Some of these established waiting lists which subsequently "fed" others like the Concord Co-op. Some maintain an active component to help start "spin-off" co-ops from growing membership lists. Some weather growth by establishing sub-co-ops or collectives. within the co-op to perform needed tasks. Open membership is a cornerstone of Rochdale gospel and an important component of co-op growth. Most co-ops find a way to accommodate people either within their group or within new co-ops.

The issue of size is not so easily taken care of by divide and multiply tactics, though, since co-ops increasingly try to work together to increase their economic power and economies of scale. The advantages of inter-co-op cooperation weigh against the needs of keeping co-ops small. Some sort of mechanism is required to balance off intimacy and participation with economic effectiveness. The best way for co-ops to cope with changes in space, staff, and overall size is with an organization that accurately reflects members' interests and needs.

COMMITMENT MECHANISMS

Social science research on utopian communities suggests that if organizers want to build a long-lasting community and are wondering how much responsibility the members should bear, a good guideline is "the more, the merrier." "To create a long-lived communal order . . . requires many fairly strict and demanding social practices," claims Rosabeth M. Kanter in *Commitment and Community*.[1] The most long-lived nineteenth-century communities benefitted from a strong commitment of members elicited through such mechanisms as renunciation of outside-commune life, full sacrifice of private money and property to the community, free love or celibacy, and acceptance of elaborate ideologies.[2]

Food co-ops probably needn't elicit such elaborate commitments, but the principle of requiring much deserves greater consideration. Some co-ops view high initial member fees as a way of extracting a commitment from new members. They feel that once a member has paid such a fee he or she is more likely to give the co-op a chance to prove that it can work, more willing to last out problems, and more willing to help out. Ronald Wolff of Oakland's Alternative Natural Foodstore reports that the Alternative may use a money-based commitment mechanism:

We may soon ask present shoppers to front us $2-$5 in order to continue to shop here, so mebbe we won't bounce as many checks in the future. . . . We also want to arouse a bit more community concern in our well-being rather than the present, "Well the Alternative's still hangin in there, and I guess it always will, even though I John Coolperson Organicfreak, don't help them survive other than by shopping there."

The Seminary Co-op, which operates out of the General Theological Seminary in New York City, has extraordinarily tough rules for members. People must show up when they're supposed to or find a replacement. No excuses are accepted, and negligent members are dropped after one mishap. The organization thrives. The Boston Food Co-op and the co-ops in the St. Louis area found that members responded well to similar, but not nearly as tough, crackdowns on seeing that all members come to work at the co-op each month. Work collectives like the Whole Earth Learning Community in Madison, Wisconsin, and the Glut co-op in Washington, D.C., have found that their organizations run more smoothly and members "feel better about their relationship to the group" when members must agree to stay with the group for at least six months at a time.

Commitment mechanisms are not an inherently good tactic, though. Ms. Kanter points out:

Up to a point the greater the number of commitment mechanisms a group uses, the stronger the commitment of its members. But past that number, commitment mechanisms may become dysfunctional for the group; they may be perceived as oppressive and may stifle the person's autonomy to the extent that he becomes less rather than more committed.[3]

Food co-ops that demand high degrees of commitment may scare off new members and isolate the old ones. Some commitment mechanisms may promote bureaucracy and/or bad feelings. An active member of the Dry Goods collective in Minneapolis remarked, "I don't want my whole life to be the co-op. It's too much. As it is now you make up a fantasy story and 'put it on the wire' in the morning and by the evening you'd be convinced it's true because you'd hear it from everybody you ran into during the day." Throughout my visit in Minneapolis I kept hearing the expression "burned out," used by many people to describe their inability to cope with the commitments their co-ops attempted to elicit.

A strongly committed co-op could be a pain in the neck for many people to work into their lives, and an organizational dictatorship. Like the food that a co-op buys, the commitment mechanisms it employs will have much influence in determining what is the overall profile of the organization. As there are tradeoffs in selling foods that appeal to different kinds of people, so there are also tradeoffs in establishing commitment mechanisms.

Beyond reasonable limits, commitment mechanisms can turn a group into a totalitarian nightmare.

ORGANIZERS: A SPECIAL CASE

In the "Getting Started" chapter of this book I pointed out that many food co-ops are initiated by one person or a small group of people. Particularly tough bureaucratic problems can emerge in such co-ops. Often these go on to become co-ops in which participation and responsibility are spread among the membership, but occasionally co-op initiators become co-op coordinators in name and co-op kings (queens) in fact. This is particularly prevalent among people who dabble with co-ops to give themselves something to do in their free time. They soon find themselves at the hub of a thriving organization which, if they've planned it properly, will place them in a key position of responsibility. Fortunately, these people usually do not last long in these positions because of basic human limitations. Too much work is involved in most co-ops to make it humanly feasible to center the work/responsibility on one person.

While dabbling organizers usually don't have the time or fortitude to keep up a time-consuming commitment to a food co-op, professional organizers often do. Some of the most uncooperative co-ops are those literally run by poverty workers or community organizers "for the good" of a community. One such organizer concluded in a report that the co-op should "face up to the situation that the store cannot operate on volunteer help. All volunteer organizations are carried by a small percentage of the membership. Thus, hire a full-time store manager...." It's as if organizers set up the co-op as something to keep themselves busy, because they often won't allow the community to take over. Paulo Friere points out in *Pedagogy of the Oppressed*: "A real humanist can be identified more by his trust in the people, which engages him in their struggle, than by a thousand actions in their favor without that trust." [4] Neighborhood people know all too well that the co-op isn't theirs in spite of posters and flyers arguing to the contrary. They know that if they don't show up, if no one shows, the co-op will go on because the organizer will be there doing all the work. Sometimes it's difficult for an organizer to pull out and let a group experience failure—the organizer may know all too well how easily people get disillusioned and drop out.

Still, if people can't be allowed to experience failure, the co-op inevitably becomes a maudlin charity that makes a joke of the cooperative ideal of self-help.

I met a woman organizer in New York City who, for a number of reasons, was unable to be present when "her" co-op distributed. To her (pleasant) surprise, neighborhood people stepped in, making the co-op infinitely stronger. As we sat in the co-op's basement distribution storage area discussing the situation, one of the older women in the co-op interrupted us, bending over and kissing the organizer in greeting. There were a few pleasantries exchanged, and when the woman left the organizer explained that the woman, who was more than seventy, had gotten involved in the early-morning buying at Hunt's Point. The organizer had worried that no one would be able to perform the buying chores, but found that the older woman and several others filled in. Women in the co-op whom I interviewed later made no bones about whose co-op they were talking about. They had been having real trouble getting a truck to make pickups and deliveries, and they assured me, "If we don't go, no co-op." They go.

Yet it is not difficult to understand the dilemma of another New York City organizer who confided, "This co-op does violence to the name co-op. There just isn't a lot of cooperation." He had tried and tried to get greater involvement, and there were a number of volunteers when I visited the co-op, but he was still very disappointed with the response. What seemed most upsetting was that the co-op could have added much to the shopping power of the people in the area, many of whom were on welfare. "My friends tell me it's counterproductive, it's like social work," he mused, "but the way we feel about it is that we're helping people eat." In that situation, the rights and wrongs are not quite so clear.

THE IRON LAW OF OLIGARCHY

The need for co-ops to strike this sort of balance is heightened by sociological evidence that all organizations, even loosely structured ones like food co-ops, are governed by forces that move them away from informality and decentralized power structures toward bureaucracy, patterned behavior, and centralization of authority. Ed Wertheim, a sociology professor at Boston University's School of Business Administration, explained the process to me. He had worked with a colleague, Ronald Curhan, on research on Boston-area food co-ops described in the first chapter of this book, so he had some experience with the issue.

"The Iron Law of Oligarchy," Wertheim explains, "was postulated by the German sociologist Robert Michels in his book *Political Parties* in 1911. It means, generally, that oligarchical tendencies move power toward the center and top of organizational structures." (Oligarchy, incidentally, is a governmental form in which a few people hold the ruling power.) In food co-ops, power moving toward the center and top means power moving away from large-scale, decentralized participation to smaller, more centralized groups or individuals. The provocative thing about the Iron Law is that it applies as much to organizations which are avowedly nonoligarchical as to organizations which are supposed to be oligarchical. "Who says organization says oligarchy," says Michels.[5] No room for exception there, not even for food co-ops.

Creeping oligarchy may occur in food co-ops when volunteers don't show up for their designated work and some members take on added responsibilities. As "regulars" emerge, they take on more work, more responsibility, and more authority. Their experience and involvement gives them power. Similarly, poor attendance at policy-making meetings may lead to the establishment and strengthen the power of steering committees. Replacing participant activities like wholesale buying and truck operations with services offered by individuals outside the co-op also weakens the broad-scale participatory base.

Recent developments in organizational theory point out other principles, some which directly strengthen the iron law and some which just make it difficult for an organization to serve its members. Jerome Murphy titled his recent study of State Departments of Education's use of flexible, nontargeted federal grant monies *Grease the Squeaky Wheel*. The title helps make the point that when organizations are confronted with an opportunity to use "no strings" assistance, they respond with short-run sorts of programs. Murphy's summary of organizational theory suggests that organizations are more interested in avoiding disorder and uncertainty than in seeking "the best solution" to a problem. Avoiding disorder and uncertainty may be in themselves important goals for some organizations, but Murphy claims they often become overriding concerns. In addition, he points out that an organization's standard operating procedures frequently become unbendable dogma, effective blockades to any innovation or change. He concludes that when organizations do change, they change slowly.[6]

Standard operating procedure worship in a food co-op can happen with any aspect of co-op operations. One example is the suburban Massachusetts co-op buyer who won't use the NEFCO buying service because "we've always dealt with the concessioner. We're used to it." It is understandable that a group of amateurs would develop an uncertainty avoidance fixation, but some co-ops immortalize their problems this way, clinging to inconvenient order forms, time-consuming distribution techniques, inefficient ways of using members' time, confusing bookkeeping systems, or wasteful food handling techniques.

In addition to all the organizational factors contributing to bureaucratization, there are some causes at the level of the individual members. Terry Molner of the Boston Food Co-op suggests that one reason co-ops must struggle to remain cooperative is that the whole cooperative concept is beyond most people's experience. "We all know how to be leaders or followers," he points out, "but not how to be collaborative."

Some psychological considerations on the nature of groups are also relevant here. Freud kept a special place in his heart for groups because he felt they were of formidable psychological concern. In *Group Psychology and the Analysis of the Ego* Freud postulates: "A group is impulsive, changeable and irritable. It is led almost exclusively by the unconscious. . . . A group is extraordinarily credulous and open to influence, it has no critical faculty, and the improbable does not exist for it. . . . The feelings of a group are almost always simple and always exaggerated." [7]

There is also some evidence that a phenomenon called groupthink is a silent but powerful participant in group processes of decision-making. Groupthink drives group members to push for consensus as well as for their particular interests. The drive for consensus can then overtake the individual motivations people bring to a group, producing a decision that no one really wanted. Food co-ops that want to keep up "good vibes" are particularly susceptible to groupthink. Unable or unwilling to admit that they have any disagreements, members quickly arrive at a state of hollow accord.

Wertheim points out that it is particularly dangerous for food co-ops to get beleaguered by bureaucracy and oligarchy. It's more than the contradiction in terms that's troublesome. In his research, Wertheim found that for a substantial number of people, saving money wasn't the major motivation for being in the food co-op. Most people were far more interested in the social aspects. Bureaucratization and oligarchy minimize the social benefits and the resultant number of reasons for people to join. If they can't enjoy participation, Wertheim feels they will take their business elsewhere.

He also pointed out that bureaucracy is not completely evil, but that co-ops should at least be aware of the forces working on their organizations. He recalled a meeting of one co-op he observed (he thought Mission Hill) where there was considerable debate over using a bookkeeping system that enabled a limited number of people to sign the checks. Members felt they couldn't have decentralized power unless all members were able to sign the checks.

A man once active in food co-ops in the Houston area felt that his co-op had suffered greatly because members didn't give in enough to bureaucracy. "Too many people have a mindless distaste for any kind of structure," he explained. His co-op had been losing money from "shrinkage," but "they couldn't bring themselves to say the words 'someone is stealing from us' or admit that they needed more accurate record-keeping." Members of the West Village Co-op in New York told me that some of their membership were "structure freaks." "There's one guy here who doesn't want *anything* permanent," a woman told me, adding, after a glance at the assortment of people putting food in bags in the cluttered basement, "but this ain't exactly a police station, is it?" Some professional organizers also take issue with advocates of nonstructure. Saul Alinsky claims, "Power and organization are one and the same." [8]

BREAKING THE IRON LAW

At an organizational level, Mr. Wertheim cited some examples of how co-ops have attempted to mitigate the effects of bureaucracy. Some disband, unable to resolve the problem. Some consciously limit themselves to small numbers of people or divide large groups into more intimate subgroups, often giving the subgroup a specific task to carry out or setting them up as blocs. Beyond these concepts, there are a number of others that can also help break the iron law of oligarchy and work against bureaucracy. *Union Democracy*, an academic work by Seymour Lipset, Martin Trow, and James Coleman, tries to identify salient reasons

why the International Typographers' Union doesn't follow the
"law." Some of their conclusions which may apply to food co-ops:

The more homogeneous the interests of the members . . . , the greater
the chances for democracy.

The more that workers . . . associate with each other off the job, . . . the
greater is likely to be their participation in the union.

The more opportunities the members of a union have to learn political
skills, the greater the chances for democracy and their union.

The greater the number of independent channels of communication to
the membership available to opposition groups, the greater the chances
for democracy. [9]

A food co-op wishing to use these principles would provide
opportunities for members to get together away from the co-op,
help members develop political skills, and keep open channels
of communication among all the members. Translating these
principles into more specific suggestions for groups brings about
some straightforward hints. Underlying these, however, is the
realization that organizations that want to prevent creeping
oligarchy can't rely on their good looks to wage the battles.
Jane Mansbridge, a political scientist at the University of
Chicago who has studied participatory democracy, states:
"Direct democracies (organizations run by member participation)
that want to spread participation must do so consciously, by
multiplying the number of ways a member can have influence." [10]
She suggests some specific tactics organizations can use to help
bring about a more democratic way of operating:
   —Distribution of responsibilities throughout the membership.
Chairperson positions can be rotated throughout the membership,
as can positions on important committees. In any case,
responsibility and authority should not be delegated by default,
but by some plan. Even position assignment by alphabetical
order will spread authority better than default. The warehouse
in Minneapolis carries this principle out by attempting to
get everyone in the collective to be able to do every job.
A member of the collective told me she was very satisfied with
the arrangement, but "there's so much of an 'everybody's got
to know how to do everything' philosophy that we ignore some
people's skills. Still, I guess that's what you have to do to
make sure that we're really a collective."
   —Encouraging small associations. The Boston Food Co-op,

for example, recently initiated a granola collective which bakes the co-op's granola at Queensberry Street Bakery, which is otherwise unused on Sundays. The Boston co-op also recently began a meat collective which meets weekly to carve up half a side of beef and learn butchering in the process (an experienced butcher leads the group). Minneapolis's Powderhorn Co-op uses a system of day groups—members come to the store weekly and work with the same people on their chosen day. Other co-ops also use the collective approach with some smaller co-ops starting one- or two-person work teams. Ms. Mansbridge points out that these groups need not be directly related to the operation of the organization, but "the [small] group initiates personal interactions that are more important for most participants than the substantive decisions governing the large institutions that affect their lives. . . . Active membership, even in a group completely unrelated to politics like a sports association, increases one's subsequent political participation." [11]

—Paying for participation. In her *Working Papers* article, Ms. Mansbridge acknowledges the common practice of food co-ops giving weekly surpluses to whichever blocs or people did the work that week. Remuneration might also take the form of covered-dish dinners or parties. There is a fine line between this kind of remuneration and the establishment of paid positions.

—Becoming participation conscious. Ms. Mansbridge advises, "If . . . a community wants to make it more likely that political decisions balance the needs of all its members relatively equally, and if it does not want to exclude any of its members from the psychological benefits of participation, it cannot accept the participative status quo." [12] Active members need to include as part of their normal range of activities an awareness of what it takes to keep the food co-op a participatory group. In *Up the Organization*, Robert Townsend describes a tactic he found successful in working against oligarchy—creating a position or designating someone as "vice president in charge of anti-bureaucratization. . . . In addition to his regular duties, it's his job to wander around the company looking for new forms, new staff departments, and new reports. Whenever he finds one that smells like institutionalization, he screams 'Horseshit!' at the top of his lungs." [13] A little of that might help break some co-ops out of the trap of unawareness so easy to wander into.

Co-ops that are aware of themselves and the structure of their organizations can maintain a democratic organization.

Outpost Co-op in Milwaukee traced the development of their
storefront away from centralization. "As the store grew and
original people dropped out," a member reports, "the management
burdens were spread to more shoulders." Mission Hill moved to
involve more people more closely in its organization when it
implemented the current system which gives over whole-co-op
operating responsibilities to one bloc each week. The prior
arrangement used a six-member council, elected monthly, which
arranged work parties, juggled orders, distributed newsletters
and order lists, and, in short, ran the co-op. Another Boston
area co-op, attempting to get more involvement from members,
published a newsletter with the heading, "Changes in Food Co-op
are Badly Needed." The newsletter communicated a reasoned
appeal:

> While in terms of size and savings, we have been very successful, we
> are beset by some very serious problems. The most important of these
> is a need for more participation by Co-op members in the tasks that
> have to get done if the Co-op is to continue. As of now, a group of
> 15-20 people do a tremendous amount of the general co-op work.
> Increasingly these people have become dissatisfied over the amount
> of time they have to put in, every week, while many Co-op members
> are getting the benefit of the Co-op without contributing any time
> or effort. This is not the way a Co-operative organization should
> function. If everyone put in just a small amount of time, every week
> or even every month, the burden that a few people have had to bear
> would be lessened and the Co-op would be very much strengthened.
> Only if this happens does the Co-op become a real Co-op, and only then
> can we be sure it will continue even if some people can no longer
> work on it. It's up to the members of the Co-op to keep it going.

There followed a list of job descriptions. I understand that the
newsletter, along with some direct telephone contact, brought
out a substantial increase.

While broader-base participation can sometimes be mandated
and enacted in food co-op operations, it may be much more
difficult to evenly distribute participation in decision- and
policy-making. Co-op meetings which are well attended may
not elicit real participation from more than a handful of
people. The all-co-op meetings in Minneapolis followed this
path and inspired a heated response in the all-co-op newsletter
from a co-oper named Mark Elliot:

All-coop meetings seem to be run by a small group of people who work a lot in the coops and have many strong, definite ideas about how they ought to be run. Once one of these coop "heavies" gets an idea in his head about how something ought to be done, he will talk and bullshit endlessly until everyone else gets sick of it and gives in. (I say "he" and "his" here because 90% of the people who dominate all coop meetings are male.) People who have different ideas have to fight their way into a discussion when they want to say something, and are very rarely listened to when they are allowed to speak. The people who do the most and the loudest talking at all coop meetings will psychologically set up a very intimidating, exclusive structure by which they dominate the meeting, regardless of what sort of form we may choose to try to run the meeting by. As long as these people are allowed to continue their dominance, the form that we choose to have the meeting follow (voting vs. consensus, 2 regular reps. from each store, etc.) won't make any difference. The solution is for all of us to become very conscious of the coercive tactics used at these meetings and demand that they be stopped. There is no point in continuing the all coop meeting unless we make it into a place where all of us can freely communicate our thoughts and ideas with each other. This won't happen all by itself, or by "good karma," it can only happen if we increase our awareness of how oppressive we are to each other at meetings, and learn how to stop it.

SEIZE THE TIME! SMASH THE DICTATORSHIP OF THE LOUD!!

Newsletters in themselves are also important ways of cutting down on oligarchy. They spread information, and in many cases, information is power. Most food co-ops produce a newsletter without a lot of extra work when they produce their price lists. Some newsletters are just concerned with co-op news, but many co-ops, finding the main work to be in getting out any sort of printed matter, add a little effort to make the newsletter a vibrant expression. Newsletters from the North Cambridge Food Co-op feature recipes (Anti-Imperialist Casserole, vegetarian dishes, etc.), social comment, and a small classified section. Using newsletters to circulate recipes is an excellent way to publicize "new vegetables," grains, and new food ideas. In a bloc co-op, newsletters can link the overall membership and coordinate interbloc activity. In a smaller co-op, a newsletter can keep up ties with people who are unable to come to the co-op for a time and explain new policies or endeavors of the co-op that might not get communicated in the commotion of people picking up their food. In storefronts, newsletters can keep people posted on meetings and activities when storekeepers are (as they often get) harried.

Newsletter production has come within reach of even the smallest groups. Small groups can usually produce a newsletter with a typewriter or legible handwriting and a five-cent copying machine available at most public libraries. Most small co-op newsletters seem to get duplicated clandestinely at some member's place of work. One of the most ingenious of these is the suburban Massachusetts architect who uses the office line printer, creating great oversized listings and notes. A cheaper method of reproduction is a Ditto machine, which uses a stencil. The stencils are cheap, and can be written or typed on. Churches and community organizations often have these gadgets and can sometimes be persuaded to allow the co-op to use them.

There are more complex ways of getting newsletters out, all well described in the "Publications" section (pp. 42-59) of a paperback called *The Organizer's Manual* (OM Collective, Bantam, 1971). *OM* also stresses: "Whatever printing method you use, be sure your leaflet is clean and clear." A smeary newsletter looks bad and may not communicate anything, and it just isn't that hard to produce something legible.

EDUCATION

Cooperative education is the time-honored way (tracing all the way back to the Rochdale principles) for co-ops to deal with problems of communication and participation. At present, only the larger co-ops are involved in co-op education programs and even they leave a lot to be desired. Education takes many forms and many co-ops engage in education programs without actually calling them programs. A newsletter is, in a sense, education, as are meetings, posters, flyers. Grouping all of these and other functions under the heading of education and formalizing the concept enough to give it permanence is one way of assuring that participation gets consistent attention. Co-ops organized into work brigades sometimes designate one collective to handle this function.

The Boston Food Co-op's approach to education was to actually establish classes. There was a general feeling at the co-op that, short of making a movie, classes would be the best way to help orient new members both to co-op operations and to a little bit of co-op history, philosophy, and organization. A battery of members volunteered to teach the one-class sessions and set up the classes so they would be given frequently, available for people with all sorts of schedules. To make sure people would attend the classes, the board of directors made attendance mandatory for new and old members.

The classes briefly review co-op history and the variety of food co-op forms possible. The latter is "taught" with an eye to enabling people to start their own co-op if (as so many BFC members do) they leave the Boston area. Then there is a store tour, with explanations of how the equipment works ("Don't stock food in front of the fans in the cooler," the "teacher" warns), and how the co-op operates. There is also usually some advice thrown in on special food items, co-op news and notes, and a plea to get "students" to make the best use of the co-op. The classes fill a special role at BFC, adding a degree of personal contact that many members in the large organization would otherwise miss. In addition, the class's explanation of co-op operations should help maximize the use of members' required two-hour monthly time requirement.

There is admittedly a paradoxical aspect of a voluntary association like a food cooperative having mandatory education classes. Yet, the classes are a minimal commitment mechanism and a not very demanding attempt to make the large co-op more personal. They help the co-op operate better and maintain stronger links with members.

OTHER TACTICS

Some other organizational tactics that co-ops use to spread participation:

—Telephone chains can decentralize the task of spreading information in a hurry. In a predetermined system, member A calls another member, B, or the member C if B is out. C then passes the information on; A is responsible for getting back to B, etc.

—Brainstorming at a meeting is a way to bring out new ideas. In a brainstorming session, everyone contributes and criticism may be outlawed to help nurse developing concepts.

—"Stacking" at meetings involves lining up potential interrupters in the same way as airplanes line up at an airport, taking turns. People who wish to speak take turns in the stacking order.

—Sponsoring social events like parties or covered-dish dinners. Roger Auerbach restated Lipset's principle at a NEFCO meeting: "If we're going to create a co-op movement, I've got to feel comfortable with you."

Growing and dividing keeps groups small and helps expand overall co-op activities. Dave Zinner explained how the beginning St. Louis co-op split when it was growing too fast, "And that was a good thing. When you're overloaded, people should be encouraged to start their own co-op. Then you end up with more co-ops and more activity." The grow-and-divide strategy is particularly well suited to co-ops that take on new functions like mills or warehouse operations. Bruce Singer, who was working on getting a Washington warehouse started, commented, "One thing that really became clear in Minneapolis was, whenever you find out that you're doing two separate things in one place, split them and get two places."

BEYOND BUREAUCRACY: CONFLICT AND RESOLUTION

A lively co-op can thrive on conflict. Conflict may be the antonym of cooperation, but cooperation is empty unless it involves some controversy and some upset. The best organizations aren't the ones that don't have any conflicts but the ones that can weather a conflict without ripping apart the group. A philosopher friend swears that the couple on his block who throw dishes at each other, slam the doors, and generally argue very loudly is also the couple that is most in love. That may be debatable, but it does help make the point that sound organizations can have serious conflicts and still be good organizations.

Not all conflicts can be resolved. Some may, some have irrevocably split co-ops. It is upsetting to see a strong co-op wither or break up, but even more upsetting to see a co-op plod on with a disgruntled membership and a bad organization. Members who had joined in search of an alternative to the supermarket end up looking for an alternative to the co-op. Putting the co-op out to pasture can be a creative act that spawns new co-ops and new growth, but it may simply end, too. If a co-op works for two or three years, it's served a real purpose for members. In fact, if the co-op works at all, it serves a real purpose for members.

Chapter Four

CO-OPS AND POLITICS

I had lunch with an incensed member of the Concord Co-op who had been at the meeting described in the "Starting a Food Co-op" chapter. It was just a day or two after the meeting and he was still outraged. "Union lettuce!" he intoned. "Who the hell cares who picks the goddam lettuce? It all tastes the same to me, and besides, I don't need to waste my time at these meetings listening about the injustices of the food corporations. I joined the co-op to get cheaper food, not hear lectures on other peoples' politics." The gentleman was quite upset that Ben had announced that the co-op would carry lettuce only when United Farm Workers' lettuce was available. "What's the point of being in the co-op if I can't get the food I want?" he demanded. But what really made him indignant was having to listen to political proselytizing. "I don't think co-ops ought to be a political vehicle," he commented. "The problem is that politics is permeating everything. At least when I go to the supermarket I'm not subjected to the owner's political views."

Linda Spero, a Somerville mother and current coordinator of the Broadway Co-op, had an experience similar to that of the man from Concord. I met with Mrs. Spero and several other co-op members over coffee at Mrs. Spero's home. Her cup informed me that "Housework is a bitch." Neither she nor her friends had had prior experience with food co-ops or anything like them. Mrs. Spero, an ex-WAC, had been a quiet member of the co-op for several months. She liked the idea of saving money on food and she enjoyed working with neighbors in the co-op. Like her neighbors, she suspected that the woman who started the co-op was interested in using it as a political vehicle. The suspicions were never borne out, though. "If she had an ulterior motive, we never found out about it," Mrs. Spero recalled. When the

93

woman who had done much of the organizing left, the group
came under the control of some young people who were involved
in antiwar activities. They ran the co-op well enough, but mixed
politics with co-op operations. They inserted leaflets in people's
food orders. "None of us thought it was right for them to
do that," Mrs. Spero recalled, "but I was the only one that
opened my mouth. I guess you could say I stole the organization
from them. It was summertime and a lot of them were traveling,
so I stepped in as coordinator." Since then the Broadway Co-op
has been notably apolitical. "I joined the co-op to save money
on food, not to do anything political," Mrs. Spero noted. The
co-op mirrors her convictions well.

The Concord and Somerville co-ops both stretched the purposes
of their organizations beyond the basic functions of distributing
food. In Concord, the stretching wasn't a big step from the
regular operation of the co-op. The group has to buy food and
can control the kind of food it buys. Similarly, co-ops have to
transport food, have some sort of organizational structure, deal
with a wholesaler, have to handle money, etc. Since the co-op
exercises control over the specifics of carrying out all these
tasks, it can choose what kind of food it buys, which wholesalers,
banks, delivery services, and adding machines it wants by whatever
criteria the group chooses. Co-op members develop an awareness
that their combined spending adds up to a considerable sum.
"All of a sudden I'm the one who's spending a couple of hundred
dollars for food every week, buying for the co-op. I can afford
to be choosy," one woman told me. Co-op buyers quickly
realize the economic clout they possess. One woman remarked,
"When I shopped in the supermarket I never considered
returning spoiled items or complaining about how the store
was run. I didn't think it would make any difference. Now that
I buy from a wholesaler, I just insist that everything is the
way I want it because I know it can be that way. The wholesaler knows, too, and he doesn't want to lose my business."

BUYING POWER

Encouraged by the control they exert over food quality,
some co-ops go on to experiment with greater influence. Food
co-ops with co-op consciousness try to help other cooperative
forms. Numerous Boston area food co-ops make a point of
doing business with the co-op-run NEFCO buying service.

Midwestern co-ops go out of their way to patronize the regional trucking collective. Food co-ops in Chicago deal with the Cornucopia warehouse. Beyond this basic sort of support for food-related operations, many food co-ops exercise discretion over other services. One Boston-area co-op member described how his group carefully chose the bank for its "business account." They wanted to avoid banks they suspected of discriminatory employment practices. Similarly, a suburban Boston co-op chose a one-person delivery service because they wanted to avoid dealing with large, impersonal businesses.

Many food co-ops try to reflect their interests, beliefs, and politics in the food items that they stock. Like the Concord group, many co-ops avoid any lettuce except UFW label. The nonunion lettuce boycott is widespread among co-ops, perhaps because of its extensive publicity and national strength. Some co-ops only begin with the lettuce boycott, though, and use their whole inventory to reflect political and social values. An example of this practice and the reasoning behind it is described well in an article in Minneapolis's Powderhorn Co-op's newsletter in late 1973 by Greg Gaut, titled, "Yes, We Have No Bananas, Pineapples or Papayas, and *WHY*":

> Recently, a number of questions have come up about our policy of not stocking bananas, pineapples and papayas in the store. People are especially curious about the absence of bananas, not only because they are wholesome, cheap food, but also because it is widely believed that the vegie group is a bunch of monkeys. Since this decision was made in March of this year, we would like to restate the rationale for the benefit of those who were not around much then, which includes most of us.
>
> In the course of the debate of this issue, two arguments were put forth in favor of the policy.
>
> First, it was argued that we have access to a great deal of produce, at good prices, because of the exploitation of countries like Guatemala and Honduras by U.S. corporations like United Fruit. Bananas are cheap because they are harvested with cheap labor, monopolistically controlled. It was felt that we should select a few blatant examples of this imperialism as symbols and boycott them as a means of self-education.
>
> And there was also the secondary argument which focused on the environmental effects of consuming produce from so far away. Considering the energy involved in transporting fruits thousands of miles, wouldn't it be better if we began to learn regional self-sufficiency through canning and other techniques?
>
> In rebuttal, it was argued that most of our produce, at least during

the winter, comes from far away and often Mexico. There was some fear that arbitrarily choosing certain items to symbolically boycott would hinder efforts to create a vital community store in the neighborhood.

The final consensus was to avoid bananas, pineapples and papayas but it was made with the understanding that we continue to educate ourselves about the imperialism of agribusiness corporations and the non-exploitive alternatives open to our community. This has never really taken place. Hopefully, the creation of an Education and Research work group will be a positive step in this direction.

There is considerable controversy within co-ops on such discretionary inventory policies. Some members react like the gentleman from Concord described above. In his case, the disagreement didn't affect the group much because he was silent and overwhelmingly outvoted anyway. In the co-op in Lynn, Massachusetts, disagreement over union lettuce policies put a serious dent in the solidarity of the group. The controversy there split the co-op, reduced the membership, reduced the co-op's economic strength, and created a lot of bad feelings. This sort of conflict usually occurs at the outset of co-op organization. There is some initial fray, as in Concord, over what items the co-op will handle. Then a policy is established and held to. Confusion arises only when new products are considered or co-op members become aware of the symbolic values of various products they had been handling. By that time, it seems harder to decide to drop an item that's been on the order lists for several months than to keep off an item that's never been on. "I know we shouldn't carry cashews," one Boston area co-op member lamented, "but when we started, we didn't know. Now people are used to eating them, and we can't see that it would do any good anyway." The same co-op actively boycotts and has never stocked nonunion lettuce.

Some co-op members believe it is not a good idea to support any boycotts. "You can't eat politics," observed Diane Brown of Washington, D.C.'s, Glut collective. She maintains that co-ops that build inventories to reflect their political beliefs actually set up a boycott of who will join the co-op. "If people can't get what they need at the co-op, they'll just get it somewhere else. They may not even come into the co-op. The co-op, and the people who want to support those political things will end up losing." Bill Coughlan, chairperson of the

Boston Food Co-op's board of directors, asserts, "Don't give me any of this purist shit. Feed the people."

Numerous co-ops are less interested in the political implications of the food than the nutritional implications. They turn up their noses at white bread, canned goods, processed luncheon meats because they feel these foods have little or no nutritional value. The motivation for nutritional boycotts differs from that for political boycotts, but the effects are much the same. When inventory is limited, people who might support the co-op if it carried the boycotted items are excluded.

Attempts to get food co-ops to support boycotts don't alienate everyone. Some co-ops attract members specifically because they sell union lettuce. A Minneapolis co-oper described his pleasure on overhearing a conversation in the neighborhood tavern. One of his neighbors declined an offer of cashews from a friend, remarking, "I stopped eating cashews. The co-op doesn't buy them because they come from Mozambique, and Portugal is giving them a lousy deal these days." A storekeeper at one of the Minneapolis-St. Paul co-ops told me how she had observed a regular woman shopper buying an increasing amount and variety of co-op food as time went on. "She started out with peanut butter, oil, flour, and some of the beans," reported the young storekeeper. "Each time she came in I'd ask her if she'd ever had, say, short grain rice, and dig out a recipe for her. Now that the co-op has a recipe notebook, she just uses that. She keeps buying more things here, so she's got to be cutting down on that junk food."

Some co-ops stock all kinds of food but conduct vigorous education campaigns to warn members of the implications of the food they're buying. When Mark Sherman of the Powderhorn Co-op toured some of the other Minneapolis co-ops with me, he expressed outrage that some of them were stocking a particular brand of packaged frozen fish. "Don't you know this stuff is rancid?" he asked the storekeepers. Finally, in one co-op he diligently wrote, "*Consumer Reports* says this stuff is rancid" on a poster over the freezer as the co-op members looked on approvingly. Other co-ops wage more organized publicity efforts, supporting or defaming various products in posters, newsletters, or flyers. The Boston Food Co-op, for example, carries a full complement of soap products, but the only one I've ever seen publicized in its newsletter is one made by a black community group in Roxbury.

Some co-ops favor handling food items with questionable nutritional value, seeing such an inventory as a measure of concern for community needs. In Minneapolis-St. Paul's All Co-op newsletter, a member of the Green Grass Co-op commented:

Green Grass is in a basically blue-collar working and lower middle class neighborhood. Green Grass has a higher degree of community participation and support than any other co-op, I feel. Thus when the majority of workers wanted to carry Taystee Bread, canned goods and luncheon meats, the co-op ordered the stuff, in addition to the "traditional" co-op foods of bulk grains, flours and nuts, milk, cheese, vegies, etc.

POLITICAL POWER

Some co-ops stretch the strength of their organizations far beyond issues that relate in any way to food. They see the group as a waiting audience for whatever political concerns may be relevant for the time. It seems that the further a co-op gets from food and issues that relate to food, the less strength its organization can muster. The experience of Linda Spero's co-op, mentioned earlier, is typical. What seems to have happened more often, though, is that neighborhood people who are not interested in the brand of politics sit back contentedly and let activist groups do the bulk of the food co-op's work. The neighborhood folk put in a cursory appearance to order and pick up food, making the activists happy, then hurry home before any real organizing can be done. The activists sit around at meetings staring at each other, wondering why the community is alienated, while the neighborhood people stay home.

Some activist or political groups have forsaken food co-ops as an organizing tool. Hard Times, a tenant organizing group in Cambridge, diverted a substantial amount of its members' energies to running a food co-op. They thought the co-op would bring more people into their storefront and could also branch off to become a self-sustaining activity. After several weeks of begging and pleading for involvement from neighborhood people and continuing oversupport from the Hard Times staff, the organization gave up the co-op experiment. "It was a waste of time," one member concluded. "Now we're concentrating on our real interest—work with tenants." Members of the New York Chapter of the New American Movement, a socialist political group, reached a similar conclusion after having a similar experience. "We are working on the theory that the co-op is a neutral activity. In and of itself, we think, it is not enough," they wrote in an issue of the NAM newspaper.

Despite this and other failures, food co-ops continue to overlap with overt political activity. As long as co-op people are involved in political work, the overlap will continue. The bulletin boards also often include notices for meetings of women's groups, day care groups, and spin-off co-op functions like parties, benefits, and more work-oriented activities like job teams. The bulletin boards are in themselves an important and much-used source of communication. I've never seen an uncluttered one.

Part of the problem confronted by NAM and Hard Times is the common problem of mobilization faced by any political group. Outside or professional organizers have a tough road to travel no matter what vehicle they choose. Food co-ops disappoint them because, as one activist put it, "Food co-ops seem like a natural thing—very uncontrived. It just shouldn't be that hard." Some of these groups complicate their already difficult position as an outsider organizer by putting up a very hard sell.

Sometimes part of the problem in extending co-op influence beyond food is that members' interests are too diverse. A woman in the West Village Co-op in New York City explained that nearly all of the co-op's members were involved in one or another kind of organization. "There's political things, spiritual things, religious kicks, sexual kicks—you name it. But it never carries over to the co-op, except very informally. The only real thing that the co-op has in common is an interest in cheap, good food. The lettuce boycott we all agree on, but as far as anything political, we're much too diverse to take a stand on most issues."

Sometimes a co-op's uniformity hinders expansion to political issues. Many suburban co-ops, for example, are run solely by women with similar backgrounds at times that make it impossible for working men to share in the work. These co-ops reinforce the role of women as shoppers and men as providers unless some members of the group consciously try to get men involved. If one or two members of the group are aware of, and try to change, the situation, they may be able to reschedule operations. They may also be able to get the group more involved in other cooperative endeavors.

Feminist issues are a prime example of the different political implications that can come of participation in co-ops. While some co-ops make no effort to consider challenging sexist assumptions,

others effect change in numerous ways. Large co-ops often sponsor
feminist organizations and awareness groups. Some co-ops make
a point of spreading responsibility among men and women. Co-ops'
placement of female buyers in the wholesale markets has challenged
the long-standing preconceptions of market workers. Overall,
though, co-op participation does not lead inevitably to a
breakdown in sex roles.

Nancy Perrelli reported that the Mission Hill Co-op doesn't
get involved in political issues because "It's really hard to do that.
And as far as putting leaflets in peoples' orders or in with the
newsletter, we've established an advisory committee that has to
approve anything that would get circulated that way. We have
a lot of different kinds of people in the co-op and we don't
want to offend anybody." Yet political action at the neighborhood
level is proceeding at an impressive rate. "The blocs are working
together more as a unit," Ms. Perrelli observed. "Blocs on the
back side of Mission Hill and in Jamaica Plain are doing a lot
of work. They started by just cleaning up the place, but now
they've got a city planner working with them and they're
getting involved in redevelopment plans." In New York City,
too, food co-ops have become linked with neighborhood-focused
issues. A woman resident of the Chelsea area described the local
food co-ops' relationship to the interests of brownstone owners
and residents in keeping up the neighborhood. "The food co-ops
are part and parcel of desperate people putting up a fight,"
she commented. In addition, she felt that the co-ops placed
long-standing neighbors together in the context of a
constructive activity. "Once you know people it means you can
do more things together," she observed. Many Minneapolis-
St. Paul co-ops also make conscientious efforts to relate to
the neighborhoods in which they're located. In addition to
stocking a variety of food, they become involved in local
political issues. Green Grass Co-op is working on a day care
center and a teen drop-in center.

Some activists are discouraged with the limited scope in
which food co-ops have been able to exert influence. They feel
not only that there is little potential in expanding food co-ops'
interests beyond food, but also that the whole cooperative
concept is of limited social import. There is, however, a
strong case to be made for the social significance of food co-ops.

The current wave of food co-op activity is a product of
national broad-scale participation. With some sociological inquiry

suggesting that such participation is not the norm for American culture (de Tocqueville notwithstanding, is the line the sociologists always use), this sort of broad-scale involvement in itself takes on some significance. One study suggests that the much-touted picture of Americans being joiners is a mirage:

In our judgment, the first conclusion to be drawn is that American adults . . . most frequently are *not* members of voluntary associations" [author's italics].[1]

This finding conflicts with the large memberships claimed by voluntary assocations like PTAs and women's clubs. Organizational theorist Charles Perrow provides perspective on this issue and on understanding "participation":

Compared to other nations we may be a nation of joiners, but we are far more likely to give our names and our money rather than our time and effort to an organization. Surveys show that the proportion of members of a voluntary association who do any more than attend an occasional meeting is quite small.[2]

Food co-ops emerge in sharp contrast to a national outlook of generally low levels of participation. The people involved are not merely giving their names and their money. Unlike PTA, church groups, or civic associations, food co-ops run an ongoing operation. They conduct business every week. They don't just meet; they work. They transact and conduct a sometimes involved operation, and on a regular basis. Many people involved with food co-ops measure their involvement in terms of hours actually worked and time spent in physical and mental labor. Attendance at meetings, the core of participation for some groups, is a supplementary activity, a mere pleasant side involvement for co-op members.

Art Danforth and others who maintain a traditional view of co-ops feel that participation should be tempered, if not replaced, by salaried managers and staff to ensure the longevity of the co-ops. Roger Auerbach and others involved in current food co-ops argue that broad-scale participation will keep co-ops alive. "Only with participation will the co-ops continue to be an alternative to the supermarkets. If people don't participate in co-ops they won't be able to start co-ops if they move. Without participation there will be a very hard time starting co-op spin-offs like bakeries and warehouses. The importance of participation makes me a little leery of work collectives, too.

I just don't see how they won't be limited to a very small
number of people. Participation is what makes food co-ops a
peoples' movement."

Participation involves members in the co-op and helps provide
the organization with a democratic decision-making process.
If members are more involved, actually operating the co-op,
driving the truck, sweeping the floor, they're much more likely
to take a more active role in the organization. In the current
wave of food co-ops, members' active role in decision-making
is anchored in their physical work commitments to the co-ops.

The principle that co-ops need to offer a real alternative
in order to be successful is at the core of the participation
controversy. If it takes bureaucratic management and a
supermarket appearance to ensure a co-op's longevity then
perhaps longevity is not a proper goal. This is not to say that
the co-op supermarkets don't pursue worthy goals—their consumer
orientation and distribution of profits to members is a far cry
from supermarket capitalism. But the goals of the supermarket
co-ops are a far cry from the goals, interests, and needs of
the new co-ops. Co-op supermarkets may differ from regular
supermarkets, but they don't differ enough to satisfy members
of the new co-ops. For members of the new co-ops, participation
is resolutely linked to membership.

Work collectives balance their lack of broad-scale participation with more in-depth participation. Work collectives
don't offer everyone who comes into contact with the group
a hand in running the operation, but they create an alternative
in a different sense. While most food co-ops involve most of
their members for several hours each month and don't much
alter the rest of their lives, work collectives offer members
an alternative to regular full-time work. Members of Stone Soup
in Washington and the support industries in Minneapolis run
the organizations without a boss, a time clock, or controls
imposed by alien management. Work collectives enable people
to break from traditional employment and set up their own work
situations. In starting their own source of employment, workers
are able to exert a degree of control and autonomy impossible
with most traditional work. They can promote any issues or
ideas that interest them and initiate changes on the job. Some
work collectives choose to pay members very low wages in
the belief that they need to set an example of nonmaterialism.

Nearly all work collectives strive to break down traditional roles of customer and storekeeper, shopper and worker.

Most of the support industries (bakeries, warehouse, trucking) for food co-ops are run by collectives because they require a full-time commitment. These collectives are possible because there are people who want to find sources of support outside the offerings of the labor market. Some food co-ops are also organized as work collectives. People in work collectives use the name interchangeably with the word co-op, but the two are really distinct and quite different forms of alternative organizations.

People have to make a conscious decision to join food co-ops quite unlike the decision they have to make in choosing a supermarket. It's not a matter of choosing among a number of different kinds of supermarkets, but a qualitative choice at a different level, a rejection of the whole supermarket approach. The new approach which co-op members take up is an expression of autonomy and greater control over the forces that shape their lives.

Food co-ops are a form of independence at a very basic level, a simple response to a system that does not offer people what they want. But taking the step from being a harassed supermarket patron to a struggling co-op member is not easy. It's almost like the cliché in the old Western movies where townspeople "took the law into their own hands." Somewhere there's a breaking point at which people stop feeling sorry for themselves and start doing something about it.

Some people argue that food co-ops advance the cause of participatory democracy by involving people in a consensual decision-making group process. This may happen, but (as discussed in Chapter Three) it can't be taken for granted. Co-ops do, however, provide members with an opportunity to express their views and interact with others. Most co-ops are responsive enough to enable members to at least bring their opinions before the group. Some co-ops respond negatively, like the Somerville group, but even there the option for discussion existed. Nearly all co-ops give members exposure to new ideas and awarenesses that they are not likely to see at home on TV.

In an article in *Win* magazine, Dave Wood notes:

Some people working in the coops would label themselves as "radicals" of one sort or another—some definitely would not! But the fact that coop shoppers know that some coop workers are radicals challenges the image of radical as agent of destruction with an image of radicals as people who are trying to provide inexpensive necessities and to build a closely-knit community. [3]

The group development chapter of this book reiterated the point that people who are involved with others, even in the most apolitical groups, are likely to become more involved in political kinds of participation. The mix of different types of people in co-ops points the way to a still greater mixing of ideas.

Money spent at a co-op also carries an inherent political value. However insignificant the total of co-op financial activity may be in the overall economic picture of the nation, the individual and local economic implication of co-op activity loom somewhat larger. Each dollar spent at a co-op is a dollar not spent at the supermarket, a dollar that doesn't get involved in a system that stakes its survival on the acquisition of new dollars. At present, all of this is little more than a symbolic gesture. Some economists argue that all healthy economic systems can support fringe activities like co-ops so long as they remain on the fringe. When I discussed recent co-op growth with Ronald Curhan, a faculty member at Boston University's Business School and ex-supermarket executive, I found him lacking in enthusiasm. "When I measure that growth against total activity in food purchasing, it comes out to be less than .0001 percent," he remarked.

The political implications of co-ops range from overt attempts to use co-ops as political vehicles through implicit political actions in small-group participation, intermixing of numerous kinds of people, psychological "inner direction," and the economic support of alternatives to the "regular" system. Dave Wood's article quoted a Minneapolis co-op member who helped point out the breadth of co-ops' political implications: "Everything is political—what you eat, what you wear, who you sleep with. . . . Limiting the word 'politics' to electoral politics or to protest politics leaves out consumer politics and lifestyle/sexual/cultural politics which seem to be ultimately at least as crucial in the exercise of power as electoral or protest activity."[4]

Theorists like historian Christopher Lasch and University of Massachusetts economics professor Herbert Gintis argue that organizations like food co-ops can never be anything but marginal. Interviewed in Studs Terkel's *Hard Times*, Mr. Lasch commented: "People who talk in terms of revolution underestimate the capacity of American capitalism, its resiliency and inventiveness. . . . Aside from its tremendous resources, American capitalism has the capacity to foreclose other alternatives."[5] A co-op delegate to a NEFCO meeting put it more bluntly: "If you don't think the capitalists are going to go with their own people first, you're crazy."

It is difficult to predict whether co-op expansion will lead ultimately to repression. Despite the warnings of social theorists thus far only minor sorts of repression have occurred. Particular health or tax inspectors have taken up strong anti-co-op stands to satisfy political pressures in some areas. City officials in St. Louis reportedly harassed one food co-op in order to please an influential grocer. The co-op in Lynn, Massachusetts, lost one of its blocs' space when a community school superintendent ordered the co-op out of the school's basement. He argued that the co-op threatened small grocery stores when in fact it hardly duplicated their inventory at all. Minneapolis's flour mill is enmeshed in a legal argument over the payment of back taxes mandated by a law that expired. Both co-ops continued on relatively unhindered despite the harassment and the mill is going ahead with plans for development. It may well be that food co-ops will inspire more repression if they gain significant economic strength. Even the older established supermarket co-ops have occasionally been the target of red baiting. But repression seems unlikely because it would create widespread backlash, especially as co-ops continue to gain support from middle-class families. And despite co-ops' growth, it seems unlikely that they will pose a serious threat to supermarkets in the near future.

Co-ops' significance lies not so much in numbers and dollars (though these are growing) as in their internal organizations and the paths they are beginning to follow. Their internal organizations establish some basic patterns: members mix with a variety of people, participate firsthand in a voluntary association, exercise greater control over a portion of their lives. Herbert Marcuse points out that the power to reject what the society attempts to force is a crucial one. He describes economic freedom as "freedom *from* the economy—from being controlled by economic forces and relationships. . . ."[6] Food co-ops begin to free members from the economics of the supermarket system.

CO-OPS AS ALTERNATIVES

Food co-ops are rooted in the sort of rejection described by Marcuse, but they go a good deal further than the establishment of a nihilistic rejection, focusing energy in developing other ways of doing things. And the other ways they promote typically differ economically, politically, and socially from the mainstream approaches. Food co-ops look and feel different from supermarkets.

At the most basic level, food co-ops are an alternative to the "regular" way people do their food shopping. Co-op prices are lower. However, numerous co-op members have told me that, while low prices attracted them to the co-op, high food quality keeps them there. "I just can't get lettuce like this at the supermarket," a woman in the Marshfield Co-op explained. "I didn't even know it came like this before I joined the co-op. I couldn't understand why it has to be this way, but the produce man at the supermarket told me it takes them quite some time to peel the outer leaves off the lettuce to make it look pretty. By that time, it's just not as fresh as we get it—right off the train." Some co-op members view their groups as providing alternatives to plastic food as well as stale food. "I never ate so many fresh vegetables before," a member of the Needham co-op told me. "They're so expensive at the supermarkets. Now that I can buy them cheaply, I feel badly about buying that canned crap."

In some ways the supermarkets have helped generate alternatives. The bad feelings that high prices and poor food publicity created have been compounded by the slick, impersonal image that supermarkets continue to propagate. They try to combat it—a Stop & Shop in our neighborhood spent a mint on posters and photos during a massive remodeling to inform shoppers how "their" store was changing. The same store . sponsors meat cutting demonstrations and buses in elderly folks who have no other way of getting to a supermarket. But the size of the store and the whole atmosphere reassure everyone but the wildest dreamers that the store is not theirs at all.

High prices also have helped create ill will toward supermarkets. The meat boycotts of 1973 were nightmares for public relations people. Supermarket cults and method-shopping techniques not unlike racetrack gambling systems have evolved to arm shoppers with a tactic to get more for their money. A few popular paperbacks describing ways to stretch shopping dollars have had considerable success. Even the most conservative of these cannot avoid depicting the supermarket as "the enemy." Much of this feeling was summed up by a softspoken middle-aged member of the Needham co-op who, when asked how she thought members felt about deserting their regular supermarkets, replied: "Nobody here has mentioned it except to say ha ha and hurray. The supermarkets don't care about us, and we certainly don't worry about them."

Shoppers see the food co-op as an alternative to the supermarket's high prices, the supermarket's kind of food, and the supermarket's atmosphere. At one time the Ma and Pa grocery store was able to provide an alternative at least in the way of atmosphere. But as Ma and Pa stores increasingly disappear under the thumb of economic pressures, and 7-11's and their kin spring up to replace them, there is less and less of an alternative to supermarket-style shopping. It's not surprising that most food co-ops strive to maintain friendly relations in their storefronts and garages. In some ways, the Minneapolis-St. Paul co-ops located in former Ma and Pa storefronts and rooted firmly in their neighborhoods are updated versions of community stores.

Co-ops offer food which is usually cheaper and of higher quality than supermarket food. This food alternative bears implications beyond supermarkets, though. By stressing fresh vegetables and grains, food co-ops work against the economics of the whole food industry. Food processors make large amounts of money by turning natural food into prepared goodies. A few potatoes, some shortening, and some equipment and labor enable a company to sell potato chips for three or four hundred percent markup over what the potatoes cost initially. The potato chip people also make it more attractive for farmers to deal with them than with fresh produce suppliers. Supported by profits and advertising, they can afford to offer high prices and firm contracts.

The pursuit of profit sometimes leads food processors away from any concern for consumers. In a *New York Review* article, "Death for Dinner," Daniel Zwerdling explains why worries about unhealthy food are justifiable. Citing Senate hearings on "Sugar in Diet, Diabetes, and Heart Diseases" conducted on April 30 and May 1-2, 1973, he observes:

Scary stories about the risks of eating are now coming from well-known
and sober university deans and government scientists. Ten of them appeared
quietly before the Senate Select Committee on Nutrition and Human Needs
last spring to testify that our daily diets of processed foods, rich in refined
sugar and modified carbohydrates like white flour, are probably major
causes of diabetes, heart and arterial disease, and intestinal cancer—
among other ailments.[7]

Processed food is big business which operates in much the
same way as any other business. It strives to create demand for
products so that companies can make a profit. Zwerdling
details the profit mechanism:

A few central manufacturers can saturate supermarket shelves across the
country with their products because there's no chance the food will
spoil. Companies can buy raw ingredients when they're cheap, produce
and stockpile vast quantities of the processed result, then withhold the
products from the supermarket for months, hoping to manipulate prices
upward and make a windfall. The food industry's savings are seldom
passed on to the consumers, which is precisely why the food industry
has embraced processed foods.[8]

Food co-ops bypass not only supermarkets but a whole
complement of support industries that supply the supermarkets.
The more co-ops support nonprocessed fresh foods, the greater
their economic significance. The way the wholesale system is
set up enables co-ops to save members substantial amounts of
money on fresh food available from local wholesalers but not
on processed food.

Some co-ops move further away from the mechanics of the
food industry by reaching into the channels of food production.
The warehouses in Minneapolis and Washington, D.C., eliminate
one type of middleman; so do the flour mill and bakery in
Minneapolis. In all of these there is much emphasis on unproc-
essed food. The ultimate reach here is in making direct links
to farmers. Once only the dream of co-op true believers,
co-op/farmer links are strengthening. The experiences in New
York, California, and the Midwest described in Chapter One
appear to be growing stronger. In addition, increasing national
unity is helping food co-ops to accumulate the buying power
they need to deal directly with farmers.

Chapter Five

CO-OP HISTORY

I n 1974 there were more than ten co-op storefronts in
Minneapolis-St. Paul, a warehouse, a bakery, a restaurant,
and a number of buying clubs that operate from backyards
and garages. Five years ago there were no storefronts, no
warehouse, bakery, or restaurant. Buying clubs were just a twinkle
in the eye of a few radicals.

Most current co-ops began in the late 1960s. Given the
current level of co-op activity, it is intriguing that there was little
activity before then and worrisome that the same thing happened
earlier in this century and in the previous one. Co-ops do have
a history, but, as Richard Margolis points out in *The New Leader*,
"Cooperatism's history in this country has not been encouraging:
After more than a century of struggle, co-ops remain weak,
marginal and in the eyes of many Americans, slightly far out."[1]

Co-op history takes on increasing importance when one realizes
that probably only 5 percent of the nearly one thousand cooperatives listed in the directory in this book existed prior to 1970.
Tracing the current wave of co-op activity to its sources provides
some insight both into why co-ops now look as they do and how
the society has changed overall. The mere fact that a large
number of people, spread across the nation, are taking a direct
hand in running a voluntary association is significant in light
of mounting sociological evidence that few Americans participate
in voluntary associations. A look at recent co-op history can
provide a fuller perspective. Moreover, a look at any co-op
history yields good stories and profiles of colorful people.

BEGINNINGS

Some co-op enthusiasts trace cooperative history to the first
attempts of human beings to work together. The more specific
cooperative history relevant for this book is a product of the
Industrial Revolution. Some current organizational forms, theories,
and practices originated then, and there is some continuity
between co-ops then and now.

The first co-op, or at least the co-op that current co-ops
look to as the first co-op, was formed in England by a group
of weavers at Rochdale in 1844. Sidney and Beatrice Webb
commented in their 1921 work, *Consumers Cooperative Movement*:

> The immediate object of the twenty-eight flannel weavers of Rochdale was
> to free themselves from the adulteration and credit system of the little
> shopkeeper and the "truck shop" of the employer; but their ultimate
> purpose was their emancipation from wage-slavery by such a reorganization
> of industry as would enable them to provide themselves with employment—
> to use their own words, so "to arrange the powers of production,
> distribution, education, and government" as to "create a self-supporting
> home colony."[2]

Like innumerable other co-ops, Rochdale was a product of hard
times. The success of the store established it as a model for
others.

"Rochdale has grown to be a sacred symbol, the Mt. Sinai
of cooperation," observes Margolis.[3] The operating principles of
the store, which was a solid success, were copied, honored,
respected, and are posted today in most co-op grocery stores.
(See Appendix A for details.) The twin pines symbol of Rochdale
has found its way into most co-op trademarks. Briefly, the
principles stress: one man, one vote, profits distributed as
patronage refunds among members, open membership, education
on co-ops, growth, and control of the organization by the
members.

Cursory co-op histories usually begin with Rochdale without
a real consideration of the circumstances surrounding it. Rochdale
did not spring full-grown from nineteenth-century English soil.
It was part of a reaction, several decades old, of frenzied response
to the Industrial Revolution. "We are pressed down by the weight
of inventions and improvements," one observer commented.[4]
It is not now easy to identify with the shock that technology

must have brought with the Industrial Revolution. Workers in the newly established factories were much at the mercy of an economic system they could not understand, much less control. George Jacob Holyoake, a historian of that era and proponent of cooperatives, observed in his *History of Cooperation*: "The tendency of competition which the introduction of machinery intensified, lowered wages, and pushed the mass of workmen with increased forced against the walls of the workhouse."[5] These were the years of child labor, the sixteen-hour work day, and the company store. The Holyoake book captures a good deal of the atmosphere of the era. It is used extensively in this chapter, but recommended to be read in full by people interested in cooperativism's beginnings. The original prose best spells out the situation which spawned the utopian and cooperative schemes, schemes which weren't the lark of some workers with time on their hands but the attempts of people in a desperate situation to improve the basic conditions of their lives.

Some could see the potential of technology to pull people out from under the pressures and weights rather than subject them to more, but there was little consensus on how to do this. Some thought the process of realizing technology's potential would be political. It is said that Karl Marx, looking at an electric locomotive on display in London in the mid-nineteenth century proclaimed: "Now the problem is solved—the consequences are indefinable. In the wake of the economic revolution the political must surely follow."[6] Others thought less in terms of revolution, more in terms of small but elaborate utopian experiments.

In the midst of all this, preceding Rochdale by several decades, there arose a charismatic fagure who crystallized and spearheaded the alternative schemes of the time. Robert Owen, born in 1771 ("Nature was in one of her adventurous moods in that period," observes Holyoake[7]), mastered the factory system in true Horatio Alger fashion. He capped a meteoric rise from draper's assistant to manager of some cotton mills at Manchester by marrying the boss's daughter and becoming a partner in the business. When the other partners began to object to his preliminary attempts at social reform (building a school), he bought the business and would accept as new partners only those who agreed with his ideas.

Owen's work began with social reform before escalating to more grandiose schemes. In a letter to the *Times* in 1834, he

summarized his work at the New Lanark mill: "For twenty-nine
years we did without the necessity for magistrates or lawyers;
without a single legal punishment; without any known poor's rate;
without intemperance or religious animosities. We reduced the
hours of labour, well educated all the children from infancy,
greatly improved the condition of the adults, diminished their
daily hours of labour, paid interest of capital, and cleared upwards
of £300,000 of profit."[8]

From the successes at the mill, he went on to propose more
elaborate concepts—community baking, laundry, and washing
services. An early issue (August 27, 1821) of the *Economist*,
published by Owen, explained: "THE SECRET IS OUT: it is
unrestrained CO-OPERATION, on the part of ALL the members,
for EVERY purpose of social life."[9]

Owen split his efforts between publicizing his ideas and
experimenting with them. He wrote letters, rubbed elbows with
the celebrities and royalty of the time. His own charisma is a
substantial part of the story. Holyoake quotes a duke character-
izing Owen:

"Mr. Owen looked to nothing less than to renovate the world, to extirpate
all evil, to banish punishment, to create like views and like wants, and
to guard against all conflicts and hostilities."[10]

His charisma carried him through some difficult times—"Much was
thought of him, much was forgiven him, much was hoped for
him," notes Holyoake.[11]

But he could not escape some problems. His criticisms trod
too heavily on the church, which he felt was encouraging the
people to remain silent. Organized religion in those days was
more powerful and sinister than now, and there are some
indications that he faced real danger because of his criticisms.
In addition, not all royalty was favorably impressed with his
efforts to make common folk dissatisfied with their lot. It just
wasn't politically expedient. Finally, he lost proportionately more
support as his plans became increasingly all-inclusive and he
became increasingly taken with them and himself. ". . . [He] was,
doubtless, later in life a somewhat tiresome reformer," comments
Holyoake. "His letters were essays and his speeches were volumes.
When he called a meeting together, those who attended never
knew when they would separate."[12] Economists were not
much impressed by his schemes because they involved planned
communities. "Anyone who read Adam Smith," notes

Richard Margolis, "knew that the road to hell was paved by planners."[13]

Still, he did get to try some actual experiments. Aside from his own mill, he did some work in the self-supporting pauper colonies of Holland and in supporting projects he thought worthy— like Robert Fulton's steamboat. His most extensive experience with an actual community was in the United States at New Harmony. Owen opened the New Harmony community on 20,000 acres of Indiana land in 1825 after addressing Congress and the President. Leaving his son in charge while he returned to England, Owen set up the "colony" as a midway sort of organization between traditional society and complete utopia with much cooperation and communal activity. He returned several years later to alter the organization to involve greater levels of communal activity, but the concentrated form failed. People weren't ready, or able, to cast aside individuals for the good of the community.

Owen's influence was, however, much increased by the New Harmony community. Its members turned up in later utopian and cooperative experiments, and it helped lay the groundwork for other American utopias. Owen's extensive publicity, socializing, and speechmaking also added to his influence. The atmosphere he established in England made it possible for the Rochdale store to happen. He himself thought little of it—he would rather have had the weavers produce collectively than buy collectively, but he was happy nonetheless to see a form of cooperative prosper.

Owen was not the first utopianist. Others before him had set out even more grandiose schemes. Charles Fourier conceptualized involved communities called phalanxes, thirty-three of which were set up in the United States with the help of Horace ("Go West, young man") Greeley. Babeuf, a somewhat more wildeyed Frenchman, had a plan to "establish a system of equality by force."[14] These and other utopianists had some influence, but the work of Owen is particularly notable for its depth and its links to ongoing concepts.

CO-OPS IN AMERICA

Immigrants to America brought with them the ideas of the utopianists and cooperators, and infused them into the organizations they set up. They were supported in their ventures by a government that billed itself as "for the people" and an economic environment that rewarded cooperation. Rochdale-type associations showed up in Philadelphia in the 1860s. Protective Union Stores that combined buying club operations with temperance interests enjoyed several decades of activity until the Civil War disrupted economic and social relationships. Numerous utopian experiments, some of which are still going strong, got a start in the developing American West.

The most stable cooperatives arose from two major sources: farmers who wanted more control over the prices they got for their produce and consumers (often immigrant groups) who wanted more control over the prices they paid for necessities. The need for such control became increasingly important as the forces of an industrialist economy took shape. Historian Samuel Hays described the situation in *The Response to Industrialism*: "Businessmen, farmers, and workers individually could not cope with the impersonal price-and-market network, but they soon discovered that as organized groups they could wield considerable power." [15] Hays also points out that in most cases, consumers failed to unite.

PRODUCERS' CO-OPS

The producers' co-ops, now large, conservative businesses indistinguishable from any other kind of business, began with the banding together of farmers with an interest in getting better prices for their goods and acquiring public services that were taking too long to spread to rural areas. Many farmers owe their acquisition of electricity to co-operatives formed by farmers who were bypassed by electric companies interested in the greater profit potentials of the cities. Producers' co-ops followed different growth patterns depending on the crops with which they were involved and the region of the country they were in. At some places for some causes, producers' co-ops were a part of general farmer unrest that produced phenomena such as the populists, the greenbackers, and the Wobblies. Free silver and Bob LaFollette were all mixed in with farmers' producer co-ops and an overall political profile which is almost the perfect opposite of the current one. S. M. Lipset reminds us, "The history of American political class consciousness has been primarily a story of agrarian upheavals." [16]

Individual producer co-op histories depict all the color and turmoil of current radical groups. One of the most extensive, and longest lasting, stories is that of the wheat farmers in

Saskatchewan. They established a network of cooperative organizations and eventually even a socialist government of the Province.
Much of the growth in the area, well described in Lipset's
Agrarian Socialism, took place in the 1920s with the settling of
the area by farmers with an "absence of strong, settled ties to
a traditional pattern of economic, social and political behavior."[17]
Many people were first-generation settlers with high hopes,
"receptive to new ideas, to panaceas that promise the opportunity
they seek." The overall situation was not unlike that in Kansas
and Nebraska a hundred years earlier. Moreover, many settlers
brought with them a tradition of acceptance of new ideas and
radical policies. For some of them the very act of settling was a
rejection of old-world practices and problems.

Once settled, the farmers soon found cooperation to be a
helpful tactic. Lipset notes:

The sparse settlement and lack of large urban centers, which made various
community and social services economically unprofitable, have also increased
local ccoperative endeavors. Farmers have been forced to unite cooperatively
to obtain telephone service, local roads, medical and hospital facilities,
and other social services.[18]

Early successes spurred the farmers on to more cooperative
endeavors, with the fickle climate and the doubly fickle market
situation for wheat farmers further reinforcing co-ops. "More than
any other group," Lipset observes, "the wheat farmer is economically naked."[19]

Cooperative action subsided with the lagging onset of economic stability and bureaucracy in the political party organizations.
Though the co-ops are no longer the seething, vibrant organizations
they once were, they continue to exert an influence on the
overall appearance of government operations and, at a more
personal level, the receptivity of many people to co-op ideas.
The situation resembled that in Minneapolis-St. Paul, where there
is also a cooperative past, perhaps even a cooperative tradition.
New co-ops are not perceived as alien or subversive forms—
the word co-op is part of most people's realm of experience. In
Boston and New York, the absence of this link for many people
causes some problems in basic recognition and acceptance.

The Saskatchewan experience combined producer and consumer
co-op activities under the greater common interest of collective
action for self-help. The combination stuck and helped support
the Socialist Party in the province until the 1950s, when the party

lost at the polls. American producers' co-ops more often than not
neglected ties with consumer interests or allowed the ties to wither
away. A major factor behind the neglect of consumer co-ops
was that, until the 1920s and the onset of mechanization on the
farms, there was little that the farmer had to consume. Fertilizer
and seeds were produced by the farms themselves. Technology
created new products which were practically unavailable yet
necessary for profitable farming, and many farmers responded by
forming buying co-ops. American producers' co-ops had a political
perspective quite unlike their Canadian cousins. Ideologies were
sorely split and finally healed by a hands-off approach to politics
that encouraged a single-viewpoint, single-interest organization.
In all, the experience of producers' co-ops in the U.S. was a
lively exercise of economic development and a colorful story
largely untold by most history books. It is more story than
history, filled with conflict and struggle. Producers' co-ops
were not exactly Sunday afternoon gentlemens' groups—their
struggle at times included "night riding" *a la* KKK to encourage
holdouts to join their federations. [20]

Producers' co-ops stand on shaky philosophical ground,
which has shifted like the dunes as the co-ops themselves have
changed. It is easy to sympathize with the struggling farmers
who try to get a fair price for their season's work, easy to see
that cooperation among them could help them control the prices.
It is not quite so easy to understand how such cooperation
can get out of hand so that the farmer's voice is lost in a
bureaucracy that he himself helped establish. A historian of
cooperatives suggested in the early twentieth century that there
is an inherently questionable aspect of producers' cooperation.
"A cooperative grain elevator is nothing more nor less than the
machinery for joint exploitation," he notes. [21]

More recently, Richard Margolis has written that cooperation
involves people "trying to get their hands on the capitalist
wheel and making it turn for them." [22] If either producers or
consumers do this independently, the other will inevitably suffer.

Producers' co-ops account for the lion's share of financial
activity among co-ops. It is reported that five out of six American
farmers are members of a co-op. The development of producers'
co-ops did not much resembled the development of consumers'
co-ops. Different people were involved; different problems
prevailed.

CONSUMERS' CO-OPS

The co-op supermarket and related services in Fitchburg, Massachusetts, present a good case study for the development of consumers' co-ops. The co-op's history is detailed in a provocative little book, *The Story of a Cooperative*, written by a member and published by the United Cooperative Society in Fitchburg.[23]

The author, Savele Syrjala, explains, "Our story begins in Finland." He describes the harsh land and climate and the still harsher political climate created by a ruthless, dominating Russian Czar. Finnish immigration (302,095 people between 1883 and 1924) brought people who were caught up in the political turmoil of the times. The turmoil included a nationalistic cooperative response to the oppression. Syrjala notes, "It was natural, therefore, that the Finnish immigrants, many of whom had been inspired by these newly organized movements, should form similar associations when they settled in America."[24] All the more so when a difficult language barrier and disappointing economic situation awaited the immigrants. Indigenous organizations formed by the Finns to help make their situation more tolerable provided material and psychological support. Organizations probably received more attention than they would have in better times.

Finns came to Fitchburg to pursue weaving work offered by the local mills, and as in other areas, the concentrations of ethnic populations attracted yet more Finns. The Finnish community established its first co-op store in 1910, one year after the failure of a previous attempt, and five years after the community's first co-op store venture. The co-op's beginning traces back to dissatisfaction with the local grocer. Founders sought to raise $5,000 capital in five-dollar member shares, and designated a $1,000 minimum reserve before any earnings could be distributed to shareholders. The store was named the Into (Finnish for Ardor) Grocery Store. Early by-laws established the one-member, one-vote principle key to cooperative operations. Later by-laws limited the investment of any one co-op member to forty shares and put a 5 percent ceiling on the rate of interest allowable on members' investments.

The grocery weathered a few shaky years, then found stability and growth in 1912 when it opened a branch store with the collaboration of Saima, an influential labor and temperance society.

The black-and-white glossy in the book showing several staunch men loading a staunch horse-drawn carriage with orders depicts an atmosphere of stability. This business is not going to soon fail.

A milk distribution co-op and a boardinghouse co-op evolved and were incorporated into the new expanded building housing the grocery (which had officially changed its name to Into Cooperative Store). The business volume in 1917, of $144,713, reflected an increase in activity since the first year of operation ($14,922) seven years earlier. The co-op experimented with cooperation with other New England Co-ops in the early 1920s, then withdrew when the "million dollar cooperative" dissolved.

The co-op also weathered a political storm in the early 1920s when the Finnish community split violently between supporters and detractors of Communism. Control of Saima and the local newspaper, *Raiwaaja*, were sought in vain by the Communists. In 1921 they even set up their own co-op, which carried on for about a year and a half before it, and prevailing interest in Communism, waned.

The Depression slowed the co-op down a bit, "but at no time did the society operate in the red." [25] In fact, the society took over the operation of the failing co-ops in Gardner, Massachusetts, and Milford, New Hampshire, running them as branch stores. During the Depression it also added a coal yard, fuel oil and gasoline sales.

Since then the Fitchburg co-op has prospered and grown, expanding its physical plant and its inventory along the way. It's branched out into cooperative education services and summer camps and strengthened its position in the community. It is only recently that the co-op has experienced substantial problems. Deficits reflect not only internal problems of the store but the diminishing of the Finnish community's strength. Older Finns are moving to Florida (a large number of the newspaper's subscribers are located in a retirement community there) and young Finns are moving out for other reasons. With plant closings due to petroleum shortages in its plastics industries, Fitchburg is not exactly a hub of economic activity these days. Even the young Finns who do stay don't feel the same commitment to their nationality as their parents did. The language barrier hardly exists any more and there is little outside oppression forcing Finns together.

At present, the store is a clean, large supermarket located in the midst of old factories in the center of town. The town has seen better days—many of the old factories appear vacant, but there are pockets of renewal. The town is noted as a host of bicycle races, and reportedly has the largest population of Finns in the U.S. It supports a twice-weekly newspaper printed in Finnish. The cooperative is closely linked to the city's Finnish background. "We're still fighting the image of being a Finns-only co-op," E. Miriam Doody, Fitchburg Co-op's public relations director, told me.

The co-op is straddling the black and red columns in the account books. Sales are off, and no patronage refund was declared in 1972 or 1973. (Unlike the new food co-ops which sell food at low prices, the co-op supermarkets sell at regular market prices and return savings to members once a year in the form of a patronage refund based on the total amount of their purchases.) These are not the best of times for any supermarket, but the Fitchburg Co-op has some additional problems. It is having difficulty competing with new, flashy supermarkets in the area.

What the co-op has to offer—a friendly atmosphere, a stodgy organization, old-time specialty and Finnish foods—just doesn't interest modern shoppers. People don't want to wait a year to collect patronage refunds. They want savings when they buy. "In this city, at this time," Mrs. Doody observed, "people are shopping 'specials.' We call them cherry pickers." The several people with whom I chatted at the checkout line confirmed Mrs. Doody's suspicions. One man stopped in for a few items "only because it's convenient. But I never shop here regularly—it's too expensive." A woman with a large order told me she was only shopping for her mother, who lived nearby. The co-op has a committee that checks up on prices in other supermarkets, but apparently doesn't get the message across to the membership.

The supermarket is plodding along on the support of elderly Finns who simply shop co-op out of habit and dedication. Mrs. Doody explained her recent efforts to involve more younger people in the co-op. She watches wedding announcements in the newspapers and sends out gift certificates to young marrieds. She is also trying to get the co-op linked more closely to the new co-ops and break down some of the barriers between the two.

Behind the out-of-date atmosphere and high prices at the co-op is an inflexible and out-of-date management. The co-op is run by a board of directors elected from the aging member-ship. Mrs. Doody thinks the board could use a shot in the arm.

"They just don't realize all the things that are being done in other places. Like Berkeley [California, where there is a thriving, successful co-op supermarket]—if you mention here the things that they do in Berkeley, the board members would get white hair and pass out cold."

Yet the co-op continues. The gift shop specializing in Scandinavian imports on the second floor of the co-op is being discontinued. But supermarket sales are stabilizing. The recently installed snack bar-luncheonette is doing well, and the other co-op enterprises (heating oil, gas stations, milk pasteurizing for area farmers, the end product of which ends up in the co-op's dairy cases) are all holding their own.

The Fitchburg Co-op at present is not in dire trouble, but its situation could be much better. Even if sales pick up so that members' patronage refunds can be paid once again and the co-op advances financially, it will have to make strides in other directions to qualify for success as a co-op. As it is, the Fitchburg Co-op has little or no member involvement. A board of directors gets elected at one of two yearly meetings, both of which bring out about 125-130 people from a membership list which is much larger. Community activity is low, and so is involvement in consumer affairs. The newsletter, an important source of unity, has cut publication back to one or two issues a year. The store looks and feels much like any supermarket, except for its signs explaining how the co-op is owned and shopping bags, which say: "Co-op: Where people get together." Mrs. Doody feels that co-op customers generally receive better treatment from co-op workers than they would get from workers in a supermarket: "You can ring the bell in the meat department and the man will answer without biting your head off."

The Fitchburg Co-op illustrates the issues facing many of the other co-op stores. Nationally, business is mixed, but there is an overall slump reflecting problems throughout the food distribution industry. Aside from straight business issues, there is also a common neglect of cooperative principles in many stores. The neglect is a disappointment to some, but to most co-op members it's just a fact of business life. Art Danforth of the Cooperative League concedes that most co-op stores are mirroring too well their supermarket competitors.

Mr. Danforth pointed out that there are two shining exceptions to the trend to supermarketism: the co-ops in Berkeley, California, and the Cooprix in Montreal. Both stress

consumer interests—impartial information on the food items is
posted along with *Consumer Reports* ratings. The Berkeley Co-op
also has extensive member participation in committees to start
new co-op enterprises and initiate related activities. Cooprix
features low prices through its "direct charge" operation and the
low prices help contribute to the store's success. Berkeley's success,
however, seems due more to good management than to the
store's cooperative structure. The store's strong consumer
orientation certainly helps, but probably not as much as the
sensible and aware management policies that prevail.

But neither co-op involves members in the actual operation
of the co-op or (except at the board of directors level) in some
of the basic decision- and policy-making issues. Because of this,
I told Art Danforth that many members of the new co-ops laugh
to think that the co-op grocery stores actually call themselves
co-ops. "The laughter," he replied, with the kind of authority that
can come only with experience, "goes both ways."

Not all co-ops fared as well as the Fitchburg example. An
accountant in St. Louis who was active in the co-ops there in
the mid-1930s described the various operations undertaken by
their group. There was a small buying club that operated out of a
basement, growing to the point where it occupied a rented cottage
and provided a small amount of compensation for two members.
At the same time, a group sold shares for a storefront which
opened and met with numerous operational problems. The co-op
finally met with real disaster when its uninsured truck was
wrecked. The storefront moved to more modest operation, but
never really recovered from the loss before the onset of World
War II.

Some earlier co-ops met with more violent opposition. In his
1891 work, *How to Cooperate*, Herbert Myrick described the
experience of a cooperative store in Lyon, Iowa:

... [T]he public in general, with a few exceptions, had put little faith
in the success of the enterprise, the expression being oft heard that
"the boys are having a little fun, but it would not last long." More or
less opposition was provoked, and the officers received a letter threatening
to blow up the store with dynamite.[26]

A key part of the old co-op/new co-op debate is that the old
co-ops now in existence are what's left of earlier efforts at
cooperation. At one time (notably in the 1930s) there was growth
and diversity much as there is now, but the only co-ops that

weathered a time and indifference are the ones that remain. If longevity is the goal of current food co-ops, there are some important lessons to be learned. But longevity may not be a proper or rational goal if the resulting organization does not meet members' interests and needs. At any rate, there are a number of long-lived co-ops and much to be learned from them. One of the more important developments in recent co-op history has been the linking up of old and new co-ops. The linking is being taken up with reluctance and suspicion on both sides, but there is also a certain shared excitement about the potentials of mutual support. The Fitchburg Co-op helped provide assembly space for a recent NEFCO conference of new co-ops and is very interested in more interaction. They invited Terry Dix of the (new) Worcester co-op to speak at one of their meetings.

Despite this diversity, despite even some blatant conflicts of interest or policy, the word "co-op" occasionally helps break the ice for new buying clubs. In some areas, co-op producers and warehouses give new food co-ops special considera-tion because of the shared co-op background. The Boston Food Co-op buys many of its groceries from the warehouse serving the co-op supermarkets in New England. Treatment from the warehouse has grown to be cordial and open. There is also some interchange with old and new co-ops on the West Coast and in the New York City area.

In a recent letter, Mark Sherman of Minneapolis described the interest and potential of meshing old and new co-ops in Minneapolis:

Went to a meeting at Mutual Service (a co-op insurance company) a couple of weeks ago with some old time cooperators who are interested in the same ideals we believe in—a rare breed around here. One refined gent wants to start quarterly meetings between us and high-level executives at Land o' Lakes and Midland (a midwestern producers' co-op and warehouse with an extensive product line). It should be interesting. We have a lot of things to say to those people and we could use a little support, mainly in the way of capital and expertise.

RECENT HISTORY

The current wave of co-ops was not in any way an offshoot of the stores established in the Fitchburg area. The only relation-ships between the two are the ones being pondered now, four or five years after the wave's beginning. Though their makeup

has changed, current co-ops appear to trace their beginnings back
to student activism in the late 1960s. In the *International Socialist
Review* (Vol. 31, No. 7) of October, 1970, George Breitman char-
acterized what happened then as the Current Radicalization. He
defined, with considerable perspective,

. . . a period of radicalization is one in which large numbers of people,
responding to material conditions and alterations in those conditions,
change their attitudes about important questions, beliefs, values, customs,
relations, arrangements and institutions—social, personal, philosophical,
political, economic, cultural. Things that were previously accepted or taken
for granted begin to be questioned or rejected.[27]

In some cases the link between antiwar organizations and food
co-ops was a direct one—The New American Movement and some
SDS groups made co-ops part of their early regular agenda in
attempting to reach greater numbers of people. At breaks in
co-op conferences now it is not uncommon to overhear reminis-
cences of protest marches against the war or for civil rights.
It seems that the sixties helped spawn both the ranks of people
who stepped in to initiate co-op activity and the larger numbers
of people willing to join in with the efforts of the former group.
    One view of the people involved with co-ops holds that they
are rebels who have by default designated co-ops as their cause
since the rug of antiwar protest has been pulled from under them.
An opposing view maintains that involvement in community
projects like co-ops is part of an evolution of organizing interests
from abstract macro issues to immediate concepts close to
people's homes. In the latter view, neighborhood organizing is
a key part of an overall, constructive approach to social reform.
Co-ops are no longer something that keep the activists happy
since the activists are outnumbered by neighborhood folk and
rapidly losing identity anyway. Terry Molner, a member of
Boston Food Co-op's board of directors, believes that although
the co-op "movement" is an outgrowth of antiwar activity in
the late 1960s, it is qualitatively different. "The antiwar movement
had leaders and followers, but co-ops are trying to do things
consensually," he notes. The people involved with co-ops
"are not the leadership of the early movement, but the gentle
people who did the work."
    The evolution of the Minneapolis area co-ops, which is fairly
representative of the initial forces spurring co-op growth, traces
back to a "People's Pantry" network in the late sixties.

Dean Zimmerman, who now works at the warehouse in Minneapolis, describes the pantry as having started "on a hippy's back porch." "Hippies" wanted to get others interested in healthy foods and to create some community interaction. They organized a co-op at a converted church based on the interest they raised by distributing foods from their back porches. The buying clubs combined their operations in a church basement which they used as home base until increasing volume and activity motivated some people to start a storefront. The storefront, named North Country, was initiated in April 1971 to service the buying clubs and increase overall co-op operations. The storefront's format, with people signing up for shifts and operating the store collectively, met with acceptance from enough people to supply a willing, if not professional, staff. The storefront was a runaway success financially and organizationally. Inspired members formed other storefronts and related services (bakery, restaurant, warehouse) based on the North Country model. Recent storefronts are strongly anchored in neighborhood interests (see notes on Green Grass in "Beginning a Storefront") and participation, and there is continuing criticism leveled at those storefronts that don't identify with community needs. Whether by intentional outreach or in spite of themselves, the co-ops are serving an increasingly mixed group of people—fewer activists and more neighborhood people.

One Minneapolis co-op member told me that community people had been put off by the co-ops because, "The people are too freaky and the food is too freaky." It seems that the freaky people are becoming less so as they are around longer and are being outnumbered by neighborhood people anyway. Similarly, some of the co-ops are offering less "freaky" food at the same time when many people are becoming interested in the "freaky" product standard in the co-op line.

In an interview in the Boston *Phoenix*, a member of the Mission Hill Food Co-op gave one interpretation of the shift in co-op support. "Back in 1970 and 1971," he says, "people believed co-ops would be 'the immediate instruments of sudden change.' They expected the revolution to come overnight. Now most people in the co-op look on it as a way to get cheap food." [28]

As in Minneapolis, recent national co-op history is marked overall by a shift to community identity and increasingly heterogeneous co-op clientele. Minneapolis's Powderhorn Co-op

takes on a whole new dimension now that it includes in its
membership the neighborhood alderman. Other co-ops are also
turning up "official" members. There seems to be more activity
in Minneapolis than in the rest of the country, but national activity
is fairly widespread and apparently growing steadily. Dave Zinner,
who helped tabulate the directory in this book, told me that he
gets an average of one listing of a new co-op every day.

The pattern in Minneapolis of new co-ops forming along the
same lines as the first successful example locally (North Country)
also parallels the experience of most other areas. In Boston,
where most early co-op activity was in large buying clubs organized
in blocs, the storefront was organized initially as a large buying
club, complete with mandatory participation and preorder systems.
In New York, there is so much diversity in co-op growth that
there's no real model.

Legacy accounts for part of the influences in the formation
of new co-ops. If co-op X is successful in an area, then it is likely
and logical that new co-ops will look like the "son of co-op X."
Geography, climate, and local business conditions also shape co-op
growth as they shape co-op formation. In the Boston area, where
there is easy access to the wholesale produce market through the
NEFCO buying service, produce is the mainstay of co-op business.
In Minneapolis, produce is a sideline after beans and grains.

Regional social and political conditions also account for part
of the influence in co-op formation. A Bostonian who visited
Minneapolis felt that its success with co-ops was due to the unique
political atmosphere there. "As close as I've ever seen in the U.S.
to a popular Maoist community," he claims. One member of the
North Country Co-op expressed surprise that food co-ops were
so much more advanced in Minneapolis-St. Paul than in Chicago.
"We're always two years behind them with everything else,"
he observed. A frustrated co-op organizer in Ann Arbor commented
last year, "Ann Arbor's loaded with dope smokers—impossible to
muster up a committed responsible work force. Demise in store
due to a flood of top-quality dope."

The first impression one gets in looking at the Minneapolis
experience is that it plots a snowballing sort of co-op growth,
with small, amateurish co-ops giving way to more organized, more
bureaucratic and less involving (at a broad base) forms. This is a
false view, because there are more amateur buying clubs now than
ever before. The relationship between buying clubs and more
visible storefronts is not one of evolution but interplay. Some

people drop out of buying clubs when they are able to do necessary shopping at a co-op storefront, but many storefronts help start and support buying clubs. Some people, having found that a large storefront doesn't provide the same social rewards as a buying club, keep up their storefront activity and return to a buying club, too. One ex-member of the Boston Food Co-op told me she rejoined the Mission Hill Food Co-op because "it has more of a neighborhood feeling." This is not to de-emphasize storefronts. If anything, the development of storefronts marked a high level in co-op organization and development and a vehicle for making new inroads into the involvement of a greater mix of people. A member of the Common Market Co-op in Denver explained that "Moving to a storefront downtown changed our membership from primarily students to working people." Co-op growth, then, has been diversified.

Terry Molner points out that "co-op growth has, until late in 1973, been unconnected regionally. Just about every food co-op started on its own." It was not until the Minneapolis conference and the Directory which came out late in 1973 that there was much regional or national cooperation among co-ops.

Many co-ops have started with more direct outside help than the Minneapolis folks had. Some were more directly related to antiwar activities, like the Gentle Strength Co-op in Tempe, Arizona, formed initially as a buying club at the Peace Center in town. Some were more closely related to college activities, like the Boston Food Co-op (as was mentioned before, it received a $10,000 start-up grant from Boston University's Student Union), and the Shanti Food Conspiracy on Staten Island, New York (which was funded by a student government staffed by its members). It seems that all of these "linked" co-ops have made efforts to unlink and strengthen ties with their respective communities.

Students' roles in co-ops have undergone a reversal since the current wave began. At the outset, most co-ops probably were supported primarily by students. Now students are decreasing not only in numbers but prestige. "We don't like students in the co-op—they're bad for the neighborhood. They only stay a little while and raise hell," one Minneapolis co-op member explained. Students' dwindling participation in co-ops is explained partly by the emphasis on neighborhoods and partly on students' dwindling participation in everything—it seems that the campuses are looking more and more like they did in the 1950s. "Metamorphosis of the Campus Radical," an article in the January 30, 1972, *New York Times Magazine*, contains two pictures of a young man. In one picture, dated 1967, titled "David Sundance, protestor," he is dressed in a hooded black robe, carrying a sickle over his shoulder and a doll in his hand, standing next to what appears to be a burning casket. In the larger picture, titled "David Sundance, day care baby-sitter," he is playing with two toddlers. The article describes the shift of protestors at the University of Iowa: ". . . [L]ast year's window busters are busy with day care centers and health-food cooperatives." [29] The article cites the waning number of activists, but points out that other forms of activity are emerging.

The influx of neighborhood people is important to the current strength of co-ops, but the concurrent absence of students strikes an ominous chord. Art Danforth of the Cooperative League worries about the future of the current "movement" if it continues to discourage student involvement. "If they can't get young people involved, they're going to wither away," he predicted. In addition, he wonders what will happen when the activists at the core of the current movement get older. "It has to happen, you know. There'll be kids, and financial worries." There are a few parents active in cooperative storefronts, but the low "people's wages" paid by collectives don't attract your typical young marrieds. Floating co-ops, on the other hand, do attract a large number of marrieds—floating co-ops don't demand a life's commitment and do serve a real purpose for them. One of the real strengths of many co-ops is the growing number of families that are joining. Perhaps it is unnecessary for co-ops to draw directly from students in schools if they can serve families directly. Also, the role of students and activists is minimized by co-ops' spreading of responsibilities among many people. Ideally, co-ops should involve students and neighborhood people.

Tracing the current co-op wave to the unrest of the late 1960s really only begins an understanding of recent co-op history. What happened in the late 1960s was complex. There is certainly no chain of events leading inevitably from war protest to food co-ops. What's important for co-ops now is that a lot of people then got involved in a lot of activities. Their activities spurred other activities at more general and abstract levels and helped contribute to an atmosphere that enabled co-ops to evolve.

Recent co-op history is also not an inevitable progression from

generalized buying clubs to neighborhood-anchored organizations.
There is much diversification and overlap. Recent trends are
interesting but the real point of recent co-op history is that,
for better or worse it will have a heavy hand in shaping co-ops'
future.

Other eras have seen co-ops come and go practically at the
whim of people's willingness to participate in them. Art Danforth
is impressed with the strength of the current wave, but skeptical
nonetheless. He and others involved with co-ops earlier on feel
that co-ops must concede more to bureaucracy, hiring paid
managers, getting away from relying on direct member participation or low-paid enthusiasts to run the co-op. Still, he concedes,
"We won't know who's right for another seven or eight years."

Danforth pointed out some basic similarities between current
co-ops and earlier ones. Organizational forms are pretty much the
same. Early co-ops also often were related to antiwar organizing.
"A lot of them were liberal and were involved in organizing in
one way or another," he recalled. A good deal of the support
from Upton Sinclair's campaign for the governorship of
California went on to help co-ops after he lost the election.
But most of the co-ops went on to disintegration. Except,
that is, for the ones that established paid positions for professional managers, of which many remained and prosper still.
There is some justified debate, especially among members of
new co-ops, regarding just how much of an alternative the
now-mammoth supermarket co-ops are.

Don Philips, another Rochdale co-op advocate, pointed out
a basic difference between the current co-ops and those of the
thirties. Mr. Philips is public relations director for Co-op City,
the massive cooperative housing project in the Bronx. He was
quick to point out that earlier co-ops were based on considerable
support from the labor unions. "Unions are vital to the co-op
movement," he observed. But unions are not at all the organizations they were in the thirties. It is characteristic of current
co-ops that they relate not at all to established unions but
rather to small work collectives. Recently, some established unions
have shown interest in the new co-ops. Mill workers in southern
Massachusetts recently invited Roger Auerbach to lecture them
on how to start food co-ops.

HISTORY LESSON?

Though it continues to influence current developments, co-op history doesn't much help point the way for new co-ops, but it does have some other values. Knowing that co-ops were active in earlier years and then withered might help introduce a note of needed skepticism in the minds of people involved in the current wave. There is some irrelevant drawing of parallels between the old and new, but there are also some lessons to be learned from past experience. Links between old and new co-ops need to be strengthened so the perspective of past experience can become clearer.

Looking at past cooperative activity should turn up differences as well as similarities. The differences give current co-ops their identity and will strongly influence their potential for growth and longevity. Analyzing the causes and effects of these differences will give co-op members some restless nights but it should help them concentrate their strengths.

Beyond considerations of the utility of co-op history, I've always enjoyed it because it captures the essence of what co-ops are about. Co-op history is not at all like the "normal" kind of history. It's not a history of movements or developments or abstractions, but, profoundly, a history of people.

With co-op history operating at a scale of small groups, rather than masses, it is not really surprising that three people-related themes emerge from co-op history over the years. The trends are interesting because of both their persistence and their contents. Co-ops do best in periods of hard times; co-ops are volatile politically; and co-ops have a way of getting linked up with social causes and utopian schemes. These three recurring themes emerge from a look at the Fitchburg co-op and are reinforced by the experiences of others.

Hard Times

Hard times helped bring the Fitchburg co-op together— Finns were hard put economically as immigrants. The initial co-op effort arose from the struggling immigrant community. Moreover, the co-op experienced one of its most impressive periods of growth during the Depression. In 1934 Orin Burley, a cooperative historian, observed:

Waves of consumer cooperation have developed in the United States
in depressed or war periods, or immediately following such periods.[30]

In 1923 James Warbasse, then president of the Cooperative
League, commented in his book *Cooperative Democracy*:

Born in poverty, adversity encourages [the cooperative movement].
When the dominant system oppresses society with injustices and war,
the people turn to themselves for relief.[31]

Even the monied producers' co-ops had their origins in stormy
economic straits. The farmers of Saskatchewan, with their
dependence on one crop, are perhaps an exaggerated example.
But the situation was not so much better for more self-reliant
and diversified farmers. Most often, the prices they received for
the crops they had taken months to raise were determined by
forces completely beyond their control. J. A. Everitt, a farmer
activist early in the nineteenth century, noted in his book,
The Third Power:

All he [the farmer] is supposed to know under the present system is how
to work sixteen hours a day and the road to market. When he gets there
he finds a man who tells him how much his produce is worth, and if
he wants to take something home the price of that also. He has no
organization. . . .[32]

Somewhere along the line this poor, struggling farmer discovered
that co-ops work and, somewhere else along the line, the
struggling co-ops turned into big business. Though economic
hardship was probably not the motivating force at the heart
of the current consumer co-op wave, the perils of inflation and
rising supermarket prices have helped add much to the more
recent increased interest in co-ops.

The link between periods of hard times and the development
of cooperatives is not a simple one. People don't automatically
turn to co-ops when previously existing organizations go sour.
But if people don't have problems there is sometimes little reason
for them to change their normal ways of doing things. Moreover,
periods of hard times have a way of bringing political and
social unrest along with the economic upset that co-ops emerge
from.

Politics
The Fitchburg Co-op confronted a political problem when

the local Communist Party attempted to take over, and failing in that, set up a competing store. The Communists eventually shriveled up and went out of business. Communism was one of several political issues that rocked co-ops. Some co-op groups became involved in actual political campaigns or in the interests of local politicians or political groups. It was only natural that political involvements of that sort would occur. As long as co-ops are responsive to the interests and needs of their members, they will continue to reflect their members' changing ideas and involvements. (More current information on this is detailed in Chapter Four, Co-ops and Politics.)

The Kansas Alliance Exchange Company, a farmers' co-op active at the end of the nineteenth century, sought political remedies in controlling economic forces beyond their reach. Co-op historian Joseph Knapp notes:

When the energies of the Alliance were absorbed by political measures after 1890, this completely drained it of vital interest in self-help cooperation, and brought on its rapid disintegration as a general farmers' organization. . . . For many years following the collapse of the Alliance, the wistful refrain could be heard in farm circles, "Politics killed the Alliance."[33]

Co-ops' political volatility has been expressed through takeover attempts by splinter interests, expansion attempts by co-ops themselves, and internal political struggles as well. The last of these is probably the most tumultuous, but the least dangerous to co-ops overall. Internal co-op struggles often strengthen the co-op in the process of their resolution. When internal struggles don't get resolved internally, they often lead to the formation of new co-ops.

Takeover attempts of co-ops by tangential interests have posed real threats to some co-ops. Outside interests are likely to be well financed and capable of devoting a lot of energy to bringing co-ops under their wing. Several political campaigns tried to use co-ops and caused formidable problems. In some cases takeovers from tangential interests were mixed with internal struggles when co-op members espoused new ideas or programs.

One form of political involvement which large co-ops found particularly useful has been (jokes about campaign contributions aside) lobbying. In order for farmers' co-ops to serve their members and survive the economic trends of time, they had to receive the same kinds of help from the government as private corporations. In the beginning, this meant only recognition, but later on it meant subsidy and support.

The Communist Party, for which a good deal of support came from the same immigrant communities that backed co-ops, posed particularly heated conflicts in co-ops in the late 1920s. Some co-ops were taken over by members with Communist sympathies. Other co-ops resisted Communist advances in ways similar to the Fitchburg Co-op group's efforts. The Communist split was overall a difficult issue for co-ops to handle because of the inherent closeness of Communist and co-op philosophies and the unflinching support of Communism provided by some of the co-ops. James Warbasse was impressed enough by Communist doctrine and the strength of the Russian cooperative movement to journey to Russia for a firsthand look in 1924. He returned with the conclusion that cooperation was a source of great hope for Russia, but that it was incompatible with the Communism being practiced there. [34]

Despite his position as president, Warbasse did not exercise unchallenged leadership in the Cooperative League. Articles appeared in the *Cooperator* in 1925 and 1926 on "Why Cooperation Is Not Enough" by the American Communist Earl Browder. In the 1928 Congress of the League, Communists withdrew an opportunity to divide the League into two competitive factions. [35] Apparently they didn't want their struggle to head in that direction.

The Communist struggles plunged the League and the individual co-ops into a resolved apolitical mold from which they have never really broken. Co-op supermarkets now are less political than regular supermarkets, and old line co-opers crinkle their noses at the mere mention of politics. Despite this steadfastness, the co-ops have not escaped the memories of early involvement with Communism which are used on occasion by some groups to conjure up re-tinted images. Richard Margolis notes:

In many states co-ops had trouble coaxing charters out of their legislatures. There was a general feeling in state capitals that co-operatives were at once "communistic" and "monopolistic," and this feeling was encouraged by that tireless defender of laissez faire: the railroad lobby. [36]

This seems quite unjustified, for the backlash among co-ops which brought about a mistrust of politics created an even stronger mistrust of Communism.

The Communist experience is recounted here as an example of co-ops' political activity and as a partial explanation of the

character of the co-op stores at present. In forcing the hands
of sympathetic co-op members, the Communist experience turned
the co-ops far away from Communism and any other form of
political involvement.

Political volatility since then has taken a similar but not quite
as heated a path with the new wave of co-ops. At present,
there are few co-ops involved in overt political activity. There is,
however, a kaleidoscope of more subtle, inherent activity which
is explored in depth in the chapter on political significance.
There was more overt political involvement when feeling about
the Vietnam war was more of an issue. The overall trend of
political involvement has been a toning down of stands on the
war and on more local issues as well. There is more concentration
on getting a mix of people involved and letting the group take
its own course than in "raising consciousness." Not that co-ops
are apolitical, but their approach to politics is different from
the approach of the earlier co-ops. Both old and new co-ops
share a predisposition for political involvements rooted in their
members' commitment to their organizations.

Co-op history underscores the depth of political activity
people brought to co-ops, the lack of direction given the activity,
and the confusing ways in which co-ops deal with politics.
The tradition of confusion traces back to Owen himself, who
while trying to help working people gain greater control over
their lives was described by Holyoake as having "no political
principles—not even in favour of liberty." [37] The Communist
takeover plots continued the confusion, and the recent experiences of activist groups (described in the next section) updated
them. Throughout, the confusion has been supplemented by
co-ops' connections with utopias involved in their own politically
confusing entanglements.

Utopianism

Despite some efforts to break from utopianism, members
with political and social predispositions help continue to bring
co-ops into an assortment of utopian schemes. Co-ops (or something
like them) are part of some utopian schemes. Another manifes-
tation of utopianism is the way in which people refer to
cooperation—it is not another simple business scheme, but something extra. Herbert Myrick begins his *How to Cooperate*, published in 1891, with, "The True Way Out of the evils that now
afflict both producers and consumers is through an agency

[cooperation] that already exists."[38] Others have spelled out
their hopes for cooperation in book titles. There's Isaac Roberts's
Looking Forward: Cooperation the Solution (1913), Emerson P.
Harris's *Cooperation: The Hope of the Consumer* (1918), Jerry
Voorhis's *The Morale of Democracy* (1941), George Boyle's
Democracy's Second Chance (1941), Toyohiko Nagawa's
Brotherhood Economics (1936), and E. R. Bowen's *The Coopera-
tive Road to Abundance* (1953). Titles like these convey some
of the feelings people brought to cooperatives.

More importantly, co-ops share much utopian philosophy,
some utopian experience, and a good deal of utopian idealism.
The first co-ops arose from utopian schemes in England. The
first American co-ops were started by participants in those
utopian schemes. Some of the strongest supporters of current
co-ops live in communes or utopian experiments of their own.
Throughout their development, co-ops have recruited people from
various aspects of utopias.

Links with utopian philosophies add a lot of color to co-op
history; reading about nineteenth-century communities that
practiced free love beats memorizing state capitals any day.
Some historians scorn utopias as aberrations or insignificant
experiments. Numerically they were insignificant, but socially
they held sway over a mass of new ideas. Their significance
lay in the uniqueness of their internal practices and the
exchange of ideas at their interface with the larger society.
Co-ops drew from both areas.

On one hand the utopianist outlook is critical of the
cooperatives that remain because they maintain a very limited
scope. "From implying concert of life in community, it
[cooperation] sank into meaning concert in shopkeeping."[39]
An opposing view holds that utopianists are frivolous and
irrelevant. Marxists have carried this view an extra step, proclaim-
ing utopias to be dangerous and harmful, particularly in their
romanticism and apoliticism.

More recently, Paula Rayman, who worked with the New
Communities Project in Boston, made a similar criticism of
recent communes:

[T]he concentrated dosage of self-centered change pervading the communal
alternative atmosphere did little to revolutionize the large causes of
our oppression much less aid others in our society struggling with
domination.[40]

Martin Buber, in *Paths to Utopia*, suggests that this view is limiting because utopias are concerned as much with structural renewal of society as with romanticism.[41] Criticisms against utopias that retreat from society are justified in that these utopias may pursue unique internal organizations and in that the act of withdrawal is in itself significant. "Tune in, turn on, drop out" caused some outrage for each of its declarations, but "dropping out" was the one viewed as the most far-reaching.

Whatever the values of utopia, it seems that utopias are destined to retain a link to cooperatives and evaluations of cooperation. "Someday we're all going to join together," a Boston co-oper recently told me, "all the work collectives and all the food co-ops, and maybe the day care co-ops and housing co-ops, too. It'll be a real, all-round alternative to everything." History doesn't point to the success of these ideas, but it doesn't show that they're terribly harmful either. A little enthusiasm, a little dreaming, can help warm the cold nights.

APPENDIX A: CO-OPS TALK ABOUT THEMSELVES,
INCLUDING "THE ROCHDALE PRINCIPLES"

I've selected the following from assorted co-op newsletters and
notices because I feel they represent key areas of co-op work.

A BIT OF CO-OP HISTORY – From "Food for Thought,"
9/10/73, New York City's Broadway Local Food Co-op
Newsletter

The Broadway Local Food Co-op was started by three high
school students in the early spring of 1971. It was just one of the
activities that a group of community people organized after
breaking into an abandoned city-owned storefront—the same
storefront the co-op now leases from the city. "Breaking and
entering" seemed natural at a time when many desperate poor
people of the Upper West Side were squatting in buildings to
save their homes from Urban Renewal.

The co-op was the only storefront activity that survived the
test of time. From a small nucleus of people we have grown to
include 200-300 families sprawled out from 72nd to 173rd Streets.
How was this achieved?

The Bloc System
When there were only 20 or 30 people in the co-op all the
food was packed right in the storefront. As more people joined
this arrangement became chaotic and a new, decentralized form of
co-op was organized—the nucleus of our present organization.

People were divided into about 5 small groups or "blocs"
based roughly on geographical location. One bloc at a time did
all the shopping for the entire co-op—a responsibility that rotated

every two weeks from bloc to bloc. Instead of breaking down the
food into individual orders in the storefront it was divided into
the bloc orders which each bloc would further subdivide into
individual orders in an apartment or community room in its
own area. This system worked and is the same one we use today
nearly 3 years later.

Progress thru Struggle

What progress have we made these last 2½ years? Most
importantly we have come a long way in the variety of foods we
can buy. In the beginning, with so few members, we could buy
only the most commonplace vegetables and fruits. As we grew,
energetic people worked to have new food items added to the
order form. First came dairy, then grains and yogurt, then meat
and bread. Now we even buy many foods directly from farmers.

We also grew to two shopping days and became large enough
for the city agencies to notice us (perhaps because of some
tattletaling by the local A&P!). To protect our rights we went
"legit" as it were and leased the storefront ($1/Mo.), got a
Health Department permit, a bank account, our own truck, and
a fine bureaucracy.

Our co-op is a $150,000 a year nonprofit business completely
owned and operated by the members. It is an achievement perhaps
to be proud of and protected, especially now when the wolves
are at the supermarket check-out counters all around us!

A SUBURBAN WEEKLY CO-OP NEWSLETTER: NEEDHAM, MASSACHUSETTS, FOOD CO-OP

Greetings to old, new, and prospective Co-op members!

We are now well into the adventure of enlarging the Co-op,
and we welcome all suggestions for our betterment. This letter
explains our present status.

Membership: You become a member by ordering food on any
Tuesday. Order forms are at Something Special, the gift shop on
Great Plain Ave. The store is open from 10-5 p.m. Food pick-up
is Thursday at the Unitarian Church in Fuller Hall, 11 a.m.-
2:30 p.m.

Money: When you pick up your first order, there will be a
$5 membership fee charged; cost of your food; and for the first
few weeks, 15% surcharge. The 15% is a sliding percentage and
is used to pay for the church, driver and van, and incidental

costs. We are nonprofit.

Food: We are essentially a fruit, vegetable and grain Co-op. Our buyer in Boston is Roger Auerbach who buys in crates and ½ crates at Chelsea Market. We also provide Arnold bread products. There is no guarantee that the food you order will be bought but we'll do our best.

Time: Each member is required to work for the Co-op. A member chooses the job s/he can best do according to his or her personal schedule.

Presently the jobs are:

1) Tabulator — This person works with individual orders, adds them together for one total order. This must be done by about 7:00 p.m. on Tuesday.

2) Editor of Orders — Person converts the total order into crates, etc., and decides what we can or can't order according to quantity. She phones order to Roger on Wed. morning.

3) Van Unloaders — 9-9:30 a.m. They unload van, open crates, arrange them according to the items that are counted or weighed.

4) Packers — They weigh, pack, and price individual orders, and initial the orders which they bag; 9:30-11:00 a.m.

5) Sitter for Packer children — 9:30-11:00 a.m. — In small nursery of church.

6) Cashiers — For the first months, the Board Members will do this so that they can sign checks and check on our organization of jobs, etc. Cashiers use the adding machine, thus do the billing.

7) Clean-up — Take stuff to dump and neaten church; 3 p.m. on.

8) Job Coordinator — Keeps card catalog of members, addresses, etc.; sets up the work assignments for each month.

9) Mimeographer — Person who donates stencils and runs them off.

10) Typist — Help with typing order forms, newsletters, etc.

11) Bread-getters — Go to Arnold store, Newton; get bread early Thurs. morning.

Prices for the previous week will be posted at Something Special if you want to use them as estimate prices.

Needed: 1) Recycled paper bags; 2) names of those who have compost heaps or rabbits, etc., so they can take our garbage.

Our extra food is given to the United Farm Workers in Boston.

AN ALL VOLUNTEER COMMUNITY STOREFRONT: GREEN GRASS GROCERY, ST. PAUL

Welcome to Green Grass Grocery. This is a community operated cooperative store. In order to provide food at the lowest possible price, we have limited packaging items whenever possible. We request that you, as a customer, bring your own sacks, egg cartons and other containers (some sacks and cartons are available, ask if you need one).

There are no paid employees here. All work is done by volunteers, people just like yourself. In return for working a minimum of three hours each month, workers receive a 10% discount on all the food they buy. Each customer can help too. Please fill your own container and weigh your own purchases. If you need help with anything, just ask; the person working is probably your neighbor. If you think you might like to work and receive the discount, please sign our book. Someone will contact you soon and explain the many different things that need to be done.

Finally, if you do not find everything you want, please be patient. We are operating with a limited amount of capital and cannot immediately stock everything we would like. Please put any suggestions about items you think we should carry, or about the operation of the store in the Suggestion Box. If you want to help us make decisions, come to our meetings. They are held in the store every Thursday at 7:00 P.M. Everyone is welcome. If we all work together, we can truly make Green Grass grow.

THE ROCHDALE PRINCIPLES – As described in James Warbasse's "Cooperative Democracy," p. 22

1. Each member shall have one vote and no more.
2. Capital invested in the society, if it receive interest, shall receive not more than a fixed percentage which shall be not more than the minimum prevalent rate.
3. If a surplus-saving ("profit") accrues, by virtue of the difference between the net cost and the net selling price of commodities and service, after meeting expenses, paying interest (wages to capital), and setting aside reserve and other funds,

the net surplus-saving shall be used for the good of the members, for beneficent social purposes, or shall be returned to the patrons as savings-returns ("dividends") in proportion to their patronage.

Warbasse also points out "certain methods which are commonly associated with . . . cooperative administration" including voluntary and unlimited membership, business done for cash, co-op expansion to other co-op activities and democratic control of the group. In other parts of the book, he discusses the need for co-operative education (pp. 108-110) and the hazards of politics (p. 147).

APPENDIX B: GUIDE TO WHOLESALERS

This appendix is a product of a mail survey I conducted in late fall 1973. I asked the co-ops surveyed to provide me with names, addresses, and comments for the wholesalers with whom they dealt. The information and comments were excerpted from the returned questionnaires.

The list is provided more as a guide to people's experiences with wholesalers than as a directory. The best way for a co-op to find a wholesaler is for the co-op to check with other co-ops in its area and in the Yellow Pages. Cooperation with other co-ops and maximal development of local resources usually yield better and cheaper food and stronger co-ops as well.

This list is included as a horizon expander for existing co-ops, a demonstration of the variety of products co-ops can handle. The list also points out the delivery distances some products travel and the outlooks of some of the co-ops on relations with the wholesalers. Finally the list may help people in parts of the country where there are no co-ops to start contact with wholesalers.

Addresses have been given wherever possible. Those not given can be found in area telephone books. Comments on wholesalers were provided by the co-ops listed as references. Wholesalers marked with an asterisk are outgrowths of local cooperative endeavors.

Arkansas

S & E Wholesale, Springdale. Product: can goods, juice. Referred by Ozark Food Co-op.

Shiloh Farms, Sulphur Spring. Product: frozen goods, dairy items. Referred by Sunflower Co-op, Sarasota, Florida. ("Delivery with own truck once a month. Must order with foresight."

Arizona

Food for Health, Indian School Road, Phoenix. Product: food items and vitamins. Referred by Amigos de Salud, El Prado, New Mexico. ("No regular deliveries, many mistakes in orders.") and Gentle Strength Co-op, Tempe, Arizona.

Granary, 526 N. 4th Avenue, Tucson. Product: grains. Referred by Gentle Strength Co-op, Tempe, Arizona.

California

Book People, 2940 7th St., Berkeley. Product: books. Referred by Capital Hill Co-op, Seattle, Washington.

Westbrae Natural Foods, 113½ Gilman St., Berkeley. Product: pasta, dry goods, fruit juices. Referred by Santa Cruz Consumers Co-op and Alternative Food Store, Oakland, California. ("Westbrae carries a full line of fruit juices . . . ; also has a wholesale bakery tho they are a hassle on this end, since they insist on selling their bread the same day and their bakers are often 'out' . . . . Their cashew granola is excellent and inexpensive. . . . They will ship anywhere in the U.S. or Canada for a $100 minimum order.")

Spiral Foods, Inc., 1144 W. First St., Chico. Product: "Limited line of macrobiotic essentials." Referred by Alternative Food Store, Oakland.

Kahan & Lessin, 3131 East Maria, Complon 90221. Product: health foods. Referred by Consumers Cooperative Society of the Monterey Peninsula. ("Account.")

Erewhon, 8454 Stellar Drive, Culver City. Product: grains and oils. Referred by Gentle Strength Co-op, Tempe, Arizona and Santa Cruz Consumers Co-op, Santa Cruz, California.

Alternative Distributing Co., 6448 Bay St., Emeryville 94608. Product: organic produce, dried fruits, oils, some seeds. Referred by Santa Cruz Consumers Co-op and Alternative Food Store. ("A collective of about 15 people distributing organic produce and other natural foods on a wholesale basis.")

Jaffe Bros., Escondido. Product: dried fruits and nuts. Referred by Sunflower Co-op, Sarasota, Florida. ("Old line reputable fruit grower and distributor. Competitive prices.")

Rock Island Line, Ignacio. Product: dairy. Referred by Alternative Food Store.

Organic Foods and Garden, 2655 Commerce Way, Los Angeles. Product: vegetables and produce. Referred by Gentle Strength Co-op.

Oroweat Bakeries, Monterey. Product: bread. Referred by Consumers' Cooperative Society of the Monterey Peninsula. ("Cash.")

Ranch Market, 1193 Fremont Ave., Monterey. Product: produce. Referred by Santa Cruz Consumers Co-op.

Andersons Egg House, Morgan Hill. Product: fertile eggs. Referred by

Santa Cruz Consumers' Co-op.

Food Mill, 3033 MacArthur Blvd., Oakland. Product: stone ground flour. Referred by Alternative Food Store, Oakland. ("A good source for all sorts of natural foods ... *very* favorable prices. ... Don't be put off if the order people seem to give you brusque treatment. ... They're a retail outlet, too, and as such are a moneymaking business. They give off all those vibes until you become a 'regular.' In other words, Be Persistent.")

Associated Coop, 4801 Central, Richmond. Product: regular supermarket nonperishables. Referred by Consumer Cooperative Society of the Monterey Peninsula, Inc. ("Tho we are the smallest Cost Plus member of Associated Cooperatives we are *not* pushed aside. Efforts are made [not always successful] to meet our needs.") and Consumers' Cooperative of Palo Alto. ("Basically no problems.")

Rainbow Pure Foods, 543 South 31st St., Richmond. Product: dairy. Referred by Santa Cruz Consumers' Co-op and Alternative Food Store, Oakland. ("Capitalist pigs, meat eaters, and cigarette smokers, but unfortunately the only wholesale outlet in the Bay Area for Al Stornetta's dairy products, which are excellent. ... Write Stornetta Dairy, Sonoma, California, for info on distributors at other West Coast points.")

Everybody's Dist. Co., 1201 San Anselmo Ave., San Anselmo 94960. Product: New Age Juices. Referred by Alternative Food Store. ("New Age Juices are unpasteurized–all are outasite. Due to rapid spoilage on these juices, outside California delivery might not be possible. Ask anyway.")

Heirschfelder, No. 1 Arkansas Street, San Francisco. Product: nuts, seeds, etc. Referred by Consumers Cooperative Society of the Monterey Peninsula. ("Account.")

Al Muti Herb Collective, San Francisco 94103. Product: herbs. Referred by Alternative Food Store, Oakland. ("Very complete stock of herbs, will ship anywhere COD. A resale number is probably necessary, unless you order for personal use only. 1 lb. minimum on all herbs.")

Giustos' Whole Grain Bakery & Natural Foods, 241 E. Harris Ave., South San Francisco 94080. Product: dry goods. Referred by Santa Cruz Consumers Co-op.

Alum Rock Cheese Co., 215 E. Alma Ave., San Jose, 95112. Product: cheese. Referred by Consumers Cooperative Society of the Monterey Peninsula. ("Cash.")

The Well, 795 W. Hedding St., San Jose 95126. Product: produce, honey, grains, oils, Referred by Santa Cruz Consumers' Co-op and Alternative Food Store, Oakland. ("These people are organic freaks and tho their prices run high, are trustworthy folks to deal with.")

Bud's Granola Shop, 550 Palm, Santa Cruz. Product: granola. Referred by Santa Cruz Consumers' Co-op.

Harmony Foods, Box 1191, Santa Cruz 95060. Product: dry goods.

Referred by Santa Cruz Consumers' Co-op. ("Local people–beautiful
suppliers with good tasting and feeling food–Great people!")

Jim and Rod Robertson, 21 S. Circle Drive, Santa Cruz 95060. Product:
honey. Referred by Santa Cruz Consumers' Co-op.

Real Truckin, 320 Dufour St., Santa Cruz. Product: dairy, yogurt.
Referred by Santa Cruz Consumers' Co-op.

Staff of Life Natural Foods Bakery, 1305 Water St., Santa Cruz. Product:
bread. Referred by Santa Cruz Consumers' Co-op.

Redwood Specialty Farm, P.O. Box 233, Sebastopol. Product: dairy.
Referred by Santa Cruz Consumers' Co-op.

Age of Foods, Inc., West Arcadia, California. Product: dairy. Referred by
Alternative Food Store, Oakland. ("The only wholesale outlet for
Altadena dairy products–raw milk and raw milk products. . . . The
only source of nonfat raw milk known to us. . . . Often they short
you on the order for several items, but they're apologetic when wrong
and eager to please wholesale customers.")

Colorado

Green Nut Herbs, Box 2369, Boulder. Product: herbs. Referred by
Amigos de Salud, El Prado, New Mexico.

Nutri-books, Denver. Product: books. Referred by Ecology Food Co-op,
Philadelphia, Pa.

Washington, D.C.

*Peoples' Warehouse. Product: grains, dry goods, beans.

Florida

Happy Health Products, Miami. Product: Arrowhead and Erewhon products,
packaged items and dairy items. Referred by Sunflower Co-op,
Sarasota, Florida. ("Truck delivery.")

Tree of Life, Inc., St. Augustine. Product: Arrowhead and Erewhon products,
packaged and dairy items. Referred by Sunflower Co-op, Sarasota.
("Truck delivery.")

Illinois

People's Food Co-op, Bloomington. Product: produce. Referred by Northside
Buyers Club, Peoria, Illinois.

Chicago Natural Food, Chicago. Referred by Outpost, Milwaukee, Wisconsin.
("No hassle.")

*Cornucopia, 2808 W. Lake St., Chicago. Product: produce. Referred by
People's Food. ("They break cases but it costs too much that way.")

Foods for Life, Chicago. Referred by Outpost, Milwaukee. ("No hassle.")

Now Foods, Chicago. Referred by Outpost, Milwaukee.

Vitamins, Inc., 401 N. Michigan Ave., Chicago 60611. Referred by Coop
League Handbook.

Food for Life, 420 Wrightwood Ave., Elmhurst, 60126. Product: grains, beans. Referred by New Pioneer Food Co-op, Iowa City, Iowa.

Gridley Cheese Co., Box 187, Gridley. Product: cheese. Referred by Northside Buyers Club, Peoria, Illinois. ("Delivers.")

C & G Wholesale Meats, 2101 S. W. Washington, Peoria. Product: meat.
Referred by Northside Buyers Club, Peoria. ("Delivers–packages to
order.")

Warren Fyre Poultry Farm, RR 2, Rt. 150 N.W., Peoria. Product: eggs.
Referred by Northside Buyers Club, Peoria. ("Member of co-op,
gives good prices.")

Peoria Cash & Carry, S. W. Washington, Peoria. Product: canned goods.
Referred by Northside Buyers Club, Peoria. ("Must pay cash–buy in
full or ½ crate lots.")

Producers Dairy, 2000 No. University, Peoria. Product: milk. Referred by
Northside Buyers Club, Peoria. ("Delivers twice weekly.")

Kentucky

Grindmaster of Kentucky, Inc., 745 W. Main St., Louisville. Product:
peanut and cashew butter grinders. Referred by Santa Cruz Consumers'
Co-op.

Maryland

Laurelbrook Farms, Bel-Air. Product: Erewhon, Arrowhead Mills, and Japan
Foods. Referred by Ecology Food Co-op, Philadelphia, Pa.

Massachusetts

Doe Sullivan & Co., 61 Faneuil Hall Market, Boston. Product: dairy goods,
cheese. Referred by Boston Food Co-op.

Erewhon, 33 Farnsworth St., Boston. Product: grains, dried fruits, oil,
granola. Referred by Yellow Sun Co-op, Amherst, and Boston Food
Co-ops.

*NEFCO Buying Service, c/o Boston Food Co-op, 12 Babbitt St., Boston.
Product: produce. Referred by 25 New England co-ops.

Minnesota

*People's Warehouse, 204 11th Ave., South, Minneapolis. Product: grains,
flour, spices. Serves co-ops only.

Missouri

Great Plains National Food, 240 Oak St., Kansas City. Product: Erewhon,
Deaf Smith, grains etc. Referred by Ozark Food Co-op.

Noogles & Co., Kansas City. Product: raisins, sorghum, etc. Referred by
Ozark Food Co-op, Arkansas.

New Jersey

Pendulum. Product: dairy products such as goat milk, honey, ice cream,
yogurt, cheese, eggs, Food for Life Delites, cream cheese, butter, and

apple and peach butter. Referred by Shanti Food Conspiracy, Staten Island, New York. ("They're a reliable company and will deliver even when our orders are quite small. They accept checks.")

New Mexico
Cliffrose, Las Vegas. Product: grains. Referred by Amigos de Salud, El Prado, New Mexico.

New York
Sherman Foods, Bronx, New York. Product: vitamins. Referred by Ecology Food Co-op, Philadelphia, Pa.

T'ai Natural Food Flow, Brooklyn. Product: juice, honey, grains, and flours, Japanese products, and tea. Referred by Shanti Food Conspiracy, Staten Island, New York. ("Their prices are fairly reasonable and they pride themselves on being a collective. Their deliveries are extremely undependable and when they do deliver they're usually out of half of order. Their allegiance seems to be to the health food stores rather than co-ops because that's where the money is. They accept checks.")

Bazzini's, New York City. Product: dried fruits and nuts. Referred by Shanti Food Conspiracy, Staten Island. ("Their selection is fantastic and their prices are competitive.")

Glenmere Farms, Greenwich Ave., New York City. Product: eggs, cheese, butter. Referred by 300 Riverside Drive Co-op, New York City. ("Cash, no deliveries.")

The Infinity Company, 173 Duane St., New York City. Product: Tamari, peanut butter, oils, flour grains, tahini and cashew butter. Referred by Shanti Food Conspiracy, Staten Island. ("They're a small, personal company who are dependable in their quality as well as their deliveries. Can pay by check.")

Mottel, New York City. Product: books, yogurt, eggs, Syrian cheese, AK-mak, dry milk, grains, cooking utensils, juices, grinders. Referred by Shanti Food Conspiracy, Staten Island. ("They're a giant company and it's a pleasure dealing with them." Delivery for orders over $150— cash only.)

Joseph A. Zaloom Co., Inc., 8 Jay St., New York City. Referred by Co-op League Handbook.

P & C Nette Division, State Fair Boulevard, Syracuse. Product: groceries. Referred by Oswego County Co-op, Fulton, New York. ("We pay cash— pick up order ourselves in a rented truck.")

Ohio
Worthington Foods, Inc., 900 Proprietors Road, Worthington, 43085. Referred by Co-op League Handbook.

Oregon
Coquille Valley Dairy Co-op, P.O. Box 515, Bandon 97411. Product: cheese.

Referred by Consumers Cooperative Society of the Monterey Peninsula. ("Account.")

Poolside, Route 1, Box 220, Monroe, Oregon. Product: Rennetless cheese, butter, yogurt, bread. Referred by Capital Hill Co-op, Seattle, Washington.

Pennsylvania

Pure Goat Products, Boyertown. Product: ice cream, cottage cheese, etc. Referred by Ecology Food Co-op, Philadelphia, Pa.

Edwards-Freeman, Conshohocken. Product: nuts. Referred by Ecology Food Co-op, Philadelphia.

Walnut Acres, Penns Creek, Pa. Product: prepared foods, fresh vegies, nuts, and seeds. Referred by Sunflower Co-op, Sarasota, Florida. ("Excellent cooks. Competitive pricing.") and Ecology Food Co-op, Philadelphia.

Beautiful Foods, Philadelphia. Product: miscellaneous; Continental Yogurt. Referred by Ecology Food Co-op, Philadelphia.

Center for the Blind, Philadelphia. Product: brooms, brushes. Referred by Ecology Food Co-op, Philadelphia.

Elk Brand Dairies, Philadelphia. Product: dry milk. Referred by Ecology Food Co-op, Philadelphia.

Greenberg's, New York, International Food Distributors, Philadelphia. Product: cheese. Referred by Ecology Food Co-op.

National Herb & Tea Co. and Pure Spice Products, Philadelphia. Product: herbs and teas. Referred by Ecology Food Co-op.

Powelton Baking Co-op, Philadelphia. Product: baked goods. Referred by Ecology Food Co-op.

W. R. Progner & Co., Philadelphia. Product: imported foods, Familia, grape juice, etc. Referred by Ecology Food Co-op.

Third-Story Bakery, Philadelphia. Product: baked goods. Referred by Ecology Food Co-op.

Honey Wheat, Inc., Richboro. Product: wheatsels. Referred by Ecology Food Co-op.

Rhode Island

Meadowbrook Herb Garden, Wyoming, R.I. Product: herbs and spices. Referred by Sunflower Co-op, Sarasota, Florida. ("Bio-dynamic grower.")

Vermont

Crowley Cheese, Healdville 05147. Product: cheese. Referred by Co-op League Handbook.

Maple Grove, 167 Portland Street, St. Johnsbury 05819. Referred by Co-op League Handbook.

Washington

Community Produce, 1510 Pike Place Market, Seattle. Product: organic produce. Referred by Capital Hill Co-op, Seattle, Washington.

Co-operating Community Grains & Mill, 4030 22nd Ave., Seattle 98199.
    Product: grains, flour, etc. Referred by Capital Hill Co-op.
Janus, 712 7th Ave., South, Seattle 98104. Product: all kinds of organic
    stuff. Referred by Capital Hill Co-op. ("Fine.")
Little Bread Co., 8050 Lake City Way, N.E., Seattle 98115. Product:
    bread. Referred by Capital Hill Co-op.

Wisconsin
*Common Market, East Side Warehouse, 1340 E. Washington Ave.,
    Madison; West Side Warehouse, 1535 Gilson St., Madison. Product:
    "most products." Referred by Madison Community Co-op.
Cedarburg Dairy, Milwaukee. Referred by Outpost, Milwaukee. ("No hassle.")
Kallas Honey, Milwaukee. Referred by Outpost, Milwaukee.

Saskatchewan (Canada)
Federated Co-operatives Ltd., Saskatoon. Product: "all products as
    possible." Referred by Mid Island Consumer Co-op, Nanaimo, B.C.
    ("Few problems. Some manufacturers will not supply us because we
    are direct charge.")

New Brunswick (Canada)
Maritime Co-op Services, Moncton. Product: food, paper products, lumber,
    and building supplies. Referred by Cape Co-op Ltd., Sydney, Nova
    Scotia.

Nova Scotia (Canada)
Sydney Co-op Society, Barren Road, Cape Breton County, Sydney. Product:
    produce and meat. Referred by Cape Co-op Ltd., Sydney.

Tabingen (West Germany)
Dr. Rolfhein K.G., Tabingen, West Germany. Product: Pustefix Magic
    Bubbles. Referred by Ecology Food Co-op, Philadelphia, Pa.

APPENDIX C: NATIONAL CO-OP DIRECTORY

This directory, adapted from the National Co-op Directory, is at best a precarious one. With co-ops changing and growing as they are it is impossible to attempt a completely accurate and timely listing. Many of the groups listed will probably go out of existence and many more will be organized even before this book is published.

But the directory is still the single most useful information resource in this book. Food co-ops can learn more from each other than from any hundred books. New co-ops would do well to track down and observe other co-ops nearby, picking up information on local political, economic, and wholesale market conditions.

Co-ops that disappear frequently leave traces that will enable them to be tracked. Most of the large co-ops will probably remain where they are. The individual people in the list can refer people to co-ops and provide some personal perspectives, too.

I am indebted to Don Goldhamer and Dave Zinner of the Food Co-op Conference, Midwest Region, Chicago American Friends Service Committee, office, for providing me with their most recent directory listing, from which the present one is adapted. Anyone with information about new groups—type of group, address, days and hours of operation, telephone numbers of contact people, etc.—should send it to them. They maintain an updated and corrected listing and publish a national newspaper for co-ops, the *Co-op Nooz*. These are available for a one-dollar contribution to Food Co-op Nooz and Directory, c/o AFSC offices located at 407 South Dearborn, Chicago, Il linois 60605.

Who Is Listed in This Directory

There are nine kinds of organizations listed in this directory, defined at the end of each entry according to the following code:

1. Buying clubs, food conspiracies, food cooperatives—unless they are willing to receive information and to be contacted through another group which is listed in the directory.

2. Distribution centers—serving many buying clubs.

3. Warehouses—storing cases and bags for co-ops—if they are run cooperatively or collectively, are anti-profit, and are accountable to the community.

4. Food stores and storefronts—if they are run cooperatively or collectively, and are anti-profit.

5. Food spinoffs (bakeries, cafes, mills)—if they are run cooperatively or collectively, and are anti-profit.

6. Cooperative brokers and marketers—if they are accountable to the community, and are anti-profit.

7. Cooperative food truckers.

8. Producer cooperatives and associations of small-scale farmers—especially if they are interested in alternative farming, nutritious/organic growing, or selling to low-income consumers. (Also some local farmers where no federation exists.)

9. Food information and coordinating groups and media groups relating to food cooperatives.

Note: To aid the reader in finding the co-op(s) nearest him, the listings are entered according to the sequence of zip codes, from the lowest to the highest.

Massachusetts

Yellow Sun Natural Foods Co-op, 35 N. Pleasant St., Amherst, MA 01002 (1)

Amherst Food Co-op, 24 Churchill St., Amherst, MA 01002 (1)

Peoples market, Student Union, University of Massachusetts, Amherst, MA 01002 (1)

Mixed Nuts, Beth Dichter, Hampshire College, Amherst, MA 01002 (1)

Belchertown Food Co-òp, Paul Bourke, Box 433, Belchertown, MA 01007 (1)

Holyoke Food Co-op, Dottie Foote, Work Inc., 652 S. East, Holyoke, MA 01040 (1)

Another Day Co-op, 42 Maple St., Florence, MA 01060 (1)

New England Food Co-op Org., Grain Coordinator Pat Davis, 56 Bradford St., Northampton, MA 01060

152 FOOD CO-OPS

Great Barrington Food Co-op, c/o Community Action Project, Great
Barrington, MA 01230 (1)
Greenfield Food Co-op, Pat Pease, 29 Devens St., Greenfield, MA 01301 (1)
Athol Peoples Food Co-op, Ed Brund, 216 Exchange St., Athol, MA 01331 (1)
Buckland Co-op, Chris Kenney, Cape St., Ashield, Buckland, MA 01336 (1)
Good Food Union, Randy Johnson, Woolman Hill, Deerfield, MA 01342 (1)
Our Daily Bread Food Co-op, 26 S. Main St., Orange, MA 01364 (1)
United Co-op Society of Fitchburg, 815 Main St., Fitchburg, MA 01420 (1)
International Independence Institute, Bob Swann, Don Newey, Box 183,
West Road, Ashby, MA 01431 (9)
Holden-Princeton Food Club, 21 Avery Hgts Dr., Holden, MA 01520 (1)
Community Stomach Food Co-op—Produce, 33 Wall St., Worcester, MA
01604 (1)
Community Stomach Natural Food Co-op, 197 Pleasant St., Worcester, MA
01609 (1)
Worcester Food Co-op, Louise Hagen, 9 Larch St., Worcester, MA 01609 (1)
Concord Food Co-op, Ben Kellman, 874 Barretts Mill Rd., Concord, MA
01742 (1)
Andover Co-op, Main St., Lois Simmonds, 127 Chestnut, N. Andover, MA
01810 (1)
Lowell Food Co-op, c/o Alan Solomon, 23 School St., Lowell, MA 01854 (1)
Lynn Co-op, Miles Rappoport, 6 Boynton Terrace, Lynn, MA 01902 (1)
Beverly-Salem Co-op, Nick McAuliffe, NSCAC, 356A Cabot St., Beverly,
MA 01915 (1)
The Food Co-op, Community Consumers United Inc., 91 Bridge St.,
Salem, MA 01970 (1)
Stoughton Food Co-op, Judy Stolow, 11 Horan Way, Stoughton, MA 02072 (1)
Columbia Point Food Association, 20 Montpelier Rd., Columbia Point
S. Boston, MA 02110 (1)
Rainbow Groceries, 72 Kilarnock, Boston, MA 02115 (1)
Mission Hill Food Co-op, John Osberg, 18 Lawn St., Boston, MA 02120 (1)
Brandywine Village Co-op, Debby Lieberman, 42 Trustman Terrace, East
Boston, MA 02128 (1)
New England Food Co-op—Produce Coordinator, Roger Auerbach,
85 Montebello Rd., Jamaica Plain, MA 02130 (9)
Allston-Brighton Food Co-op, 158 Harvard St., Allston, MA 02134 (1)
New England Food Co-op, Don Lubin, 8 Ashford St., Allston, MA 02134 (9)
Beansprout II, Charles Lerrige, 80 Nottinghill Rd., Brighton, MA 02135 (1)
Fresh Pond Co-op, Mary Bularzic, 234 Lakeview, Cambridge, MA 02138 (1)
Political Education Project, 65A Winthrop, Cambridge, MA 02138 (9)
Rising Earth, Limin Mo, 96 River St., Cambridge, MA 02139 (1)
Cambridge South Food Co-op, Red Book Store, 91 River St., Cambridge,
MA 02139 (1)
Vocations for Social Change, Steve, 351 Broadway, Cambridge MA 02139 (9)
Beansprout I, Joyce Thompson, 12 Douglas St., Cambridge, MA 02139 (1)
Pearl Street Co-op, Regina Flaherty, 53 Pearl St., Cambridge, MA 02139 (1)

Cambridgeport Food Co-op, Holly Sue Angier, 65 Pleasant St., Cambridge, MA 02139 (1)

Communications, P.O. Box E, MIT Branch P.O., Cambridge, MA 02139 (9)

Center for Community Economic Development Library, 1878 Massachusetts Ave., Cambridge, MA 02140 (9)

Prentiss St. Co-op, Murray Denofsky, 73 Frost St., Cambridge, MA 02140 (1)

North Cambridge Food Co-op, Harriet Browenstein, 20 Waldo Ave., Somerville, MA 02143 (1)

West Somerville Food Co-op, Chris and Rae Burns, 14 Park Ave., W. Somerville, MA 02144 (1)

East Somerville Food Co-op, Betty McLain, 500 Mystic, Somerville, MA 02145 (1)

Resources, P.O. Box 490, Somerville, MA 02144 (9)

Broadway Food Co-op, Karen Faler, 99 Puritan Rd., Somerville, MA 02145 (1)

HGS Co-op, Ann Goldberg, 110 Angleside, No. D8, Waltham, MA 02154 (1)

Tufts Food Co-op, Catherine Mulholland, 128 Professors Row, Medford, MA 02155 (1)

Newton Center Co-op, Rita Richmond, 833 Commonwealth, Newton Center, MA 02159 (1)

Peace and Beans Food Co-op, Elliot Church, Jill Dardick, 522 Commonwealth, Commonwealth, Newton Corner, MA 02159 (1)

West Newton Food Co-op, Ruth Heesplink, 45 Pleasant St., Newton Centre, MA 02159 (1)

Boston College Food Co-op, Boston College, Chestnut Hill, MA 02167 (1)

New England Food Co-op Organization—Newsletter Coordinator Spike DeHaven, 116 Vine St., Newton, MA 02167 (9)

Quincy Community Food Co-op, Southwest Community Center, 372 Granite St., Quincy, MA 02169 (1)

Cambridge Central Food Co-op, Ken Alper, 44 Cottage, Watertown, MA 02172 (1)

Lexington Food Co-op, Leah Vetter, 30 Woodcliff Rd., Lexington, MA 02173 (1)

Free Co-op, Leonie Flannery, 22 Vine St., Lexington, MA 02173 (1)

Arlington Food Co-op, Peter Callaterra, 38 Bartlett Ave., Arlington, MA 02174 (1)

Jason Food Co-op, Judy & Steve Sadow, 8 Parker St., Arlington, MA 02174 (1)

Needham Food Co-op, Betsy Oliver, 130 Grosvenor Rd., Needham, MA 02192 (1)

Weston Food Co-op, Paul & Julie Redstone, Rice Spring Lane, Wayland, MA 02193 (1)

Boston Food Co-op, 12 Babbitt St., Boston, MA 02215 (1)

South End Food Co-op, Karen Crestman, c/o Help Program, Boston, MA 02216 (1)

Hyannis Food Co-op, Delores Santos, 195 Lincoln Rd., Hyannis, MA 02601 (1)

Yarmouth Co-op, Box 379, Dennisport, MA 02639 (1)

Rhode Island

Food Co-op, University of Rhode Island, Student Senate Office,
   Kingston, RI 02881 (1)
Alternative Food Co-op, Eleanor Carpenter, 78 Biscuit City Rd., Kingston,
   RI 02881 (1)
Family Food Co-op, David Evans, 16 Prospect Ave., Narragansett, RI 02882 (1)
Divine Food Co-op, 421 Orms St., Providence, RI 02907 (1)

New Hampshire

Nesenkeag Co-op Farm, RFD 1, Hudson, NH 03051 (1)
Milford Food Co-op, Operation Help Office, Putnam St., Milford, NH
   03055 (1)
Volunteers Organized in Community Education, Tacy House, 2 Shattuck St.,
   Nashua, NH 03060 (1)
Manchester Food Co-op, Operation Help Office, 227 S. Main St., Manchester,
   NH 03102
Keen Learning Co-op, 681 Court St., Keene, NH 03431 (1)
Franconia Food Co-op, c/o Tatwamasi Natural Foods, Franconia, NH 03580 (1)
Natural Organic Farmers Assoc., Samuel Kaymen, Box 6, Cornish Flat, NH
   03746 (8)
Natural Organic Farmers Assoc., 52 Main St., W. Lebanon, NH 03746 (8)
Hanover Consumers Co-op Society, Inc., Arthur Gerstenberger, 45 S. Park
   St., Hanover, NH 03755 (1)
Listen Food Buying Club, Listen Center, 92 Hanover St., Lebanon, NH
   03766 (1)
Nepcoop South Co-op, Do It Store, 52 Main St., W. Lebanon, NH 03784 (1)
Go Up Front Organic Market, 50 S. School St., Portsmouth, NH 03801 (1)
Essence Restaurant, Rte. 153, Eaton Center, NH 03832 (5)
Valley Food Co-op, c/o Mark Reis, Eaton Center, NH 03832 (1)
New Market Food Co-op, Big Food Buying Club, Chris Logan, Grant Rd.,
   Newmarket, NH 03857 (1)

Maine

Tritown Food Assoc, 21 Washington Ave., Old Orchard Beach, ME 04064 (1)
Sanford-Springvale Co-op, 8 Bradeen St., Springvale, ME 04083 (1)
Committee for Coordination of Maine Co-ops, 14 Perkins, Topsham, ME
   04086 (9)
Portland Food Co-op/Good Day Market, 343 Fore St., Portland, ME 04111 (1)
Rap Place, Inc., 145 Park St., Lewiston, ME 04240 (1)
Maine Organic Foods Assoc., Jim Luthy & Abby Page, 1 Jackson Rd.,
   Poland Springs, ME 04274
Division of Economic Opportunity, Executive Dept., State of Maine,
   Frank Hample, Augusta, ME 04330 (9)
Vernon Valley Co-op, Mount Vernon, ME 04352
Co-op Extension Service, U. of Maine, Court House Annex, Bangor, ME (9)

Food Buying Co-op, c/o Dave Davis, University and Community Resource
    Co., 100 E. Annex, U. of Maine, Orono, ME 04473 (1)
Friends Food Co-op, Lise Herold, 448 Twitchell Hall, Freedom, ME 04941

Vermont
Black Mountain Press, Box 1, Corinth, VT 05039 (9)
Wild Farm, Georgy & Ann Clay, Arlington R.D. 2 VT 05250 (8)
Good Food Restaurant, Common Ground, 25 Eliot St., Brattleboro,
    VT 05301 (5)
Putney Consumers Co-op, Carlie Fabian, P.O. Box 55, Putney, VT 05346 (1)
Union River Food Co-op, 77 Archibald St., Burlington, VT 05401 (1)
Addison County Buyers Club, 15 Main St., Bristol, VT 05443 (1)
Food for Thought, RFD 4, Enosburg Falls, VT 05450 (1)
Food for Thought, Frank Berliner, Montgomery Center, VT 05471 (1)
Aclamont Food Co-op, Cindy Martin, Aclamont, VT 05640 (1)
Franklin County Food Co-op, Pat Silva, 157 Province, Richford, VT 05476 (1)
Plainfield Co-op, Box 157, Plainfield, VT 05667 (1)
NOFA, RFD 1, Plainfield, VT 05667 (8)
Rutland Natural Foods Co-op, P.O. Box 137, Chittendon, VT 05735 (1)
Middlebury Co-op, Ann Fox, 19 Waybridge, Middlebury, VT 05753 (1)
Northeast Kingdom Cooperative, Box 272, Barton, VT 05822 (1)

Connecticut
Consumers Co-op Assoc., Inc., 461 Flatbush Ave., Hartford, CT 06106 (1)
Food Co-op, 16 Maplewood Ave., W. Hartford, CT 06119 (1)
Stowe Village Cooperative, 66 Hampton St., Hartford, CT 06120 (1)
Alternative Press Collection, Wilbur Cross Library, U. of Connecticut,
    Storrs, CT 06268 (9)
North End Community Action Consumers Co-op, 183 N. Matin St.,
    Ansonia, CT 06401 (1)
Middletown Co-op, 113 College St., Middletown, CT 06451 (1)
New Haven Food Co-op, 490 Greenwich Ave., No. 1, New Haven, CT
    New Haven, CT 06519 (1)
N.O.W. Buying Club, c/o New Opportunities for Waterbury, 769 N. Matin
    St., Waterbury, CT 06704 (1)

New Jersey
Mid Eastern Cooperatives, Frank Anastasio, 75 Amor Ave., Carlstadt, NJ
    07072 (1)
Against the Wall, P.O. Box 4444, Westfield, NJ 07091 (9)
Cooperative Institute Assoc., Aileen Paul, 121 Gladwin Ave., Leonia, NJ
    07605 (9)
New Jersey Natural Food & Farm Cooperative, 216 Belmont Ave.,
    Ocean, NJ 07712 (1)

New York

Council for Cooperative Development, John Gauci, 465 Grand St., New
    York, NY 10002 (9)
Federation of New York Cooperatives, Matthew Reich, 465 Grand St.,
    New York, NY 10002 (9)
Shri Hans Foods, 33 St., Marks Pl., New York, NY 10003 (1,9)
Lower East Side Co-op, Ann Evans, 270 E. 2nd St., New York, NY 10003 (1)
Peoples Warehouse, Christy Young, 307 Bowery, New York, NY 10003 (3)
5th Street Co-op, 219 E. 5th St., New York, NY 10003 (1)
Lower East Side Economic Development Assoc. for Cooperatives, Inc.,
    Jose Guzman, 44 Ave. B or 214 E. 2nd St., New York, NY 10009 (9)
Good Food Co-op, 58 E. 4th St., New York, NY 10003 (1)
6th Street Co-op, 518 E. 6th St., New York, NY 10009
Wholesome Foods, 191 E. 3rd St., New York, NY 10009 (1)
The New Leader, 212 Fifth Ave., New York, NY 10010 (9)
Sabrina Food Conspiracy, 243 W. 20th St., New York, NY 10011 (1)
Integral Yoga, 227 W. 13th St., New York, NY 10011 (1)
Wild Rice Co., Inc., 325 W. 16th St., 2nd Fl., New York, NY 10011 (1)
Liberation, 339 Lafayette St., New York, NY 10012 (9)
West Village Co-op, 135 W. 4th St., New York, NY 10012 (1)
Natural Life Co-op, 1111 E. 34th St., New York, NY 10016 (1)
The Consumer Gazette, Bill Wolf, 466 Lexington Ave., New York, NY
    10017 (9)
Greenhouse Assoc., 466 Amsterdam Ave., New York, NY 10024 (1)
Sun & Sons, Cirella, 40D, 128 W. 82nd St., New York, NY 10024 (1)
Broadway Local Food Co-op, 95th and Columbus, New York, NY 10025 (1)
Liberation News Service, 160 Claremont Ave., New York, NY 10025 (9)
West Side Food Buying Club, 1050 Amsterdam Ave., New York, NY 10026 (1)
Natural Foods Center, Room 105, Earl Hall, Columbia University, New
    York, NY 10027 (1)
Food Research & Action Center, 25 W. 43rd St., New York, NY 10036 (9)
Project Able, 15 St. James Pl., New York, NY 10038 (1)
Shanti Food Conspiracy of St. George, 104 Westervelt Ave., Staten Island,
    NY 10301 (1)
Natural Foods Co-op, 12 S. Second Ave., Mt. Vernon, NY 10550˙(1)
Consumer Action Project of Bedford Stuyvesant, Adolfo Alayon, 301
    Marcy Ave., Brooklyn, New York 11206 (1)
Ossining Community Cooperative, Inc., 47 Spring St., Ossining, NY 10562 (1)
Mongoose, 782 Union St., Brooklyn, NY 11211 (1)
Brownsville Cooperative Buying Club, 388 Rockaway Ave., Brooklyn,
    NY 11212 (1)
Family Buying Club, 202 Rocky Hill Rd., Bayside, Queens, NY 11361 (1)
Organic Energy, 68-06 Fresh Meadow Lane, Flushing, NY 11365 (1)
South Ozone Park Community Buying Club, 14205 Rockaway Blvd,
    S. Ozone Park, NY 11436 (1)

Bay Co-op, 11 Linder Ct., Brookhaven, NY 11719 (1)

Huntington Collective, Box 81, Huntington, NY 11743 (1)

People's Town Hall Food Co-op, 488 New York Ave., Huntington, NY
    11743 (1)

Sound Food Co-op, 541 Lake Ave., St. James, NY 11780 (1)

Stony Brook Freedom Foods Co-op, Jack Sogro, Stage XII Cafeteria,
    State University of New York, Stonybrook, NY 11790 (1)

Cohoes Cooperative Buying Club, c/o Cohoes Community Action Program,
    Inc., 98 Mohawk St., Cohoes, NY 12047 (1)

South End Food Cooperative, 142 S. Pearl St., Albany, NY 12202 (1)

Good Food Restaurant, 18 Church St., New Paltz, NY 12561 (5)

Real Food Store, 53 Main St., New Paltz, NY 12561 (1)

Grocery Co-op, Lois Proiette, 7 Whitaker Rd., Fulton, NY 13069 (1)

Oswego County Co-op Store, W 3rd Vorheas, Fulton, NY 13069 (1)

Oswego County Co-op Store, East Bridge St., Oswego, NY 13126 (1)

Cheap Food Ltd., Chapel House, Office R., 711 Comstock Ave., Syracuse,
    NY 13210 (1)

Glenfield Food Cooperative, Rural Route, Glenfield, NY 13343 (1)

New York Organic Farmers, Nick Veeder, RD 1, Jordanville, NY 13361 (8)

Lowville Food Buying Club, Rural Route, Lowville, NY 13367 (1)

South Lyons Food Buying Club, Rural Route, Lyons Falls, NY 13368 (1)

Beaver Falls Food Buying Club, Rural Route, Castorland, NY 13620

North Family Fair, Andrew Shelton, RFD 1, Gouverneur, NY 13642 (1)

North Valley Buyers Club, Rural Delivery 2, P.O. Box 200, Newark
    Valley, NY 13811

Richford Pennypinchers, Rural Delivery, Richford, NY 13835

Alternate Cultures Reading Room, P.O. Box Drawer 8, SUNY Binghampton,
    Vestal Parkway East, Binghamton, NY 13901 (9)

Off Center, 73 State St., Binghamton, NY 13905 (1)

Barn Farm, Howard Chezar, Genesee Rd., Arcade, NY 14009 (8)

Fredonia Co-op, Bob Winslow, SUC, Fredonia, 53 W. Main St., Fredonia,
    NY 14063 (1)

East Side Community Cooperative, 300 Williams St., Buffalo, NY 14204 (1)

North Buffalo-Community Co-op, 3225 Main St., Buffalo, NY 14214 (1)

Divine Food Co-op, 681 Linwood, Buffalo, NY 14215 (1)

Lexington Real Foods Co-op, 224 Lexington Ave., Buffalo, NY 14222 (1)

Harlem River Consumers Co-op, 2555 147th St., New York, NY 14226 (1)

Brockport Food Co-op, 37 Main St. South, Brockport, NY 14420 (1)

Blessed Thistle Bakery, 510 Lake Rd., Webster, NY 14580 (5)

Clear Eye and Genesee Co-op, 713 Monroe Ave., Rochester, NY 14607

Vocations for Social Change, 713 Monroe, Rochester, NY 14607 (9)

Cattaraugus Buyers Cooperative, Inc., 22 W. Washington St., Ellicottville,
    NY 14731 (1)

Birdsfoot Farm, Bob Grubel, Box 44 RD 3, Addison, NY 14801 (8)

Consumer Protection Service Store, 140 W. State St., Ithaca, NY
    14850 (1)

Guava Jelly & Community of Communes; Real Food Co-op, 412 Linn St.,
    Ithaca, NY 14850 (1)
Somadhara Bakery, c/o Ananda Marca Yoga Society, Ithaca, NY 14850 (5)
Spencer Buyers Club, Rural Delivery 2, Spencer, NY 14883 (1)

Pennsylvania
Mireille, Revolutionary Europe, P.O. Box 4288, Pittsburg, PA 15203 (1)
Oakland Co-op, Phil Peters, 3601 Blvd. of Allies, Pittsburgh, PA 15213 (1)
Semple Street Food Cooperative, 3459 Ward St., Pittsburgh, PA 15213 (1)
Divine Food Co-op, 1364 Denniston Ave., Pittsburgh, PA 15217
Meat Buyers Club, Westmoreland County Conference for Economic
    Opportunity, 128 E. Pittsburgh St., Greensburg, PA 15601 (1)
Solomon Homes Marketing Co-op, Community Building, Solomon Homes,
    Johnstown, PA 15902 (6)
Erie Edinboro Food Co-op, 522 Shenley Ave., Erie, PA 16505 (1)
JFK Neighborhood Action Team Org. Food Cooperative, 2024 Buffalo Rd.,
    Erie, PA 16510
Pennsylvania Assoc. of Farmers Co-ops, Hal Doran, 41068 Agricultural-
    Education Building, Pennsylvania State University, University Park, PA
    16802 (8)
Adams County Buying Club, P.O. Box 205, Gettysburg, PA 17325 (1)
Pennsylvania Organic Farmers Assoc., Kevin Carroll, 601 W. Lemon St.,
    Lancaster, PA 17604 (8)
Food Co-op H, Haverford College, c/o Eric Sterling, Haverford, PA 19041 (1)
Princeton Food Co-op, Wayne Moss, 217 Pine Tree Rd., Radnor, PA 19087 (1)
Central Committee of Correspondence, 310 N. 33rd St., Philadelphia, PA
    19104 (9)
Community Food Co-op of West Philadelphia, c/o Crady Abney, 3907 Spruce
    St., Philadelphia, PA 19104 (1)
Divine Food Co-op, 3519 Lancaster, Philadelphia, PA 19104 (1)
Ecology Food Co-op, 210 N. 36th St., Philadelphia, PA 19104 (1)
Life Center Food Co-op, 1006 S. 46th St., Philadelphia, PA 19104 (1)
Philadelphia Food Co-op Federation, Ed Place, 3214 Winter St., Philadelphia,
    PA 19104 (9)
Peoples Co-op of Mt. Airy, c/o Summit Presbyterian Church, Westview
    and Greene St., Philadelphia, PA 19119 (1)
The Weavers Way Co-op, 555-559 W. Carpenter Ln., Philadelphia, PA 19119 (1)
Wharton Center, 1708 N. 22nd St., Philadelphia, PA 19121 (1)
Temple Community Food Co-op, 1439 Norris St. W., Philadelphia, PA 19122
West Oak Lane Co-op, Lamont A.M.E. Church, 1500 Cheltenham Ave.,
    Philadelphia, PA 19125 (1)
Manayunk Food Co-op, St. Davids Episcopal Church, Dupont & Kransau,
    Philadelphia, PA 19127 (1)
Good Earth, City Line and Conshohocken, Philadelphia, PA 19131 (1)
Cross Roads Community Center, 2916 N. 6th St., Philadelphia, PA 19133 (1)
Open, Inc., 2431 N. 6th St., Philadelphia, PA 19133 (1)

Spring Garden Community Center, 1812 Green St., Philadelphia, PA 19136 (1)
Life Center Food Co-op, 1006 S. 46th St., Philadelphia, PA 19143 (1)
Maripasa, 4726 Baltimore Ave., Philadelphia, PA 19143 (1)
Movement for a New Society, 1006 S. 46th St., Philadelphia, PA 19143 (9)
Stonehouse, 1006 S. 46th St., Philadelphia, PA 19143 (1)
Food Conspiracies, 165 W. Harvey St., Philadelphia, PA 19144 (1)
Germantown Peoples Food Co-op, Germantown Presbyterian Church, Greene
    and Tulpehocken, Philadelphia, PA 19144 (1)
Philadelphia Citywide Co-op Org., 5108 Newhall St., Philadelphia, PA 19144 (9)
Togetherness House, 32 E. Armatt, East Germantown, PA 19144 (1)
South Street Community Co-op, 624 S. 4th St., Philadelphia, PA 19147 (1)
Greenwich Neighbors Food Co-op, 2029 S. 8th St., Philadelphia, PA 19148 (1)

District of Columbia
Community Warehouse, 2010 Kendall St., N.E., Washington, DC 20002 (3)
Finder Associates II, Margaret Ward, 3918 W St., N.W., Washington, DC
    20007 (1)
Adams-Morgan Community Food & Drug Store, 2447 18th St., N.W.,
    Washington, DC 20009 (1)
Movement for Economic Justice, Poverty Rights Action Center, 1609 Conn-
    ecticut Ave., N.W., Washington, DC 20009 (9)
Strongforce, 1830 Connecticut Ave., N.W., Washington, DC 20009 (9)
Stone Soup Community Market, 1801 18th St., N.W., Washington, DC
    20009 (1)
Divine Food Co-op, 3235 Mckinley St., N.W., Washington, DC 20015 (1)
Yellow Sun Food Co-op, 2911½ E. Jacks   Sub. "B," p 4   2 lines

National Milk Producers Federation, Young Cooperator Program, 30 F St.,
    N.W., Washington, DC 20036 (9)
Rural Advancement Fund, National Sharecroppers Fund, Fay Bennett &
    Art Mullen, 1145 19th St., N.W., Washington, DC 20036 (9)
Freedom Trucking Collective, Pat Else, 2134 O St., N.W., Washington, DC
    20036 (7)

Maryland
Glut Food Co-op, 4005 34th St., Mount Ranier, MD 20822 (1)
Rainbow Bridge, 5604 Kenilworth, Riverdale, MD 20840 (1)
Greenbelt Consumer Services, Inc., Donald Lefevre, 8547 Piney Branch Rd.,
    Silver Spring, MD 20901 (1)
School of Living, Bob Merrick, Heathcote Community, R.R. 1, Box 129,
    Freeland, MD 21053 (9)
Spring Bottom Natural Foods, Rt. 1, Belair, MD 21213 (1)
Waverly Peoples Food Co-op, 3019 Independence, Baltimore, MD 21218 (1)

Virginia
Carrot Seed Co-op, Box 224, Flint Hill, VA 22627 (1)

Charrlettsville Food Co-op, c/o Wesley Hubbard, Rt. 1, Box 45A, Roseland,
    VA 22967 (1)
Twin Oaks, Louisa, VA 23093 (9)
Forte Foundation, P.O. Box 403, Virginia Beach, VA 23458 (3)
Southwest Virginia Growers Co-op, P.O. Box 303, Rt. 2, Nickelsville,
    VA 24271 (8)
Pittsylvania County Community Action Inc. Buying Club, P.O. Box 936,
    Chatham, VA 24531 (1)
Southern Agricultural Assoc. of Virginia, Box 734, S. Boxton, VA 24592 (8)

West Virginia
Freeman, Wolf, & Assoc. Communities Buying Club, Freeman, WV 24724 (1)
Small Earth Associates, Small Earth Farm, Union, WV 24983 (8)
Growing Tree Country Store, 128½ Court St., Spencer, WV 25276 (1)
Big Nickel, Fairmont State College, Fairmont, WV 26554 (1)

North Carolina
Country Co-op, Box 111, Pittsboro, NC 27312 (1)
Chapel Hill Food Co-op, Ilene Lee, 38 Holloway Land, Chapel Hill, NC
    27514 (1)
Peoples Intergalactic Food Co-op, Box 4763, Duke Station, Durham, NC
    27706 (1)
Chowan Cooperative Produce Exchange, P.O. Box 398, Edenton, NC 27932 (1)
Rural Advancement Fund, Jim Peirce, 1947 Lansdale Dr., Charlotte, NC
    28205 (9)
Coastal Growers Assoc., P.O. Box 490, Rose Hill, NC 28458 (8)
Mother Earth News, P.O. Box 70, Hendersonville, NC 28739 (9)
Southwestern North Carolina Farmers Co-op, P.O. Box 674, Murphy, NC
    28906 (8)

South Carolina
Woodland Community Progress Group, Rte. 1, P.O. Box 353, Georgetown,
    SC 29440 (1)
Peoples Community Cooperative, Rivers St. Extension, Walterboro, SC
    29488 (1)
Piedmont Organic Movement Assoc., Charles Parrott, 714 S. Line St.,
    Greer, SC 29651 (8)
Hampton County Buying Club, P.O. Box 706, Hampton, SC 29924 (1)

Georgia
Stone Soup Co-op, 996 Virginia, Atlanta, GA 30300 (1)
Federation of Southern Co-ops, Don Speicher, 20 Marietta St., N.W.
    Rm. 1200, Atlanta, GA 30303 (1)
New Morning Food Co-op, 862 Rosedale, Atlanta, GA 30306 (1)
Sun-Mec Buying Club, c/o Sun-Mec Neighborhood Service Center, 71 Georgia
    Ave., S.W., Atlanta, GA 30315 (1)

Food Co-op, 2030 Cliff Valley, N.E., Atlanta, GA 30329 (1)
Eastern Georgia Farmers Co-op, Box 35, Waynesboro, GA 30830 (8)

Florida
Yellow Sun Food Co-op, 2911½ E. Jackson, Pensecola, FL 32503 (1)
Divine Food Co-op, 518 N.E. 4th Ave., Gainesville, FL 32601 (1)
Our Daily Bread, 1214 N.W. 5th Ave., Gainesville, FL 32601 (1)
DeLand Buying Club, 259 W. Voorhis St., De Land, FL 32720 (1)
Rhoda, Free Press, Box 676, Coconut Grove, FL 33133 (9)
Sunshine Cooperative Assoc., Inc., P.O. Box 115, Edison Center Station,
    Miami, FL 33151 (9)
Alternative Vittles, Stan Altland, 1478 Gulf to Bay, Clearwater, FL 33515 (1)
Sunflower, The Sarasota Food Store, Tim Snyder, 1549 Main St.,
    Sarasota, FL 33577 (1)

Alabama
Federation of Southern Cooperatives, Training Institute, James Jones,
    Box 95, Epes, AL 35460 (8)

Tennessee
Neighborhood Service Center Buying Club, 1116 8th Ave. S., Nashville, TN
    37203 (1)
The Paper Bag Co-op, East Sevier Ave., Kingsport, TN 37660 (1)

Mississippi
Oxford Consumer Cooperative, 512 Jackson Ave., Oxford, MS 38655 (1)
Education/Training for Cooperatives, Ian Tomlin, Poor People's Corporation
    of Mississippi, Box 3345, Jackson, MS 39207 (9)

Kentucky
Manly Area Cooperative, 800 W. Catherine St., Louisville, KY 40222 (1)
Good Foods Co-op, 314½ S. Ashland Ave., Lexington, KY 40502 (1)
Bluegrass Organic Assoc., Jean Warrimer, 137 Eastover Dr., Lexington,
    KY 40504 (8)
Harlan Buying Club, c/o Harlan County Community Action Agency,
    314 S. Main St., Harlan, KY 40831 (1)
Cumberland Farm Products, Inc., P.O. Box 296, Monticello, KY 42633 (8)

Ohio
Racoon Valley Food Friends Co-op, Ann Hagedorn, 17 Samson Place,
    Granville, OH 43023 (1)
OSU Food Co-op, Harvey Forstag, 2377 N. 4th St., Columbus, OH
    43201 (1)
Golden Flower Seed Co., 431 W. 6th Ave., Columbus, OH 43201 (1)
Southside Food Co-op, 363 Reeb Ave., Columbus, OH 43207 (1)
Columbus Community Food Co-op, Box 3259, Columbus, OH 43210 (1)

Twin Pines Food Co-op, 3494 N. High St., Columbus, OH 43214 (1)

Divine Food Co-op, 851 Neil Ave., Columbus, OH 43215 (1)

Oberlin Good Food Co-op, c/o Co-op Bookstore, 37 W. College St.,
   Oberlin, ÒH 44074 (1)

Painesville Food Co-op, John Updike & Jerry King, St. James Episcopal
   Church, Painesville, OH 44077 (1)

Political Education Project, 2022 W. 98th St., Cleveland, OH 44102 (9)

Fruit and Vegetable Co-op, North Presbyterian Church, 4001 Superior,
   Cleveland, OH 44103 (1)

Inner City Co-op, Hough Ave. United Church of Christ, 65th St. and
   Hough, Cleveland, OH 44103 (1)

The Food C.O.O.P., Community Organization of People, c/o Hillel
   Foundation, 11291 Euclid Ave., Cleveland, OH 44106 (1)

Glenville Afro-American Co-op, c/o Audrey Jeter, Glenville Opportunity
   Center, 1073 E. 105th St., Cleveland, OH 44108 (1)

Fremont Organization Against Hunger, Fremont Food Co-op, 802 Literary,
   Cleveland, OH 44113 (1)

Metropolitan Co-op Services, Inc., Metro Meats, Inc., 2624 Detroit Ave.,
   Cleveland, OH 44113 (1)

Near West-Side Food Co-op, 3004 Clinton, Cleveland, OH 44113 (1)

Broadway Food Co-op, 4640 Broadway, Cleveland, OH 44127 (1)

Kent Food Co-op, Unitarian Universalist Church, 228 Gougler, Kent, OH
   44240 (1)

Community Action Council Food Co-op, 230 West Center St., Akron, OH
   44302 (1)

Rosy Cheeks Community Store, Jackie Johnston, 459 E. Exchange,
   Akron, OH 44304 (1)

Whole Wheat & Honey COOP, 87 W. State St., Akron, OH 44308 (1)

Wisc Food Co-op, 224 S. Market St., Wooster, OH 44691 (1)

Hollywood Community Center Food Buying Club, 101 Walnut St.,
   Franklin, OH 45005 (1)

East End Co-op (BC), c/o Carters, 2624 Eastern, Cincinnati, OH 45202 (1,9)

Vocations for Social Change, Joel Stevens, 1314 Race St., Cincinnati,
   OH 45210

Cincinnati Food Co-op, 245 W. Mcmillan, Cincinnati, OH 45219 (1)

Greene County Buying Club, 132 N. Detroit St., Xenia, OH 45385 (1)

Community Services, Yellow Springs, OH 45387 (9)

Earth Free School, Box 297, Yellow Springs, OH 45387 (9)

Real Good Food Co-op, Antioch College Union, R. R. 1, Yellow Springs,
   OH 45387 (1)

Athens Organic Food Co-op, Box 1094, Athens, OH 45701 (1)

Community Food Co-op Store, c/o Lima-Allen County Community Action
   Council, Memorial Hall, Elm and Elizabeth Sts., Lima, OH 45801 (1)

Indiana

Northside Food Co-op, 46th and Wintrhop, Indianapolis, IN 46205 (1)

Divine Food Co-op, 115 S. Audubon Rd., Indianapolis, IN 46219 (1)
Peace and Freedom Food Co-op, Tim Curtain, 471 State St., No. 2,
    Indianapolis, IN 46229 (1)
Peoples Buying Club, 2502 Winter St., Fort Wayne, IN 46803 (1)
Peoples Pantry, Bob Bucher, 104 Maple St., N. Manchester, IN 46962 (1)
Earlam Eat, Reid Bailey, Box 31, Richmond, IN 47374 (1)
Bloomington Food Co-op, Rush Robinson, 1407 S. Lincoln, Bloomington,
    IN 47401 (1)

Michigan

Lake Orion Food Co-op, c/o Karen Moore, 1230 Orion Rd. Lake Orion,
    MI 48035 (1)
Sylvan Lake Food Co-op, 1755 Lakeland, Pontiac, MI 48053 (1)
Carrot Patch Co-op, c/o Marilyn Schmidt, 15 Clayburn, Pontiac, MI 48054 (1)
Hominid Services, Inc., c/o Pat Lyons or Doug Brown, 1114 Doris Rd.,
    Pontiac, MI 48057 (1)
Michigan Federation of Food Co-ops, Peoples Wherehouse, 404 W. Huron,
    Ann Arbor, MI 48103 (3)
Ann Arbor Itemized Produce Co-op, Janet Handy, 908 Greene, Ann Arbor,
    MI 48104 (1)
Neighborhood Action Center Food Co-op, Greg Simpson, 543 N. Main,
    Ann Arbor, MI 48104 (1)
People's Food Co-op, 722 Packard, Ann Arbor, MI 48104 (1)
Ann Arbor People's Produce, Peggy Taube, Julie Carroll, 1006 Lincoln,
    Ann Arbor, MI 48104 (1)
Aoxomoxa, 428 Hamilton Pl., Ann Arbor, MI 48104 (1)
NASCO, Journal of the New Harbinger, Box 1301, Ann Arbor, MI 48106 (9)
National Switchboard List, Roy Harper, Box 424, Manchester, MI 48158 (9)
Plymouth Food Co-op, c/o Center for Young People, Box 115, Plymouth,
    MI 48170 (1)
Ypsilanti Food Co-op, c/o John Abeli, 604 Emmett, Ypsilanti, MI 48197 (1)
Cass Corridor, 4200 Cass, Detroit, MI 48201 (1)
California Sunshine, 129 California, Highland Park, MI 48203 (1)
Three for Three Food Co-op, 17714 John, Detroit, MI 48203 (1)
Masjid, 8850 Grand River, Detroit, MI 48204 (1)
Franklin Dairy Co-op, 3360 Charlevoix, Detroit, MI 48207 (1)
Big Rapids Trucking Co., 6100 Vernon, Detroit, MI 48209 (7)
Rainbow Grocery, 20536 W. Seven Mile Rd., Detroit, MI 48219 (1)
Karma Co-op, Judy Dudek, 708 S. Jefferson, Saginaw, MI (1)
Karma Co-op of Bay City, 1184 W. Hampton Rd., Essexville, MI 48732 (1)
Community Market, 933 W. Grand River, East Lansing, MI 48823 (1)
Green Earth Food Co-op, c/o Barb Clark, 311B Student Services Building,
    Michigan State University, East Lansing, MI 48823 (1)
Mountain People, 1 Franklin, Mount Pleasant, MI 48850 (1)
Mount Pleasant Food Co-op, c/o David Dixon, Bud Lange, Rte. 3, Mount
    Pleasant, MI 48858 (1)

Wolf Moon Bakery, c/o Tome Leone, 714 S. Hayford, Lansing, MI 48912 (5)
New Life Environmental Designs Institute, Box 645, Kalamazoo, MI 49005 (9)
Divine Food Co-op, 305 Stuart St., Kalamazoo, MI 49007 (1)
People's Food Co-op of Kalamazoo, 817 W. North St., Kalamazoo,
    MI 49007 (1)
Wild Bills Walk on Water Bakery, 141 Burr Oak, Kalamazoo, MI 49007 (5)
Full Circle Farm, David Adams, 466 Farrand Rd., Rte. 3, Bronson, MI
    49028 (8)
Circle Pines Center, Delton, MI 49046 (9)
Organic Growers of Michigan, Maynard Kaufman, Bangor, MI 49064 (8)
Sunshower Co-op Farm, Eileen Kreutz, Rte. 1, Box 26, Lawrence, MI
    49064 (8)
Michigan Organic Growers Assoc., John R. Yaeger, Rte. 1, Box 188,
    Lawton, MI 49065 (8)
Twin Cities Food Co-op, Sandy Holmes, YMCA, 508 Pleasant, St. Joe,
    MI 49085 (1)
Boones Farm, Rte. 4, Box 181-3, Big Rapids, MI 49307 (8)
Freemont Food Co-op, c/o Jim Austin, Rte. 2, Freemont, MI 49412 (1)
Saugatuck Food Co-op, c/o Susan Redcliffe, Bridge Street Curio, 802 Bridge
    St., Saugatuck, MI 49453 (1)
Happy Farmer Co-op, c/o Jean Demski, Rte. 3, Shelby, MI 49455 (8)
Eastown Food Co-op, 2218 Lake Dr., Grand Rapids, MI 49506 (1)
Oryana Food Co-op, 818 E. 8th St., Traverse City, MI 49864 (1)
Grain Train Natural Foods Co-op, 311½ E. Mitchell, No. 8, Petoskey,
    MI 49770 (1)
Marquette Organic Food Co-op, c/o Linda Niemi, 230 W. Ohio St.,
    Marquette, MI 49855 (1)
Karma Cafe, Sheldon Ave., Houghton, MI 49931 (5)

Iowa

Ames Peoples Co-op, c/o Little Read Book Shop, 110 S. Hyland, Ames, IA
    50010 (1)
Iowa Institute of Cooperation, Gerald R. Pepper, P.O. Box 668, Ames, IA
    50010 (9)
National Catholic Rural Life Conference, Father John McRaith, 3801 Grand
    Ave., Des Moines, IA 50312 (9)
Des Moines Food Co-op, 1535 11th St., Des Moines, IA 50314 (1)
Cedar Falls Buying Club, 3815 W. 12th St., Cedar Falls, IA 50613 (1)
Sunshine Farm Co-op, Sunshine, Inc., Rte. 1, Traer, IA 50675 (8)
National Farmers Organization, Corning, IA 50841 (8)
New Pioneer Co-op Society, 518 Bowery St., Iowa City, IA 52240 (1)
Good News General Store, 206 Fourth St., S.E., Cedar Rapids, IA 52401 (4)
Divine Light Mission, 1518 Harrison St., Davenport, IA 52803 (1)
Good Earth Foods, 1518 Harrison St., Davenport, IA 52803 (1)

Wisconsin

Hartford Food Co-op, 29 S. Main, Hartford, WI 53027 (1)

W.S.A. Store, 720 State, Madison, WI 53103 (1)

Wisconsin Organic Growers, Joseph Plesko, 10780 S. 92nd St., Franklin, WI 53132 (8)

Beans & Barley, 2340 N. Murray, Milwaukee, WI 53211 (1)

Outpost Natural Foods Co-op, 833 E. Locust, Milwaukee, WI 53212 (1)

Liberated Zone Cooperative, 800 Clark, Milwaukee, WI 53212 (1)

Westside Egg Co-op, 2926 W. Galenast, Milwaukee, WI (1)

Milwaukee Co-op Foods, 2027 W. Kilbourn, Milwaukee, WI 53233 (1)

Head Start Food Co-op, 1315 N. Wisconsin Ave., Racine, WI 53402 (1)

Racine Alternative High School, 620 Lake Ave., Racine, WI 53403 (1)

Common Market, Ltd., 1340 E. Washington, Madison, WI 53703 (3)

Cooperative Education/Training, Inc., Wayne H. Weidmann, 14 N. Carroll St., Rm. 415, Madison, WI 53703 (8)

Intergalactic Co-op, 119 W. Gorham, Madison, WI 53703 (1)

Miflin Street Co-op, 32 N. Bassett, Madison, WI 53703 (1)

Nature's Bakery, 800 Williamson St., Madison, WI 53703 (5)

University Center for Cooperatives, Mary Jean McGrath, Frank Groves, University of Wisconsin, Madison, WI 53703 (9)

Whole Earth Learning Community, 817 E. Johnson St., Madison, WI 53703 (1)

Wisconsin Federation of Cooperatives, Glenn M. Anderson, 122 W. Washington Ave., Madison, WI 53703 (9)

Eagle Heights Co-op, 611 Eagle Heights, Madison, WI 53704 (1)

Green Lantern Eating Co-op, 604 University Ave., Madison, WI 53715 (5)

Intra-Community Cooperative, 1335 Gilson St., Madison, WI 53715 (7)

Madison Community Co-op, 1001 University Ave., Madison, WI 53715 (9)

Boscobel Marketing Co-op, Michael O'Bannon, Rte. 4, Boscobel, WI 53805 (8)

Whole Earth, c/o Roger Browne, Rte. 3, River Falls, WI 54022 (8)

Menominee County Co-op, Keshena, WI 54135 (1)

Quercus Alba Bakery, Oregon, WI 54303 (5)

Stevens Point Area Food Co-op, 2501 Welsby Ave., Stevens Point, WI 54481 (1)

MFCC Cooperative Cookbook, Gena, 2501 Welsby, Stevens Point, WI 54481 (9)

Consumers Cooperative of Eau Claire, 2221 Highland Ave., Eau Claire, WI 54701 (1)

Connorsville Co-op, Rte. 2, Box 110, Boyceville, WI 54725 (8)

Organic Growers and Buyers Assoc., Paul Helgeson, Winding Road Farm, Boyceville, WI 54725 (8)

Menominee Buying Club, c/o Doug Sommers, 1814 E. 7th Ave., Menominee, WI 54751 (1)

Al Kurki & Friends, Rte. 2, Box 309, Ashaldn, WI 54806 (8)

Rice Lake Co-op, 1103 W. Knapp St., Rice Lake, WI 54868 (1)

Superior Food Buying Club, 904 Tower Ave., Superior, WI 54880 (1)

166

FOOD CO-OPS

Good Life Natural Foods, 600 N. Main, Oshkosh, WI 54901 (1)

Minnesota

Green Grass Grocery, 928 Raymond, St. Paul, MN 55113 (1)
Northfield Buyer's Club, Bos 24, Northfield, MN 55057 (1)
Steele County Buying Club, c/o Dodge-Steele-Waseca Citizens Action Council,
    Owatonna, MN 55060 (1)
Selby Food Co-op, 516 Selby, St. Paul, MN 55102
Minnesota Association of Cooperatives, Edward E. Slettom, Suite 205,
    55 Sherburne Ave., St. Paul, MN 55103 (9)
Saint Anthony Park Foods, 1435 N. Cleveland, St. Paul, MN 55108 (1)
Lake Region Enterprises, Annandale, MN 55302 (1)
Glencoe Savers Buying Club, Glencoe, MN 55336 (1)
Clear Lake Food Buying Club, Watkins, MN 55389 (1)
Good Grits, 15th and Spruce, Minneapolis, MN 55403 (1)
New Riverside Care, Cedar and Riverside, Minneapolis, MN 55404 (5)
Mill City Co-op, 2552 Bloomington Ave. S., Minneapolis, MN 55404 (1)
North Country Co-op, 2129 Riverside, Minneapolis, MN 55404 (1)
Powderhorn Co-op, 3440 Bloomington Ave. S., Minneapolis, MN 55404 (1)
Seward Co-op, 2201 Franklin Ave. E., Minneapolis, MN 55404 (1)
Whole Foods, 2500 First Ave., Minneapolis, MN 55404 (1)
Peoples Farm Co-op, 2224 Emerson St. S., Apt. 10, Minneapolis, MN
    55404 (8)
Divine Food Co-op, 734 E. Lake St., No. 200, Minneapolis, MN 55407 (1)
People's Company, 1534 E. Lake, Minneapolis, MN 55407 (5)
The Beanery, 3008 Lyndale Ave. S., Minneapolis, MN 55409 (1)
Southeast Co-op, 1023 Eighth St. S.E., Minneapolis, MN 55414 (1)
Minnesota Organic Growers/Buyers Association, c/o E.L.M., 1222 S.E. 4th
    St., Minneapolis, MN 55415 (8)
People's Warehouse, 123 E. 26th St., Minneapolis, MN 55415 (3)
Hibbing Buying Club, Box 114A, Star Rte. 4, Hibbing, MN 55746 (1)
East Central Farmers, Inc., Rutledge, MN 55778 (8)
Midland Cooperatives, Food and Clothing Dept., Allen Bradway, 217 Lake
    Ave., Duluth, MN 55802 (1)
Whole Foods Community Co-op, Lorena Gothard, 631 E. 6th St., Duluth,
    MN 55805 (1)
Organic Growers and Buyers Assoc., Bailey Farm Community, Box 112,
    R. R. 1, Altura, MN 55910 (8)
La Crescent Buying Club, Rte. 2, P.O. Box 152, La Crescent, MN 55947 (1)
Spring Valley Buying Club, Spring Valley, MN 55975 (1)
Famine Foods, 162 E. 2nd, Winona, MN 55987 (1)
Winona Buying Club, 723 E. 4th St., Winona, MN 55987 (1)
Organic Growers and Buyers Assoc., 307 S. Broad St., Mankato, MN 56001 (9)
Sustenance Shoppe, 205 N. Ermina Ave., Albert Lea, MN 56007 (1)
Waseca County Buying Club, Waseca Community Center, Waseca, MN
    56093 (1)

Prairie Dog Store, Christus House, 408 E. 4th, Morris, MN 56267 (1)
Penny Pinchers Buying Club, Olivia, MN 56277 (1)
Organic Growers and Buyers Assoc., John and Edyth Enestvedt, Sacred
    Heart, MN 56285 (8)
St. Cloud Food Co-op, Neuman Center, Box 1032, St. Cloud, MN 56301 (1)
Organic Growers and Buyers Assoc., Irene and Norman Seppanen, Rte. 3,
    Alexander, MN 56308 (8)
Organic Growers and Buyers Assoc., Kenneth Morgan, Deerwood, MN
    56444 (8)
Staples Peoples Pantry, R.R. 2, Staples, MN 56479 (1)
Organic Growers and Buyers Assoc., Jim and Joan Kohan, Meadow Farm,
    Rte. 1, Erhard, MN 56534 (8)
Heirloom Galleries, 213 E. Summit, Fergus Falls, MN 56537 (4)
Fort Fredd, Inger Rte., Deer River, MN 56636 (8)
Good Foods Store, Lengby, MN 56651 (1)
John Salmi Memorial Co-op, Lake Cabetobama, Ray, MN 56669 (1)

South Dakota
Organic Growers and Buyers, Geradt Schmeichel, Parker, SD 57053 (8)
Harvest Moon Foods, 9 W. National, Vermillion, SD 57069 (1)
Cooperative Buying Club, Inc., 1024 Quincy St., Rapid City, SD 57701 (1)
Stoneground Natural Foods, 517 7th St., Rapid City, SD 57701 (1)
Sturgis Buying Club, Meade County Community Center, 1130 Main St.,
    Sturgis, SD 57785 (1)

North Dakota
GF Co-op, 120 2nd Ave. N., Grand Forks, ND 58201 (1)
Something of Value, Organic Foods and General Store, Brian Saunders,
    618 N.E. 3rd, Minot, ND 58701 (1)

Montana
Friendship Center Meat Buying Club, 1503 Gallatin St., Helena, MT 59601 (1)
The Good Food Store, 642 Woody, Missoula, MT 59801 (1)
The New Little Food Co-op, Box 854, Libby, MT 59923 (1)

Illinois
Park Plaines, Carol Temple, 801 Laurel, Desplaines, IL 60016 (1)
Little Ladles, Kathy Slocum, 10026 Lamon St., Skokie, IL 60076 (1)
Mother Jones, Peg Dublin, 826 S. Lincoln, Waukegan, IL 60085 (1)
Karlin Family, Margaret Karlin, 7201 Adams, Forest Park, IL 60130 (1)
Maywood, Diane Nichols, 604 S. 5th St., Maywood, IL 60153 (1)
Natures Way, Jan North, 127 W. Ash, Lombard, IL 60181 (1)
West End, Barbara Meerdink, 310 E. Union, Wheaton, IL 60187 (1)
Bean Pot, Pam Brasch, 2215 Payne, Evanston, IL 602001 (1)
Dwarf, F.R. Ellis, 1518 Sherman, No. 3, Evanston, IL 60201 (1)
Sherman Street, Fred Green, 1631 McDaniel Ave., Evanston, IL 60201 (1)

Poor Richards, Joan and Bert Schomer, 1019 Seward, Evanston, IL 60202 (1)
Reba Place Church, Pat Harris, 836 Elmwood, Evanston, IL 60202 (1)
Chicago Heights, June Mosby, 302 E. 16th St., Chicago Heights, IL
    60411 (1)
Evanston Food Buying Club, Willa Jennings, 1554 Florence, Evanston,
    IL 60201 (1)
Honey Bear, Philip Gonzales, 1334 Asbury, Evanston, IL 60201 (1)
North Chicago, Jeanne Fitzpatrick, 2633 Broadway, Evanston, IL 60201 (1)
Alley, Robert Quackenbush, 826 Madison St., Evanston, IL 60202 (1)
Tinley Park, David Bagby, 5200 121st St., Tinley Park, IL 60477 (1)
Food, Diane Grung, 533 Eldon, Downers Grove, IL 60515 (1)
Recoop, Ann Biechler, 701 Hitchcock, Lisle, IL 60532 (1)
Earth Mothers, Caroline Trees, 214 Scottswood, Riverside, IL 60546 (1)
Acacia, Ralph Riedesel, 4307 N. Oriole, Norridge, IL 60600 (1)
Self Help Action Center, Dorothy Shavers, 11013 Indiana, Chicago, IL
    60600 (1)
American Friends Service Committee, Co-op Rural Project, Paul Schultz,
    407 S. Dearborn, Chicago, IL 60605 (9)
Twang, Victoria, 907 S. Carpenter, Chicago, IL 60607 (1)
Beacon House, Idella Tyler, 1440 S. Ashland, Chicago, IL 60608 (1)
Black Market, Carl Lewis, 16 S. California, Chicago, IL 60612 (1)
Browns Co-op, Mike Brown, 2903 W. Wilcox, Chicago, IL 60612 (1)
Cornucopia, 2808 W. Lake St., Chicago, IL 60612 (1)
Susan B., Eunice Militante, 3730 N. Broadway, Chicago, IL 60613 (1)
Amazing Grace Reconstituted, Kathy Danzy, 505 W. Fullerton, Chicago,
    IL 60614 (1)
Amazing Lemon, Lori Weiner, 816 Lill, Chicago, IL 60614 (1)
Fullerton Irregulars, Charles Autenrieth, 325 Fullerton Parkway, Chicago,
    IL 60614 (1)
Magnolia Street, Bruce K. Bahrmasel, 2712 N. Magnolia, Chicago, IL
    60614 (1)
McCormick, Marcia Kinzie, 900 W. Belden, Chicago, IL 60614 (1)
Webster Co-op, 2218 N. Kenmore, Chicago, IL 60614 (1)
Xanadu, Dave Biller, 1951 N. Seminary, Chicago, IL 60614 (1)
Chateau, Julia Zacharopoulos, 4858 Dorchester, Chicago, IL 60615 (1)
Divine Light Food Co-op, 5026 S. Greenwood, Chicago, IL 60615 (1)
Feed the Penguins, John Laing, 4850 S. Lake Park Blvd., No. 1605,
    Chicago, IL 60615 (1)
Friendship, Adrien Beldstein, 5459 S. Hyde Park Blvd., Chicago, IL 60615 (1)
Hyde Park Cooperative Society, Gilbert Spencer, 1526 E. 55th St.,
    Chicago, IL 60615 (1)
LSTC, Roger Anderson, 1100 E. 55th St., Chicago, IL 60615 (1)
Organic Fasters, Lee Bruce, 5448 S. Cornell, Chicago, IL 60615 (1)
Pennysavers, Libby Jones, 4850 S. Lake Park, No. 1110, Chicago, IL
    60615 (1)
Schneider, Carol Schneider, 5436 East View Park, Chicago, IL 60615 (1)

United Co-op Project, Richard Boyajian, 1315 E. 52nd St., No. 1,
    Chicago, IL 60615 (1)
CTMC, Ralph E. Peck, 3100 S. Michigan, Chicago, IL 60616 (1)
The Eaters, Jacob Carruthers, 2617 S. Michigan, Chicago, IL 60616 (1)
Emerson House, Helen Strzalka, 645 N. Wood, Chicago, IL 60622 (1)
Washtenaw, Mary Turck, 1250 N. Washtenaw, Chicago, IL 60622 (1)
Peoples Pantry, Theresa Soloma, 3061 W. Augusta, Chicago, IL 60622 (1)
F & W, W. Fontenot, 3743 W. Cermak, Chicago, IL 60623 (1)
Parent-Child Center, Karen Ivey, 3121 W. Jackson, Chicago, IL 60624 (1)
Harvest, Vicki Mitchell, 1650½ Juneway, Chicago, IL 60626 (1)
Plier Co-op, Julie Plier, 7068 N. Ashland, Chicago, IL 60626 (1)
Shin Sun Co-op, Rudy DeSoto, 5632 N. Wayne, Chicago, IL 60626 (1)
Chlamy, Eva Eves, 920 E. 58th St., Rm. 401, Chicago, IL 60637 (1)
Confooderation, Stephen Maquire, 837 E. 56th St., Chicago, IL 60637 (1)
Cop-out, Woody Poskanzer, 5741 S. Maryland, Chicago, IL 60637 (1)
Eskimo, Ruth Sorgal, 5548 S. Blackstone, Chicago, IL 60637 (1)
Hyde Park II, Marcia Rothenberg, 5716 S. Dorchester, Chicago, IL 60637 (1)
Hyde Park Distribution Center, 5655 S. University, Chicago, IL 60637 (2)
Survivors, Pat Bradley, 5611 S. Blackstone, Chicago, IL 60637 (1)
Roseland, Suzanne Yauk, 5336 N. Winnebago, Chicago, IL 60640 (1)
Uptown Food Co-op, Warren Kmiec, 4611 N. Beacon, Chicago, IL 60640 (1)
Sledd, Andrew Sledd, 10027 S. Damen, Chicago, IL 60643 (1)
Acorn, Don Wheat, 5748 W. Race, Chicago, IL 60644 (1)
Hummel Gardens, Helen Bilotta, 1132 S. Mayfield, Chicago, IL 60644 (1)
Third Unitarian, Esther Radinsky, 5822 W. Race, Chicago, IL 60644 (1)
Holy Order of Man, Rev. Thomas, 2328 N. Oakley, Chicago, IL 60647 (1)
Chicago Economic Development Corporation, Arthur Barbour, 1711 E. 71st
    St., Chicago, IL 60649 (6)
Crandon House, Dale Fischer, 7831 Saginaw, Chicago, IL 60649 (1)
Crib, Jerry Lincoln, 7427 South Shore Dr., Chicago, IL 60649 (1)
Phase II, Dante Lanzetta, 6928 S. Oglesby, Chicago, IL 60649 (1)
Redeemer Buying Club, 1406 N. Laramie, Chicago, IL 60651 (1)
Community Thrift Club, Silas Brown, 4035 S. Michigan, Chicago, IL 60653 (1)
Ujmaa, Dorothy Robertson, 4521 S. Oakenwald, Chicago, IL 60653 (1)
Ceres, Margaret Morrissey, 1020 W. Oakdale Ave., Chicago, IL 60657 (1)
Circle Grocery, Ben Burrows, 1347 W. Wolfram, Chicago, IL 60657 (1)
Kenmore, Kathy Devine, 3226 N. Kenmore, Chicago, IL 60657 (1)
Second Unitarian, Rebecca Hyatt, 654 W. Wellington, Chicago, IL 60657 (1)
Association of Food Co-ops, Faith Rich, Box 1642, Chicago, IL 60690 (9)
Pembroke Farmers Co-op, P.O. Box 62, Hopkins Park, IL 60954 (8)
Friendly Food Co-op, Doris Peter, 1217 Michigan, Rockford, IL 61102 (1)
Tompkins Street Co-op, 488 W. Tompkins St., Galesburg, IL 61401 (1)
Macomb Community Co-op, c/o Joann Cartwright, 803 Bobby Ave.,
    Macomb, IL 61455 (1)
Jo Ann Knuppel, R. R. 5, Canton, IL 61520 (8)
Alice and Bert Raabe, R. R. 1, Dunlap, IL 61525 (8)

Northside Buyers Club, 410 Wayne, Peoria, IL 61603 (1)
People's Food Co-op, Pat Allen, 36 Whites Place, Bloomington, IL 61701 (1)
Dick-Freeman Trucking Collective, 1004A W. Washington, Bloomington,
        IL 61701 (7)
Brad and Will Giudi, R. R. 1, Mackinaw, IL 61755 (8)
Earthworks & Metamorphis Restaurant, 1310 W. Main, Urbana, IL 61801 (1)
Homestead Community Bakery, St. Joseph, IL 61873 (5)
Peoples Cooperative Buying Club, 1015 Liberty, East St. Louis, IL 62201 (1)
North End Consumers Co-op, 1507 N. 13th St., East St. Louis, IL 62205 (1)
Metro East Co-op, 4 West C St., Belleville, IL 62221 (1)
Spoon River Co-op, 122 S. 4th St., Springfield, IL 62701 (1)
King Harvest Food Co-op, Lynn Kienzler, 1441 N. 5th St., Springfield,
        IL 62702 (1)
Springfield and Sangamon County Buying Club, 1310 E. Adams St.,
        Springfield, IL 62703 (1)

Missouri

Laclede Co-op, Peacock Community Center, Laclede and Ewing Sts.,
        St. Louis, MO 63103 (1)
Compton-Grand Meat Co-op, 3504 Caroline, St. Louis, MO 63104 (1)
Divine Food Co-op, 3237 Geyer St., St. Louis, MO 63104 (1)
Food Buyers Assoc., 28 Benton Place, St. Louis, MO 63104 (1)
Demun Community Center Food Co-op, 700 Demun, St. Louis, MO 63105 (1)
Midtown Food Buying Club, 4204 Folsom, St. Louis, MO 63110 (1)
Peoples Produce, 5899 Delmar, St. Louis, MO 63112 (1)
K-W Co-op, 201 Cough, Kirkwood, MO 63122 (1)
Community Collectives Combine Co-op, 554 Limit, St. Louis, MO
        63130 (1)
Midwest Cooperating Consumers Assoc., 554 Limit, St. Louis, MO 63130 (9)
Midwest Co-op Warehouse, c/o Lea Russell, 4487 Laclede, St. Louis,
        MO 63130 (3)
Water Tower Food Co-op, 4522 N. 9th St., St. Louis, MO 63147 (1)
Missouri Delta Ecumenical Ministry, Box 524, Hayti, MO 63851 (9)
Hace Co-op Supermarket, Howardville, MO 63869 (1)
Live Center Food Co-op, Brian McInerney, 915 W. 17th St., Kansas City,
        MO 64108 (1)
Divine Food Co-op, 2911 Campbell, Kansas City, MO 64109 (1)
Redstar Food Co-op, 3130 Olive, Kansas City, MO 64109 (1)
Westport Co-op, Esther Markus, 4830 Campbell, Kansas City, MO 64110 (1)
Columbia Foods Co-op, 915 E. Broadway, Columbia, MO 65201 (1)
Graduate Institute Co-op Leadership, Randall Torgerson, Agricultural
        Economics Dept., University of Missouri, 200 Mumford Hall,
        Columbia, MO 65201 (9)
Paquin Street Cafe, 1100 Paquin St., Columbia, MO 65201 (5)
Springfield Natural Foods Co-op, P.O. Box 1642, Springfield, MO
        65805 (1)

Kansas

Western Wyandotte Mini Market, 121 Allcutt St., Bonner Springs, KS
   66012 (1)
Lawrence Milk Run, Paul Johnson, 788 Locust, Lawrence, KS 66044 (1)
Linn County Food Growers Assoc., P.O. Box 447, Pleasanton, KS 66075 (8)
Bethel-Riverview Action Group Buying Club, 73 S. 7th St., Kansas City,
   KS 66101 (1)
Northeast Action Group Buying Club, 950 Quindero Blvd., Kansas City,
   66101 (1)
Total Action Group Buying Club, 1620 S. 37th St., Kansas City, KS 66101 (1)
Rainbow Foods, 3950 Rainbow, Kansas City, KS 66103 (1)
Parsons Buyers Club, 2530½ Main St., Parsons, KS 67357 (1)

Nebraska

Cornhuskers Co-op, 1319 R St., Lincoln, NB 68501 (1)

Louisiana

Food Co-op Office, 2nd floor, Central City Economic Opportunity Corpora-
   tion, 1626 Dryades St., New Orleans, LA 70113 (9)
Food Co-op, c/o Switchboard, 1212 Royal St., New Orleans, LA 70116 (1)
Department of Agricultural Economy/Agribusiness, Ewell P. Roy, Louisiana
   State University, Baton Rouge, LA 70803 (9)
Natchitoches Area Action Assoc., Farm Program-Vegetable Co-op, P.O. Box
   944, Natchitoches, LA 71457 (8)

Arkansas

Eureka Springs Food Co-op, 4 N. Main, Eureka Springs, AR 72632 (1)
Ozark Access Catalog, Box 506, 55 Spring St., Eureka Springs, AR
   72632 (9)
Boston Mountain Co-op, Murray, AR 72666 (1)
Ozark Food Conspiracy, 347 N. West, Fayetteville, AR 72701 (1)
Bill Harwood, Pettigrew, AR 72752 (8)

Oklahoma

Lone Wolf Co-op, Mark Chalom, 214 W. Symmes, Norman, OK 73069 (1)
Lovelight, 755 Jenkins, Norman, OK 73069 (1)
Tulsa Food Co-op, Box 1072, Tulsa, OK 74101 (1)

Texas

Como Assoc. of Economic Development, 2125 Littlepage St., Fort Worth,
   TX 76107 (9)
Divine Food Co-op, 35 Avondale, Houston, TX 77006 (1)
Community of Bread, Mark Matry, Dept. of Sociology, University of
   Houston, 3801 Cullen, Houston, TX 77004 (1)
Family Farmers, Malcom Beck, R. R. 13, Box 210, San Antonio, TX 78218 (8)

172   FOOD CO-OPS

Woody Hills Food Store, 1200 W. Lynn, Austin, TX 78702 (1)
Austin Community Project, 608 Oakland, Austin, TX 78703 (1)
Clarksville Bakery, 1013 W. Lynn, Austin, TX 78703 (5)
Sattua, 2532 Guadalupe, Methodist Student Center, Austin, TX 78705 (5)
The Food Co-op, Dennis Fortassin, The Ark, 2000 Pearl St., Austin,
    TX 78705

Colorado

College Press Service, John Ghrist, 4152 Pennsylvania St., Denver, CO
    80203 (9)
Common Market Food Co-op, 1100 Champa, Denver, CO 80204 (1)
Westside Action Center, Adelante Market, Craig Hart, 1100 Santa Fe Dr.,
    Denver, CO 80204 (1)
Eastside Action Center Buying Club, 2420 Welton St., Denver, CO 80205 (1)
Divine Light Mission, Divine Food Coordinator, Mark Retzloff, Box 6495
    Denver, CO 80206 (1)
Rainbow Grocery, P.O. Box 6495, Denver, CO 80206 (1)
Colorado Grower/Marketer Assoc., c/o Judd and Terry Blaine, Ft. Lupton,
    CO 80621 (8)
Peoples Market, 132 7th Ave., No. 4, Greeley, CO 80631 (1)
Us Too, Inc., Cooperative Extension Service, 27 E. Vermijo, Colorado
    Springs, CO 80903 (1)
Rocinante Grocery Store, Gardner, CO 81040 (1)

Wyoming
Laramie Peoples Market, 111 Ivinson St., Laramie, WY 82070 (1)

Idaho
Garden Cooperative, c/o S. Central Community Action Agency, P.O. Box
    531, Twin Falls, ID 83301 (8)
Co-op, c/o Good Food Store, 112 E. 2nd St., Moscow, ID 83843 (1)

Utah
Peoples Co-op, Max Aragon, 554 N. 35th St., Salt Lake City, UT 84116 (1)
Todahaidekani Nalyehe Bahooghan, Beeahodta, Inc., P.O. Box 402,
    Bluff, UT 84512 (1)
Halchiita Nalyehe Bahoogan, Inc., P.O. Box 45, Mexican Hat, UT 84531 (1)

Arizona
Divine Food Co-op, 91 W. Lynwood, Phoenix, AZ 85003 (1)
Kosmic Gardens, 2234 N. 24th St., Phoenix, AZ 85008 (1)
Gentle Strength Co-op, Tom Manheim, 1310 S. Sunset, Tempe, AZ
    85281 (1)
Food Conspiracy, 412 N. 4th Ave., Tucson, AZ 85705 (1)
Na-Ah-Tee Co-op, Inc., Indian Wells Rural Branch, Indian Wells, AZ
    86031 (1)

Tood-Dine Benalyebahowan, P.O. Box 410, Star Route, Winslow, AZ
    86047 (1)
Rough Rock Black Mesa Enterprise, Rough Rock Demonstration School,
    Chinle, AZ 86503 (1)
Ganado Feed and Consumer Co-op, P.O. Box 767, Ganado, AZ 86505 (1)
Dineh-Bi-Naa-Yei Cooperative, P.O. Box 566, Pinon, AZ 86510 (1)
Blue Gap Food Cooperative, Pinon, AZ 86515 (1)

New Mexico

Acoma Food Cooperative, P.O. Box 67, San Fidel, NM 87038 (1)
Torreon Food Stamp Co-op Assoc., P.O. Box 193, Cuba, NM 87103 (1)
Organic Growers Assoc., David Rowley, 1312 Lobo Pl., N.E., Albuquerque,
    NM 87106 (8)
Osha Co-op, Gordon Andrews, 8812 4th St., N.W., Albuquerque, NM
    87114 (1)
Eastern Navaho Feed Store Co-op Assoc., P.O. Box 104, Crownpoint,
    NM 87313 (1)
New Life Cooperative, S. Reilly, 140B W. Berger St., Santa Fe, NM 87501 (1)
Amigos de Salud Cooperative, Box 453, El Prado, NM 87529 (1)

Nevada

Midway Buyers Club, Old Junior High School, Lead St., Henderson,
    NV 89015 (1)
Community Action Self-Help, 960 W. Owens St., Las Vegas, NV 89106 (1)
Action Over 55 Cooperative, 1632 Yale St., Las Vegas, NV 89107 (1)

California

Divine Food Service, 316 N. Larchmont Blvd., Los Angeles, CA 90004 (1)
Operation Recapture, Richard Foos & Levi Kingston, 701 W. 34th St.,
    Los Angeles, CA 90007 (1)
Chicano Americanor Servicios Assoc., Bert N. Corona, 214 Echandia, Los
    Angeles, CA 90023 (1)
Community Service Organization, Tony Rids, 2820 E. Whittier Blvd.,
    Los Angeles, CA 90023 (1)
KVST-TV, 1633 Westwood Blvd., Los Angeles, CA 90024 (9)
Resource Tie Line Newsletter, P.O. Box 24006, Los Angeles, CA 90024 (9)
School of Liveing West, Green Revolution, Richard Fairfield, 442½
    Land Fair Ave., Los Angeles, CA 90024 (1)
Barrington Co-op Market, 2021 South Barrington Ave., Los Angeles,
    CA 90025 (1)
ESP Co-op/The Good Herb, P.O. Box 295, Los Angeles, CA 90025 (1)
Echo Park/Silverlake Food Conspiracy, Derek Fuchs, 947½ Vendome St.,
    Los Angeles, CA 90026 (1)
Immaculate Heart Co-op, c/o Marie Gamboa, Immaculate Heart College,
    2021 N. Western Ave., Los Angeles, CA 90027 (1)
Sunrise Natural Foods, 3817 Sunset Blvd., Los Angeles, CA 90026 (1)

Oriental Food Co-op, Jeff Ta, c/o Oriental College, Box O, Los Angeles, CA 90041 (1)

Highland Park Food Co-op, Jackie Davis, 6243 Strickland Ave., Los Angeles, CA 90042 (1)

Westsdie Co-ops, c/o Gail Williamson, 11973 Dorothy St., West Los Angeles, CA 90049 (1)

The Gathering, John Dugas, 4506 S. Western Ave., Los Angeles, CA 90062 (1)

Los Angeles Natural Foods Co-op, Carole Roberts, 6665½ Franklin Ave., Hollywood, CA 90068 (1)

Bell Gardens Buyers Club and Community Service, P.O. Box 2160, Bell Gardens, CA 90201 (1)

Head Start Food Co-op, Janet Robinson, 6713 Florence Pl., Bell Gardens, CA 90201 (1)

Topanga Canyon Food Co-op, Sherna Gluck, 19988 Observation Dr., Topanga, CA 90290 (1)

Free Venic Co-op, c/o Marvena Kennedy, 440 Venice Way, Free Venice, CA 90291 (1)

Together, 1043 W. Washington, Free Venice, CA 90291 (1)

San Pedro Food Co-op, Louis Wright, 714 N. Meyler, San Pedro, CA 90731 (1)

Dominguez Hills Food Co-op, Bill Myers, 1516 W. 19th St., No. C, San Pedro, CA 90732 (1)

Carson Natural Foods Co-op, Barry Brouillette, c/o The General Store, 21808 Avalon Blvd., Carson, CA 90745 (1)

Beach Organic Foods Co-op, 1747 E. 2nd St., Long Beach, CA 90802 (1)

Long Beach Food Conspiracy, 1747 E. 2nd St., Long Beach, CA 90802 (1)

Poor and Simple Food Co-op, 3322 E. Anaheim, Long Beach, CA 90815 (1)

Altadena Food Co-op, Bill Fenwick, 3737 Canyon Crest Rd., Altadena, CA 90110 (1)

Pasadena Natural Foods, Don Smith, 1625 East Walnut, Pasadena, CA 91106 (1)

Valley State Food Co-op, Fred Morris, 19044 Parthenia St., Northridge, CA 91324 (1)

Van Nuys Food Co-op, Leon Greenberg, 5835½ Woodman Ave., Van Nuys, CA 91401 (1)

Alhambra/Peoples Cornucopia, Jon Schuck, 3082 W. Main St., Alhambra, CA 91801 (1)

Positive Pole Produce, P.O. Box 11, Rainbow, CA 92028 (8)

Ramona Nutritional Information Center, 875 Major St., Ramona, CA 92065 (9)

Universal Co-op, 311A Pleasant Way, San Marcos, CA 92069 (1)

Encinitas Collective, Peoples Food Co-op, 503 N. Highway, No. 101, Solano Beach, CA 92075 (1)

Golden Hills Co-op, Randy Lunomaric, 3354 Lincoln, San Diego, CA 92104 (1)

Ocean Beach Peoples Store, Tom Kozden, 4859 Voltaire, San Diego, CA (1)

Mission Beach General Store, 3837 Mission Blvd., San Diego, CA 92019 (1)
San Diego State College, Muriel and Clinton Jenks, 4905 Art St.,
    San Diego, CA 92115 (1)
San Francisco Common Operating Warehouse, Mark Ritchie, 1559 Bancroft,
    San Francisco, CA 92124 (3)
Ecology Club of Laguna Beach, 2141 Laguna Canyon Rd., Laguna Beach,
    CA 92651 (1)
Peoples Union Co-op Farm, Art Zack, 8734 W. Manning Ave., Fresno,
    CA 93706 (8)
Carmel Co-op, Room 29, Bernadelli Square, Carmel, CA 93921 (1)
Carmel Valley Co-op Buying Assoc., Bernadelli Square, Carmel Valley, CA
    93924 (1)
Consumers Co-op Society of Monterey Peninsula, Inc., Box 1427,
    Monterey, CA 93940 (1)
The Granary, 1124 Forest, Pacific Grove, CA 93950 (1)
Evergreen Co-op, Ms. Broenkow, 2935 Sloat Rd., Pebble Beach, CA 93953 (1)
Berkeley Food Co-op, Randy Elliot, 1920 Berkeley Way, Berkeley, CA
    94054 (1)
Sunnyvale Buying Club, Robin Clute, 667 Toyon Ave., Sunnyvale, CA
    94086 (1)
Zen Co-op, 319 Page St., San Francisco, CA 94102 (1)
Naturally Good Buying Club No. 2, 787 22nd Ave., San Francisco,
    CA 94107 (1)
Divine Food Co-op, 300 Van Ness Ave., San Francisco, CA 94109 (1)
Bernal Heights Community Co-op, 320 Winfield, San Francisco, CA 94110 (1)
Free Food Co-op, 41 Nevada St., San Francisco, CA 94110 (1)
Inner Mission Co-op, 837 S. Van Ness, San Francisco, CA 94110 (1)
St. Peter's Food Buying Club, 1200 Forida St., Florida and 24th Sts.,
    San Francisco, CA 94110 (1)
Seeds of Life, 3021 24th St., San Francisco, CA 94110 (1)
Earth News Service, 24 California St., Suite 400, San Francisco, CA
    94111 (9)
Healthy Hunza Buying Club, 233 Brunswick St., San Francisco, CA 94112 (1)
San Francisco Food Buying Program 239 Vienna St., San Francisco,
    CA 94112 (1)
Eureka Valley Food Chain, 4529 18th St., San Francisco, CA 94114 (1)
Rose Hips Buying Club, 107 Noe St., San Francisco, CA 94114 (1)
Community Food Club, 2590 Sacramento St., San Francisco, CA 94115 (1)
Ongoing Picnic Co-op, 2234 20th Ave., San Francisco, CA 94116 (1)
Western Addition Food Buying Club, 457 Haight St., San Francisco,
    CA 94117 (1)
Common Market Buying Club, Haight Ashbury Food Conspiracy, 1446 Cole
    St., San Francisco, CA 94117 (1)
Eat Good Buying Club, 1310 Haight St., San Francisco, CA 94117 (1)
Grouphead Buying Club, 977 Clayton St., San Francisco, CA 94117 (1)

176   FOOD CO-OPS

Haight Food Conspiracy, c/o Dorothy and Dennis, 284 Frederick St.,
    San Francisco, CA 94117 (1)
Naturally Good Buying Club No. 1, 200 Cherry St., San Francisco, CA
    94118 (1)
Common Good Buying Club, 1259 46th Ave., San Francisco, CA 94122 (1)
Inner Sunset Food Co-op, 24 Irving St., San Francisco, CA 94122 (1)
PFP Food Co-op, 417 Lawton St., San Francisco, CA 94122 (1)
Seaside One Buying Club, 1370 40th Ave., San Francisco, CA 94122 (1)
Palo Alto Tenant Union Food Conspiracy, Roberta Kane, 626 Webster St.,
    Palo Alto, CA 94301 (1)
Consumer Co-op Society, Jud Reeves, 164 S. California Ave., Palo Alto, CA
    94306 (1)
Ecology Action/Common Ground, 2225 El Camino Real, Palo Alto,
    CA 94306 (1)
The Fourth Estate, P.O. Box 11176, Palo Alto, CA 94306 (1)
Ma Revolution's Natural Foods, 2566 Telegraph Ave., Berkeley, CA
    94604 (1)
Alternative Distributing Co., 6448 Bay St., Emeryville, CA 94608 (3)
Edible Dry Goods Conspiracy, 363 62nd St., Oakland, CA 94618 (1)
Oakland Food Co-op, c/o Peoples Food Market, 5520 College Ave., North
    Oakland, CA 94618 (1)
The Peoples Alternative Food Store, 55520 College Ave., Oakland, CA
    94618 (1)
Berkeley Food Conspiracy, Daryl McLeod, 1317 Cornell, Berkeley, CA
    94702 (1)
Loaves and Dishes, 2314 Bancroft Way, Berkeley, CA 94704 (1)
One World Family Restaurant, 2455 Telegraph, Berkeley, CA 94704 (5,9)
Ramparts Magazine, Derek Shearer, 2054 University Ave., Berkeley, CA
    94704 (9)
Center for Rural Studies, 1195 Sterling Ave., Berkeley, CA 94708 (9)
Consumers Co-op of Berkeley/Associated Cooperatives, Robert Neptune
    and Don Rothenberg, 4801 Central Ave., Richmond, CA 94804 (1)
Mr. Naturals, P.O. Box 148, Brookdale, CA 95007 (1)
Villa Roma Buying Club, Ann Mandel, 840 Quince Ave., Santa Clara, CA
    95051 (1)
Central Coast Organic Growers Co-op, 1920 Maciel Ave., Santa Cruz,
    CA 95060 (8)
Farm Co. Associates, 1875 17th Ave., Santa Cruz, CA 95060 (8)
Neighborhood Development Corporation, Community Action Board, Santa
    Cruz, CA 95060 (9)
Santa Cruz Consumers Co-op, 527 Seabright Ave., Santa Cruz, CA 95060 (1)
Kings Mountain Co-op, Pink Pastry Shop, Santa Cruz, CA 95060 (1)
Kresge Food Co-op, Leonard Armstrong, Kresge College of the University
    of California, Santa Cruz, CA 95060 (1)
Integral Yoga Institute, 817 Pacific, Santa Cruz, CA 95068 (1)
Arcata Co-op, 957 H St., Arcata, CA 95521 (1)

Peoples Food Conspiracy, 437 F St., Davis, CA 95616 (1)
Alternative Agricultural Resources, Isao Fugimoto, Applied Behavioral
    Sciences, Univ. of California at Davis, Davis, CA 95616 (9)
Divide Community Action Council, P.O. Box 11 Kelsey, CA 95643 (1)
Odyssey Orchards, Rte. 1, Box 56, Winters, CA 95694 (8)
Sipapu, Noel Peattie, Rte. 1, Box 216, Winters, CA 95694 (8)
Live Oak Farm, Box 11, Cottonwood, CA 96022 (8)
Cal Certified Organic Farmers, Cal Slewing, S & H Organic Acres, P. O. Box
    27, Montgomery Creek, CA 96065 (8)

Hawaii
Way Inn Co-op, P.O. Box 527, Kealakekua, HI 96750 (1)
Garden of Eden, 1910 Vineyard, Wailuku, Maui, HI 96793 (1)
Kokua Country Foods, Inc., 2357 S. Beretania St., Honolulu, HI 96814 (1)
People Not Profits, Steve Morris, Nuama House, 2930 Nuama Rd.,
    Honolulu, HI 96819 (1)

Oregon
Peoples Food Store, 3029 S.E. 21st St., Portland, OR 97202 (1)
Food Front Co-op, 1618 N.W. 23rd St., Portland, OR 97210 (1)
Divine Food Co-op, Rte. 1, Box 92, Portland, OR 97231 (1)
First Alternative, 644 N. 4th St., Corvallis, OR 97330 (1)
Lincoln Cracker Barrel Co-op, 1640 N. Hwy 101, Lincoln City, OR
    97367 (1)
Sweet Home and Neighbors Food Co-op, 1325 N. 18th St., Sweet Home,
    OR 97386 (1)
Community Natural Foods, 444 Lincoln, Eugene, OR 97401 (1)
Amrit Family Bakery, Blair St., Eugene, OR 97402 (5)
Willamette Peoples Co-op, 1391 E. 22nd, Eugene, OR 97403 (1)
Starflower, 1936½ Willamette, Eugene, OR 97405 (1)
Emily Food Co-op, 4930 Coyote Creek, Wolf Creek, OR 97497 (1)
Forest Acres Co-op, 3362 Table Rock Rd., Central Point, OR 97501 (1)
Ashland Peoples Food Co-op, 88 N. Main St., Ashland, OR 97520 (1)
Takilma Food Co-op, 10008 Takilma Rd., Cave Junction, OR 97523 (1)
Fields of Merit, 1615 N.E. 6th St., Grants Pass, OR 97526 (1)
Wonder Natural Foods, 11711 Redwood Highway, Wonder, OR 97543 (1)
Oregon Co-op Coalition, VSI, 18930 S.W. Boones Ferry Rd., Tualitin,
    OR 97602 (1)

Washington
Clovergreen Co-op, Steven Tachera, 23017 45th Ave., S.E., Bethell, WA
    98011 (1)
Community Produce, 1510 Pike Pl., Seattle, WA 98101 (1)
Corner Produce, 90 Pike St., Seattle, WA 98101 (1)
Almost Eden, 1510 Pike Pl., Seattle, WA 98101 (1)
Soup & Salad Restaurant, Lower Pike Pl., Seattle, WA 98101 (5)

Open, Northwest Resource Network, 8610 Aurora Ave., N., Seattle, WA
    98103 (9)
Phinney St. Co-op, 43rd and Phinney (Freemont Dist.), Seattle, WA
    98103 (1)
Mother Morgan's Gumbo/Live-in Honey, 431 15th Ave. E., Seattle, WA
    98112 (5)
Open, 608 19th E., Seattle, WA 98112 (9)
Upfront Cafe, Little Bread Co., 8050 15th Ave., N.E., Seattle, WA 98115 (5)
Puget Consumers Co-op, 2165 65th Ave., N.E., Seattle, WA 98115 (1)
Capitol Hill Co-op, 1835 12th Ave., Seattle, WA 98122 (1)
Rainbow Grocery, 1607 Summit, Seattle, WA 98122 (1)
Cooperating Community Grains, 4030 22nd Ave., W., Seattle, WA 98199 (1)
Low-Income Meat & Produce Co-op, 2512 Eldridge Ave., Bellingham,
    WA 98225 (1)
Community Food Co-op, 1000 Harris St., Bellingham, WA 98225 (1)
Skagit Valley Food Co-op, 619 2nd St., Mount Vernon, WA 98273 (1)
The Food Co-op, 617 Tyler St., Porttownsend, WA 98368   (1)
Food Bag, 914 Broadway, Tacoma, WA 98402 (1)
The Food Co-op, 904 E. 4th, Olympia, WA 98506 (1)
Community Communications Center, Rte. 1, Box 778, Winlock, WA
    98596 (9)
Northwest Organic Food Producers, Pat Langan, Rte. 2, Box 163,
    Toppenish, WA 98948 (8)
Pullman Food Co-op, N.E. 850 A St., Pullman, WA 99163 (1)
The Store, 1919 W. 2nd, Spokane, WA 99204 (1)

Canada

Karma Food Co-op, Dupont St., Toronto, Ontario (1)
Nature's Way, Etherea Natural Food, 341 Bloor, Toronto, Ontario (1)
Neill Wyck Food Co-op, Bob Luker, Registrar N.W. College 22nd floor,
    96 Gerrard St. E., Toronto, Ontario (1)
Cooperative D'ailments, naturales et macrobiotiques, 4614 Panieau, Montreal,
    Quebec (1)
Montreal Co-op, 4800 St. Domonique, Montreal, Quebac (1)
Banyan Tree, c/o Keith, 474 Jesse St., Winnepeg, Manitoba (1)
Cooperative College of Canada, 141 105th St. W., Saskatoon, Saskatchewan

England

BCM-O Scenes, London WVIC, U.K.
The Commonweal Library, 112 Wincheombe St., Cheltenham Glos,
    GL52, 2N.W., England (9)

NOTES

CHAPTER ONE

1. Curhan and Wertheim, p. 9.
2. Briscoe, p. 14.
3. Crocker, pp. 10-13.

CHAPTER TWO

1. Alinsky, pp. 88-89.
2. Fager, p. 12.
3. "Packet for the Bride."

CHAPTER THREE

1. Kanter, p. 127.
2. *Ibid.,* pp. 126-27.
3. *Ibid.,* p. 132.
4. Freire, p. 47.
5. Roberto Michels, *Political Parties,* in Lipset, *Union Democracy*, p. 2.
6. Murphy, pp. 22-29.
7. Freud, p. 13.
8. Alinsky, p. 113.
9. Lipset, *Union Democracy*, pp. 465-67.
10. Mansbridge, p. 11.
11. *Ibid.,* p. 11, citing Herbert Maccoby, "Differential Political Activity of Participants in a Voluntary Association," p. 524; and Verba and Nie, *Participation in America*, p. 185.
12. *Ibid.,* p. 12.
13. Townsend, p. 68.

CHAPTER FOUR

1. Hyman and Wright, p. 195.
2. Perrow, p. 105.
3. Wood, p. 7.
4. *Ibid.,* p. 6.
5. Terkel, p. 392.
6. Marcuse, p. 4.
7. Zwerdling, p. 22.
8. *Ibid.,* p. 22.

CHAPTER FIVE

1. Margolis, p. 3.
2. Webb, p. 1.
3. Margolis, p. 5.
4. Holyoake, p. 16.
5. *Ibid.,* p. 16.
6. Goodwin, p. 57.
7. Holyoake, p. 52.
8. *Ibid.,* p. 57.
9. *Ibid.,* p. 67.
10. *Ibid.,* p. 72.
11. *Ibid.,* p. 75.
12. *Ibid.,* p. 80.
13. Margolis, p. 4.
14. Holyoake, p. 39.
15. Hays, p. 48.
16. Lipset, *Agrarian Socialism*, p. 17.
17. *Ibid.,* p. 41.
18. *Ibid.,* p. 54.
19. *Ibid.,* p. 47.

20. Knapp, *The Rise of the American Cooperative Enterprise*, p. 187.
21. Sonnichsen, p. 178.
22. Margolis, p. 7.
23. Syrjala.
24. *Ibid.*, p. 12.
25. *Ibid.*, p. 31.
26. Myrick, p. 86.
27. Breitman, p. 7.
28. Waugh, p. 5.
29. Leggett, p. 14.
30. Burley, p. 289.
31. Warbasse, p. 14.
32. Knapp, *The Rise of American Cooperative Enterprise*, p. 183.
33. *Ibid.*, p. 68.
34. *Ibid.*, p. 179.
35. *Ibid.*, p. 184.
36. Margolis, p. 5.
37. Holyoake, p. 93.
38. Myrick, p. 1.
39. Holyoake, p. 68.
40. Rayman, p. 8.
41. Buber, p. 139.

BIBLIOGRAPHY

I hope readers will use this bibliography as a reference for getting more information on co-ops. In several instances, I've included details on how to order particularly interesting books or articles. The works by Margolis, Knapp, Syrjala, and Mansbridge are especially good. The Cooperative League of the USA, 1828 L Street, N.W., Washington, D.C., has booklets and pamphlets on many aspects of co-op operations. The best resources for most new co-ops are the people at the other co-ops nearby—check the directory, Appendix C.

Alinsky, Saul, *Rules for Radicals* (NY: Vintage, 1971).

Breitman, George, "The Current Radicalization," *International Socialist Review*, Vol. 31, No. 7, October 1970.

Briscoe, Robert, *Traders and Idealists*, dissertation, Harvard Graduate School of Business Administration, June 1971.

Buber, Martin, *Paths to Utopia* (Boston: Beacon Press, 1958).

Burley, Orin E., *The Consumers' Cooperative as a Distributive Agency* (NY: McGraw-Hill, 1939).

Crocker, Ken, "Trucking on the Ann Arbor Trade Route," *Network*, Summer 1973, pp. 10-13.

Curhan, Ronald C., and Edward Wertheim, "Consumer Cooperatives: A Preliminary Report," April 1972. Available from Boston University Graduate School of Business Administration, 212 Bay State Road, Boston, MA. Later published as an article in the *Journal of Retailing*.

Fager, Chuck, "The Food Co-op Crisis," *The Real Paper*, October 17, 1973.

Freud, Sigmund, *Group Psychology and the Analysis of the Ego* (NY: Bantam, 1960).

Freire, Paulo, *Pedagogy of the Oppressed* (NY: Herder & Herder, 1971).

Goodwin, Richard N., "Reflections—The American Condition," *The New Yorker*, January 21, 1974.

Hays, Samuel, *The Response to Industrialism* (Chicago: U. of Chicago Press, 1957).

Holyoake, George Jacob, *History of Cooperation* (London: Trubner and Co., 1875).

Hyman, Herbert H., and Charles Wright, "Trends in Voluntary Association Memberships of American Adults: Replication Based on Secondary Analysis of National Sample Surveys," *American Sociological Review*, Vol. 36, No. 2, April 1971.

Kanter, Rosabeth M., *Commitment and Community* (Cambridge: Harvard U. Press, 1972).

Knapp, Joseph G., *The Rise of American Cooperative Enterprise, 1620-1920* and *The Advance of American Cooperative Enterprise, 1920-1945* (Danville: Interstate Printers and Publishers, 1969 and 1972). Knapp is a former Administrator of the Farmer Cooperative Services for the U.S. Department of Agriculture. The books are backed with extensive and meticulous notes.

Leggett, John, "Metamorphosis of the Campus Radical," *New York Times Magazine*, January 30, 1972.

Lipset, Seymour, *Agrarian Socialism* (Berkeley: U. of California Press, 1971).
—, *Union Democracy* (Garden City, N.Y.: Doubleday & Co., Inc., 1956).

Maccoby, Herbert, "Differential Political Activity of Participants in a Voluntary Association," *American Sociological Review*, 23.

Mansbridge, Jane, "Town Meeting Democracy," *Working Papers*, Vol. 1, No. 2, Summer 1973. This excellent quarterly journal covers numerous issues relevant to co-ops. For more information, write Working Papers, 123 Mt. Auburn Street, Cambridge, MA 02138.

Marcuse, Herbert, *One-Dimensional Man* (Boston: Beacon Press, 1964).

Margolis, Richard, "Coming Together the Cooperative Way," *The New Leader*, Special Issue, April 17, 1972. This summary of cooperative activity in the United States can be purchased from The New Leader reprint department, 212 Fifth Avenue, New York, NY 10010 for fifty cents a copy.

Murphy, Jerome, *Grease the Squeaky Wheel*, doctoral dissertation, Harvard Graduate School of Education, 1972.

Myrick, Herbert, *How to Cooperate* (NY: Orange Judd Co., 1891).

OM Collective, *The Organizer's Manual* (NY: Bantam, 1971).

"Packet for the Bride," available from the Superintendent of Documents, Government Printing Office, Washington, D.C. 20402 for $4.65 (order No. A1.2:B 76/3 S/N 0100-02849. It includes the booklets *How to Buy Fresh Vegetables, How to Buy Fresh Fruits, Vegetables in Family Meals*, etc.

Perrow, Charles, "Members as Resources in Voluntary Organizations," in W. Rosengren and M. Lefton, *Organizations and Clients: Essays in the Sociology of Service* (Columbus, Ohio: Charles E. Merrill, 1970).

Rayman, Paula, "The Commune Movement: The Need to Revolutionize," *Win*, December 6, 1973.

Sonnichsen, Albert, *Consumers' Cooperation* (NY: The MacMillan Co., 1919).

Syrjala, Savele, *The Story of a Cooperative* (Fitchburg, MA: The United Cooperative Society, 1947). This excellent little book can be purchased from the Society at 815 Main Street, Fitchburg, MA 01420.

Terkel, Studs, *Hard Times* (NY: Avon Books, 1970).

Townsend, Robert, *Up the Organization* (NY: Fawcett, 1970).

Verba, Sidney, and Norman H. Nie, *Participation in America* (NY: Harper & Row, 1972).

Warbasse, James, *Cooperative Democracy* (NY: The MacMillan Co., 1923).

Waugh, Steve, "The Great Food Co-op Conspiracy," *The Boston Phoenix*, June 19, 1973.

Webb, Sidney and Beatrice, *Consumers' Cooperative Movement* (London: Longmans, Green and Co., 1921).

Wood, Dave, "Working in the Coops," *Win*, December 6, 1973.

Zwerdling, Daniel, "Death for Dinner," *New York Review*, February 21, 1974.

Technical consultants to the Broadway Food Co-op in
Somerville, Massachusetts. Photo by Jacki Schmerz.

INDEX